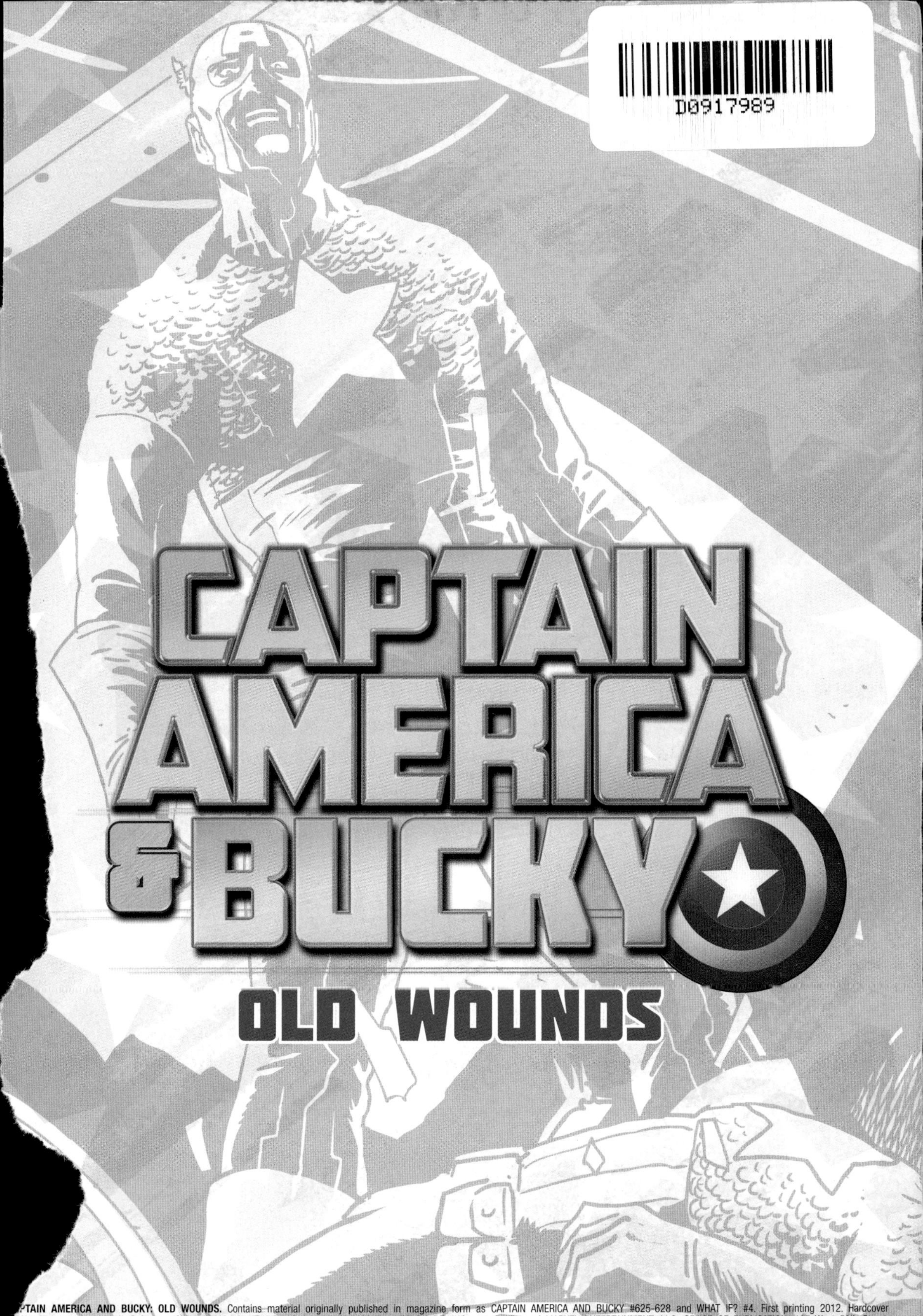

CAPTAIN AMERICA
& BUCKY
OLD WOUNDS

CAPTAIN AMERICA AND BUCKY: OLD WOUNDS. Contains material originally published in magazine form as CAPTAIN AMERICA AND BUCKY #625-628 and WHAT IF? #4. First printing 2012. Hardcover ISBN# 978-0-7851-6083-0. Softcover ISBN# 978-0-7851-6084-7. Published by MARVEL WORLDWIDE, INC., a subsidiary of MARVEL ENTERTAINMENT, LLC. OFFICE OF PUBLICATION: 135 West 50th Street, New York, NY 10020. Copyright © 1977, 2011 and 2012 Marvel Characters, Inc. All rights reserved. Hardcover: $19.99 per copy in the U.S. and $21.99 in Canada (GST #R127032852). Softcover: $16.99 per copy in the U.S. and $18.99 in Canada (GST #R127032852). Canadian Agreement #40668537. All characters featured in this issue and the distinctive names and likenesses thereof, and all related indicia are trademarks of Marvel Characters, Inc. No similarity between any of the names, characters, persons, and/or institutions in this magazine with those of any living or dead person or institution is intended, and any such similarity which may exist is purely coincidental. Printed in the U.S.A. ALAN FINE, EVP - Office of the President, Marvel Worldwide, Inc. and EVP & CMO Marvel Characters B.V.; DAN BUCKLEY, Publisher & President - Print, Animation & Digital Divisions; JOE QUESADA, Chief Creative Officer; TOM BREVOORT, SVP of Publishing; DAVID BOGART, SVP of Operations & Procurement, Publishing; RUWAN JAYATILLEKE, SVP & Associate Publisher, Publishing; C.B. CEBULSKI, SVP of Creator & Content Development; DAVID GABRIEL, SVP of Publishing Sales & Circulation; MICHAEL PASCIULLO, SVP of Brand Planning & Communications; JIM O'KEEFE, VP of Operations & Logistics; DAN CARR, Executive Director of Publishing Technology; SUSAN CRESPI, Editorial Operations Manager; ALEX MORALES, Publishing Operations Manager; STAN LEE, Chairman Emeritus. For information regarding advertising in Marvel Comics or on Marvel.com, please contact John Dokes, SVP Integrated Sales and Marketing, at jdokes@marvel.com. For Marvel subscription inquiries, please call 800-217-9158. Manufactured between 4/16/2012 and 5/14/2012 (hardcover), and 4/16/2012 and 11/12/2012 (softcover), by R.R. DONNELLEY, INC., SALEM, VA, USA.
10 9 8 7 6 5 4 3 2 1

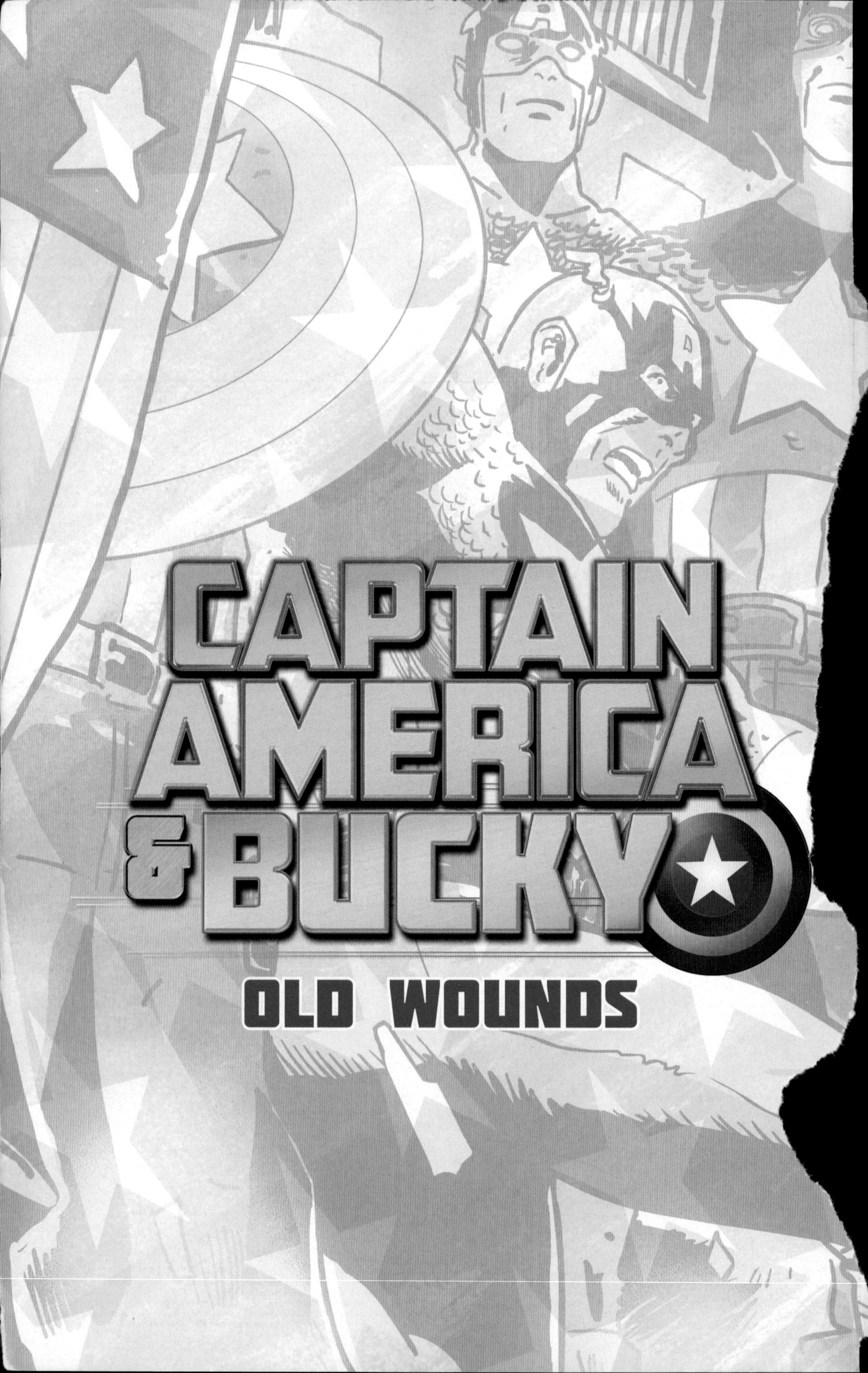

CAPTAIN AMERICA & BUCKY

OLD WOUNDS

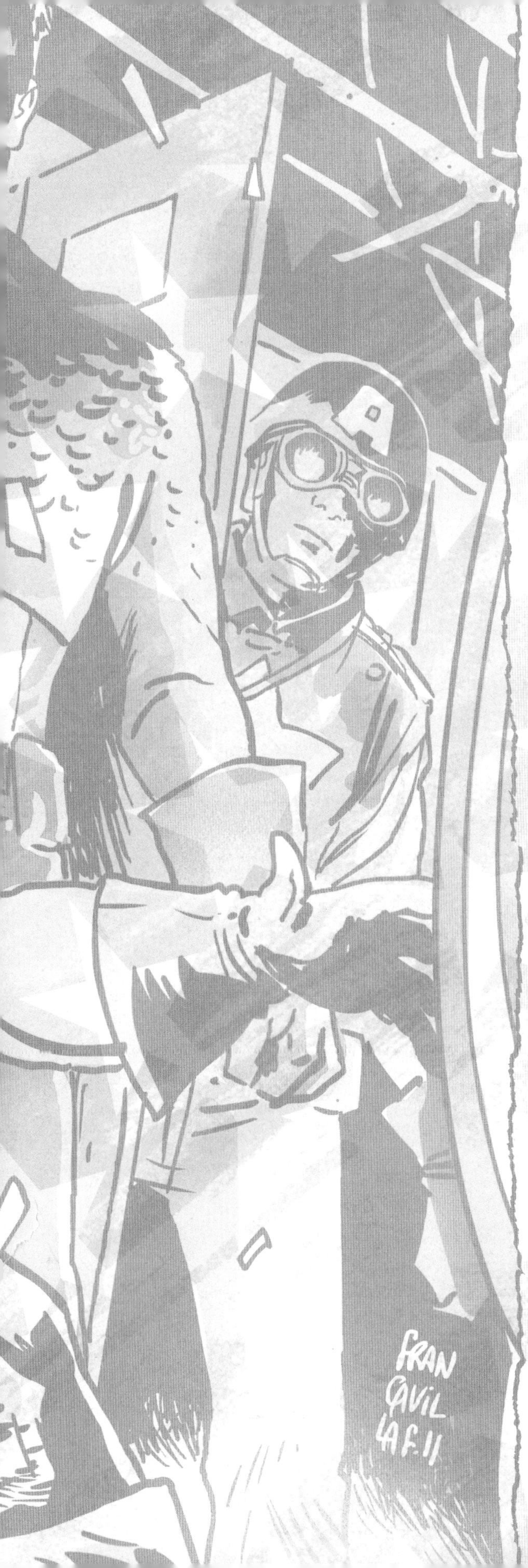
FRAN
CAVIL
LA F. 11

STORY
JAMES ASMUS & ED BRUBAKER

SCRIPT
JAMES ASMUS

ARTIST & COVER
FRANCESCO FRANCAVILLA

LETTERER
VC'S JOE CARAMAGNA

ASSISTANT EDITOR
JOHN DENNING

EDITOR
LAUREN SANKOVITCH

WHAT IF? (1977) #4

WRITER
ROY THOMAS

PENCILER
FRANK ROBBINS

INKER
FRANK SPRINGER

COLORIST
GEORGE BELL

LETTERERS
JOE ROSEN & JOHN COSTANZA

CAPTAIN AMERICA CREATED BY
JOE SIMON & JACK KIRBY

COLLECTION EDITOR
JENNIFER GRÜNWALD
ASSISTANT EDITORS
ALEX STARBUCK & NELSON RIBEIRO
EDITOR, SPECIAL PROJECTS
MARK D. BEAZLEY
SENIOR EDITOR, SPECIAL PROJECTS
JEFF YOUNGQUIST
SENIOR VICE PRESIDENT OF SALES
DAVID GABRIEL
SVP OF BRAND PLANNING & COMMUNICATIONS
MICHAEL PASCIULLO
BOOK DESIGN
JEFF POWELL

EDITOR IN CHIEF
AXEL ALONSO
CHIEF CREATIVE OFFICER
JOE QUESADA
PUBLISHER
DAN BUCKLEY
EXECUTIVE PRODUCER
ALAN FINE

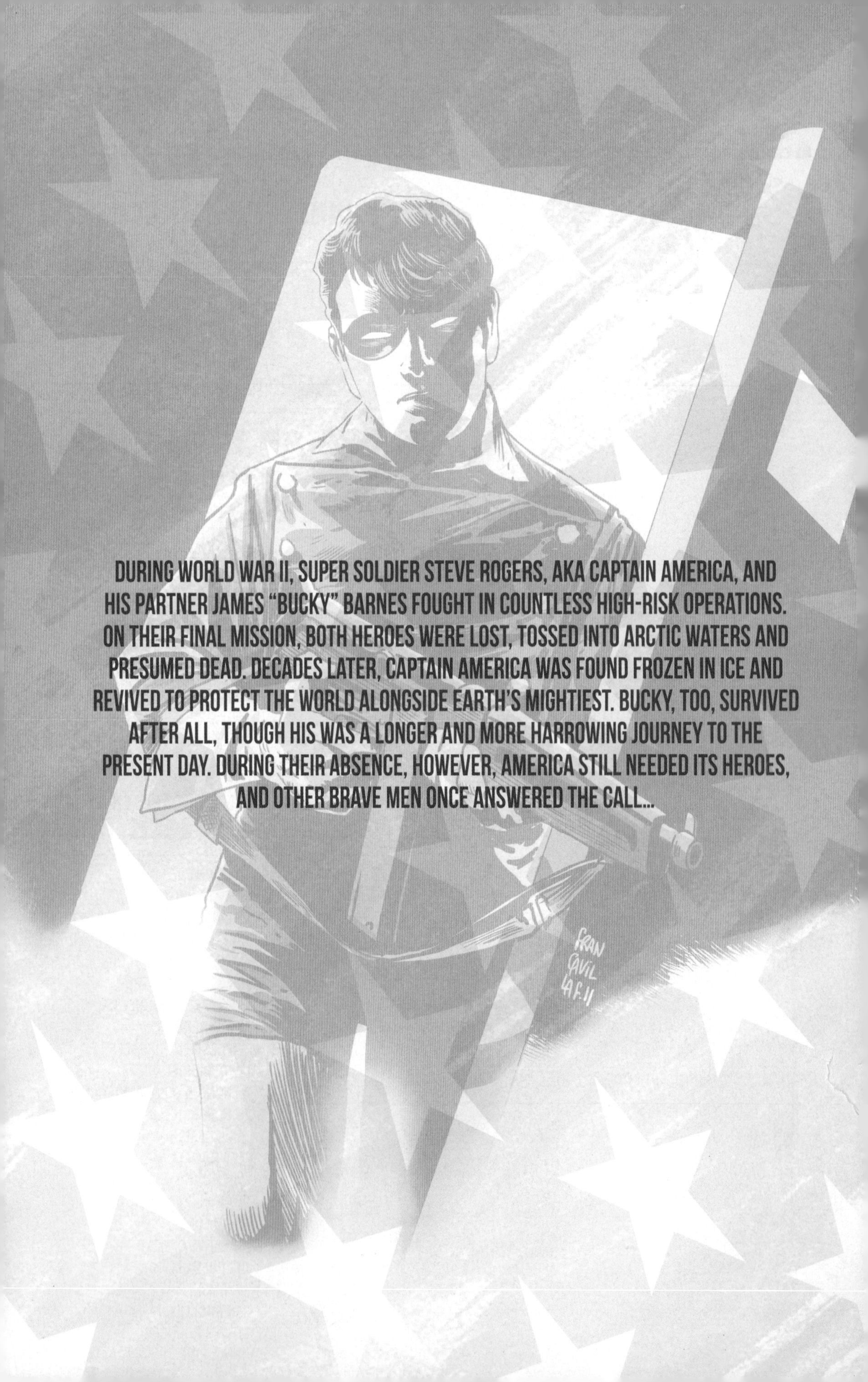

DURING WORLD WAR II, SUPER SOLDIER STEVE ROGERS, AKA CAPTAIN AMERICA, AND HIS PARTNER JAMES "BUCKY" BARNES FOUGHT IN COUNTLESS HIGH-RISK OPERATIONS. ON THEIR FINAL MISSION, BOTH HEROES WERE LOST, TOSSED INTO ARCTIC WATERS AND PRESUMED DEAD. DECADES LATER, CAPTAIN AMERICA WAS FOUND FROZEN IN ICE AND REVIVED TO PROTECT THE WORLD ALONGSIDE EARTH'S MIGHTIEST. BUCKY, TOO, SURVIVED AFTER ALL, THOUGH HIS WAS A LONGER AND MORE HARROWING JOURNEY TO THE PRESENT DAY. DURING THEIR ABSENCE, HOWEVER, AMERICA STILL NEEDED ITS HEROES, AND OTHER BRAVE MEN ONCE ANSWERED THE CALL...

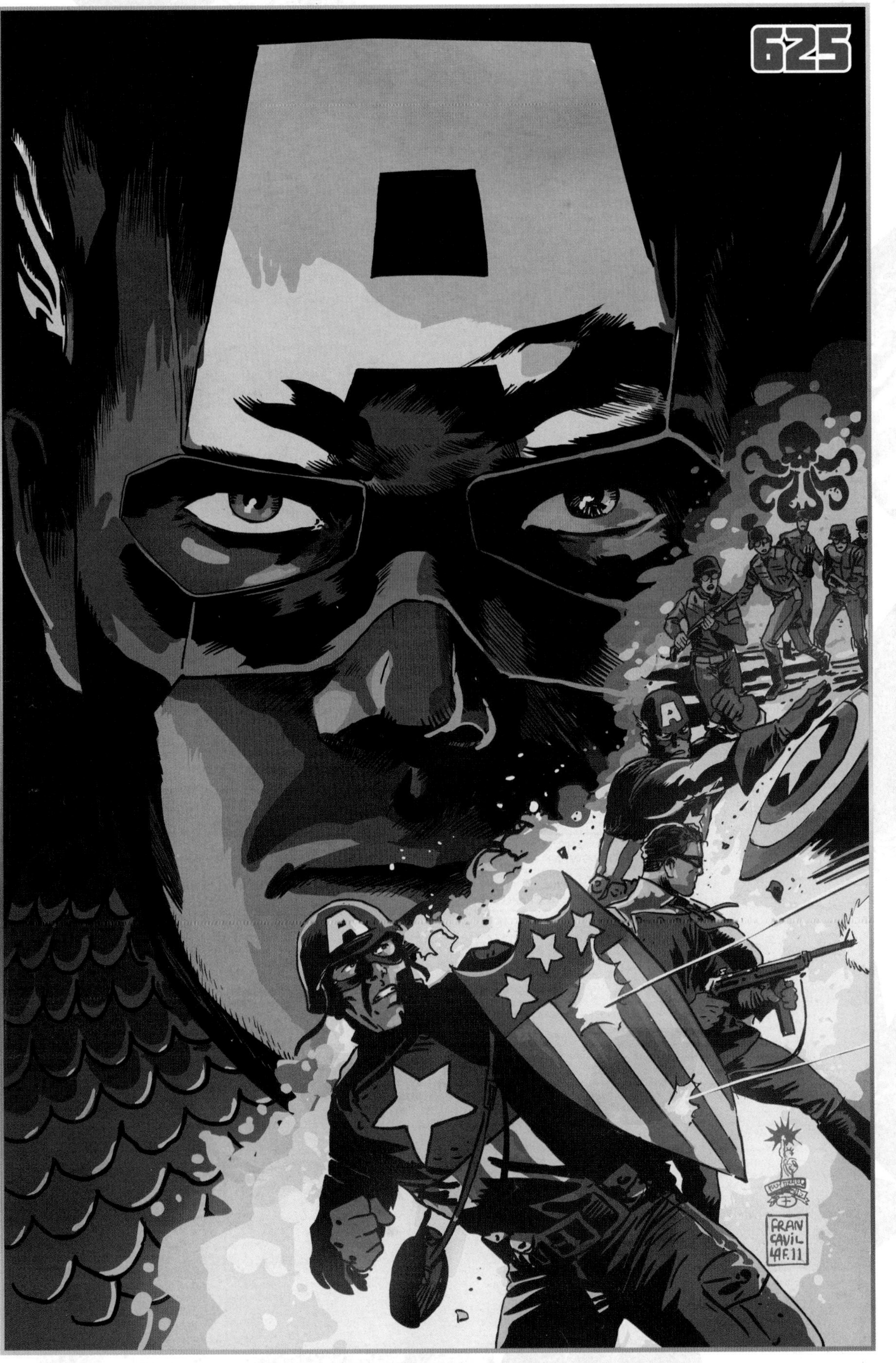
625
FRAN
CAVIL
LAF.11

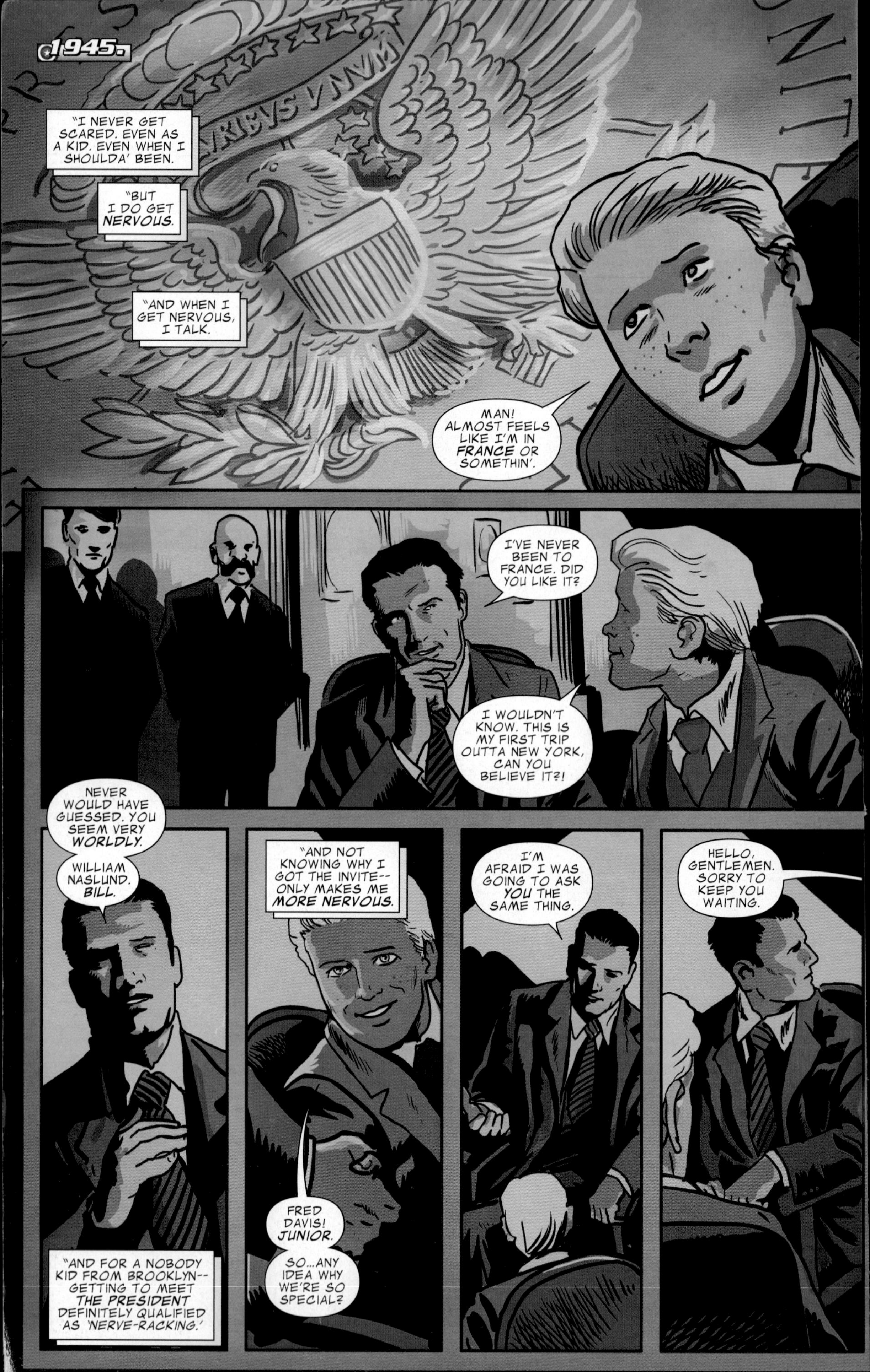
1945.
"I NEVER GET SCARED. EVEN AS A KID. EVEN WHEN I SHOULDA' BEEN.
"BUT I DO GET NERVOUS.
"AND WHEN I GET NERVOUS, I TALK.
MAN! ALMOST FEELS LIKE I'M IN FRANCE OR SOMETHIN'.
I'VE NEVER BEEN TO FRANCE. DID YOU LIKE IT?
I WOULDN'T KNOW. THIS IS MY FIRST TRIP OUTTA NEW YORK, CAN YOU BELIEVE IT?!
NEVER WOULD HAVE GUESSED. YOU SEEM VERY WORLDLY.
WILLIAM NASLUND. BILL.
"AND FOR A NOBODY KID FROM BROOKLYN--GETTING TO MEET THE PRESIDENT DEFINITELY QUALIFIED AS 'NERVE-RACKING.'
"AND NOT KNOWING WHY I GOT THE INVITE--ONLY MAKES ME MORE NERVOUS.
FRED DAVIS! JUNIOR.
SO...ANY IDEA WHY WE'RE SO SPECIAL?
I'M AFRAID I WAS GOING TO ASK YOU THE SAME THING.
HELLO, GENTLEMEN. SORRY TO KEEP YOU WAITING.

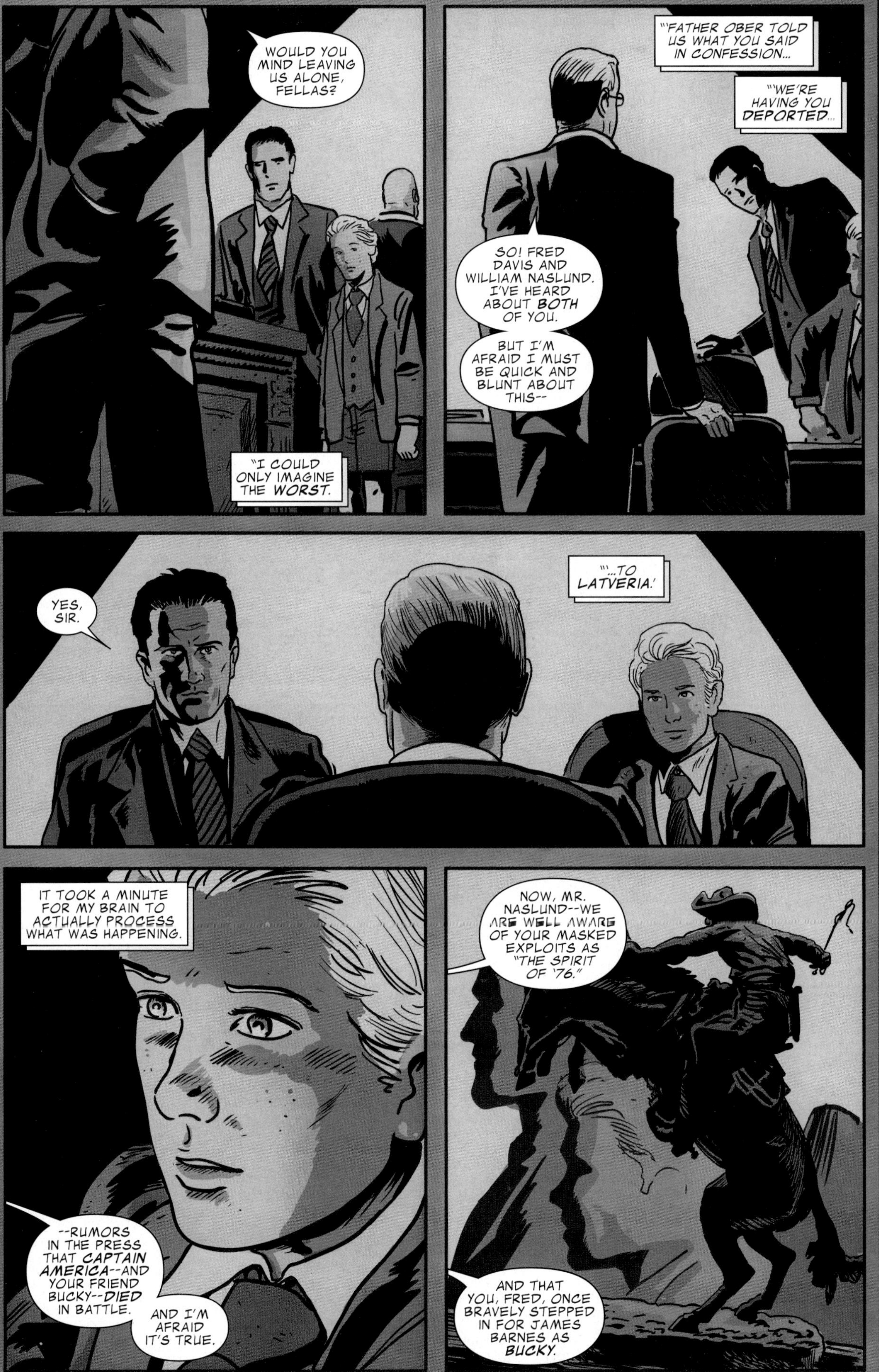
WOULD YOU MIND LEAVING US ALONE, FELLAS?
"I COULD ONLY IMAGINE THE WORST.
"FATHER OBER TOLD US WHAT YOU SAID IN CONFESSION...
"'WE'RE HAVING YOU DEPORTED...
SO! FRED DAVIS AND WILLIAM NASLUND. I'VE HEARD ABOUT BOTH OF YOU.
BUT I'M AFRAID I MUST BE QUICK AND BLUNT ABOUT THIS--
YES, SIR.
"'...TO LATVERIA.'
IT TOOK A MINUTE FOR MY BRAIN TO ACTUALLY PROCESS WHAT WAS HAPPENING.
--RUMORS IN THE PRESS THAT CAPTAIN AMERICA--AND YOUR FRIEND BUCKY--DIED IN BATTLE.
AND I'M AFRAID IT'S TRUE.
NOW, MR. NASLUND--WE ARE WELL AWARE OF YOUR MASKED EXPLOITS AS "THE SPIRIT OF '76."
AND THAT YOU, FRED, ONCE BRAVELY STEPPED IN FOR JAMES BARNES AS BUCKY.

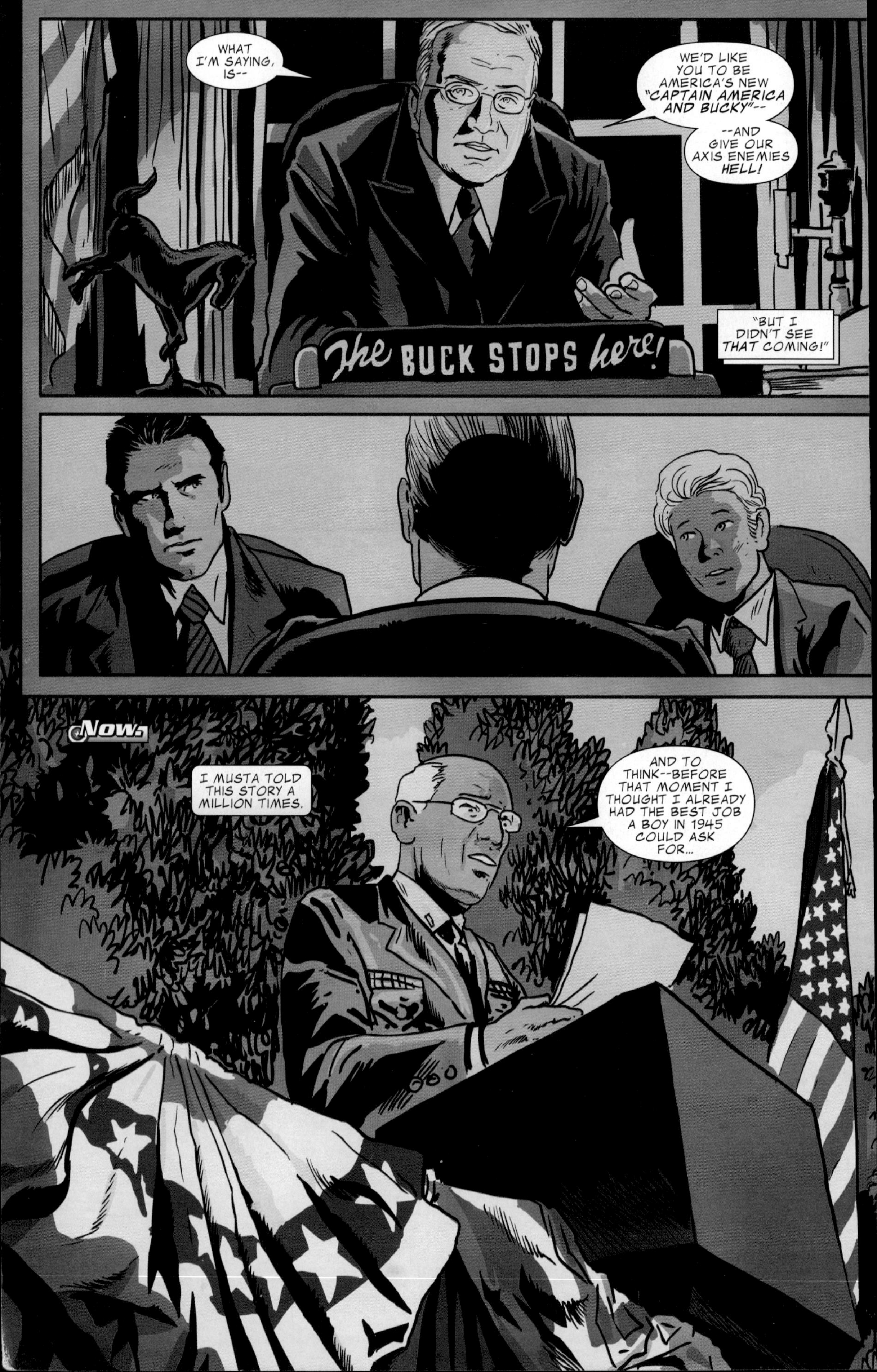
WHAT I'M SAYING, IS--
WE'D LIKE YOU TO BE AMERICA'S NEW "CAPTAIN AMERICA AND BUCKY"--
--AND GIVE OUR AXIS ENEMIES HELL!
The BUCK STOPS here!
"BUT I DIDN'T SEE THAT COMING!"
Now
I MUSTA TOLD THIS STORY A MILLION TIMES.
AND TO THINK--BEFORE THAT MOMENT I THOUGHT I ALREADY HAD THE BEST JOB A BOY IN 1945 COULD ASK FOR...

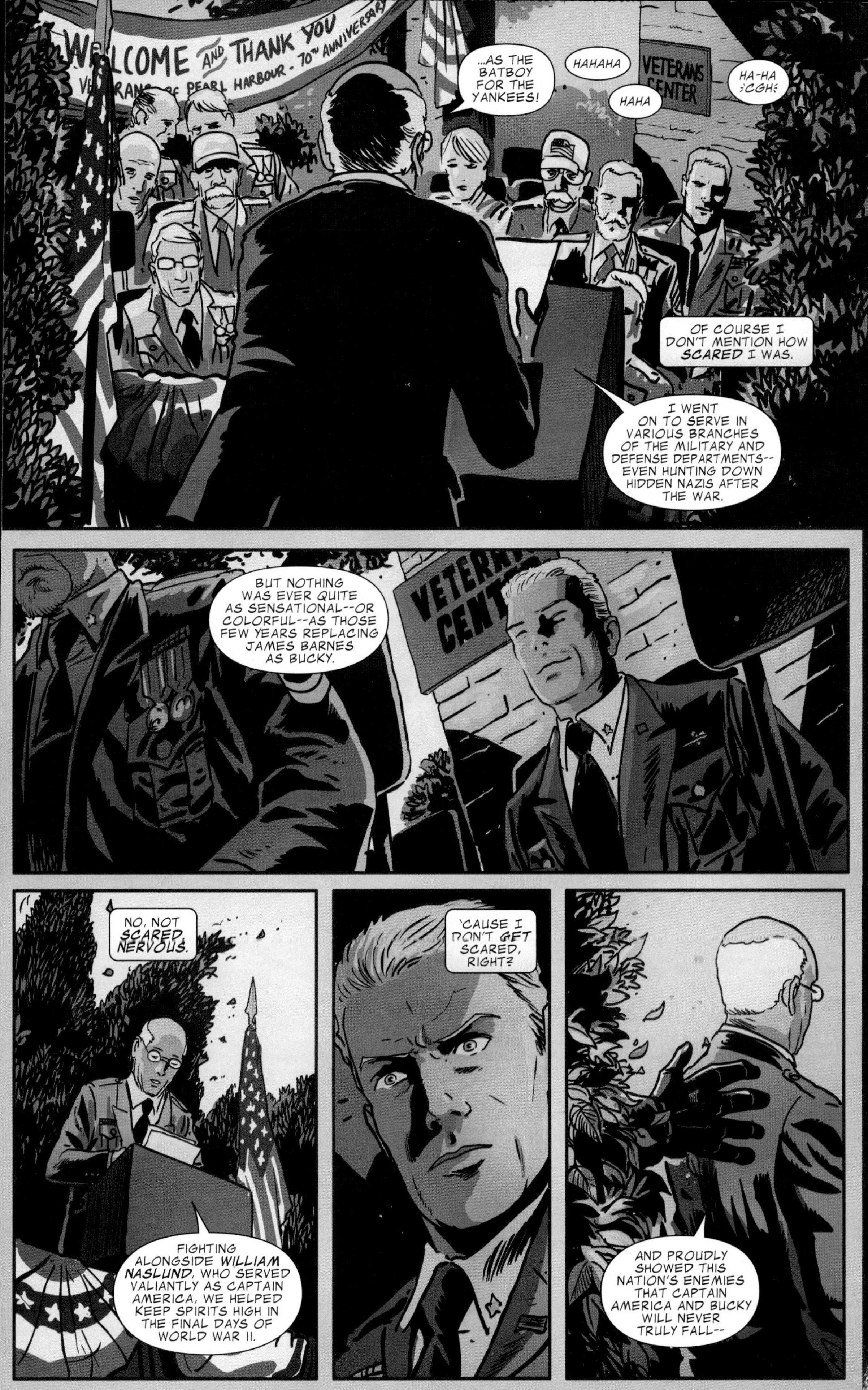
WELCOME AND THANK YOU
VETERANS OF PEARL HARBOUR - 70TH ANNIVERSARY
...AS THE BATBOY FOR THE YANKEES!
HAHAHA
VETERANS CENTER
HAHA
HA-HA *CGH*
OF COURSE I DON'T MENTION HOW SCARED I WAS.
I WENT ON TO SERVE IN VARIOUS BRANCHES OF THE MILITARY AND DEFENSE DEPARTMENTS--EVEN HUNTING DOWN HIDDEN NAZIS AFTER THE WAR.
BUT NOTHING WAS EVER QUITE AS SENSATIONAL--OR COLORFUL--AS THOSE FEW YEARS REPLACING JAMES BARNES AS BUCKY.
NO, NOT SCARED. NERVOUS.
FIGHTING ALONGSIDE WILLIAM NASLUND, WHO SERVED VALIANTLY AS CAPTAIN AMERICA, WE HELPED KEEP SPIRITS HIGH IN THE FINAL DAYS OF WORLD WAR II.
'CAUSE I DON'T GET SCARED, RIGHT?
AND PROUDLY SHOWED THIS NATION'S ENEMIES THAT CAPTAIN AMERICA AND BUCKY WILL NEVER TRULY FALL--

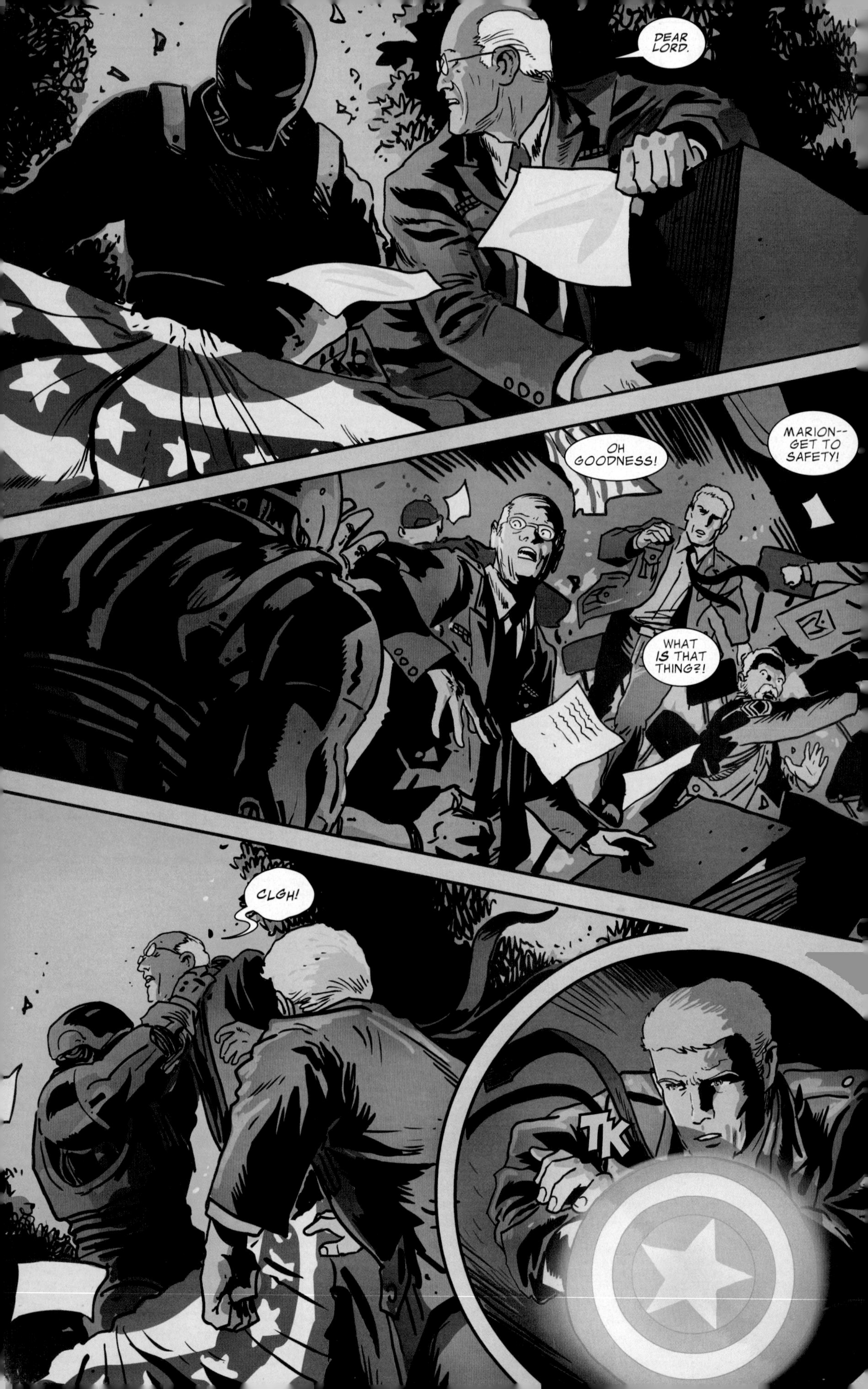
DEAR LORD.
OH GOODNESS!
MARION-- GET TO SAFETY!
WHAT IS THAT THING?!
CLGH!
TK

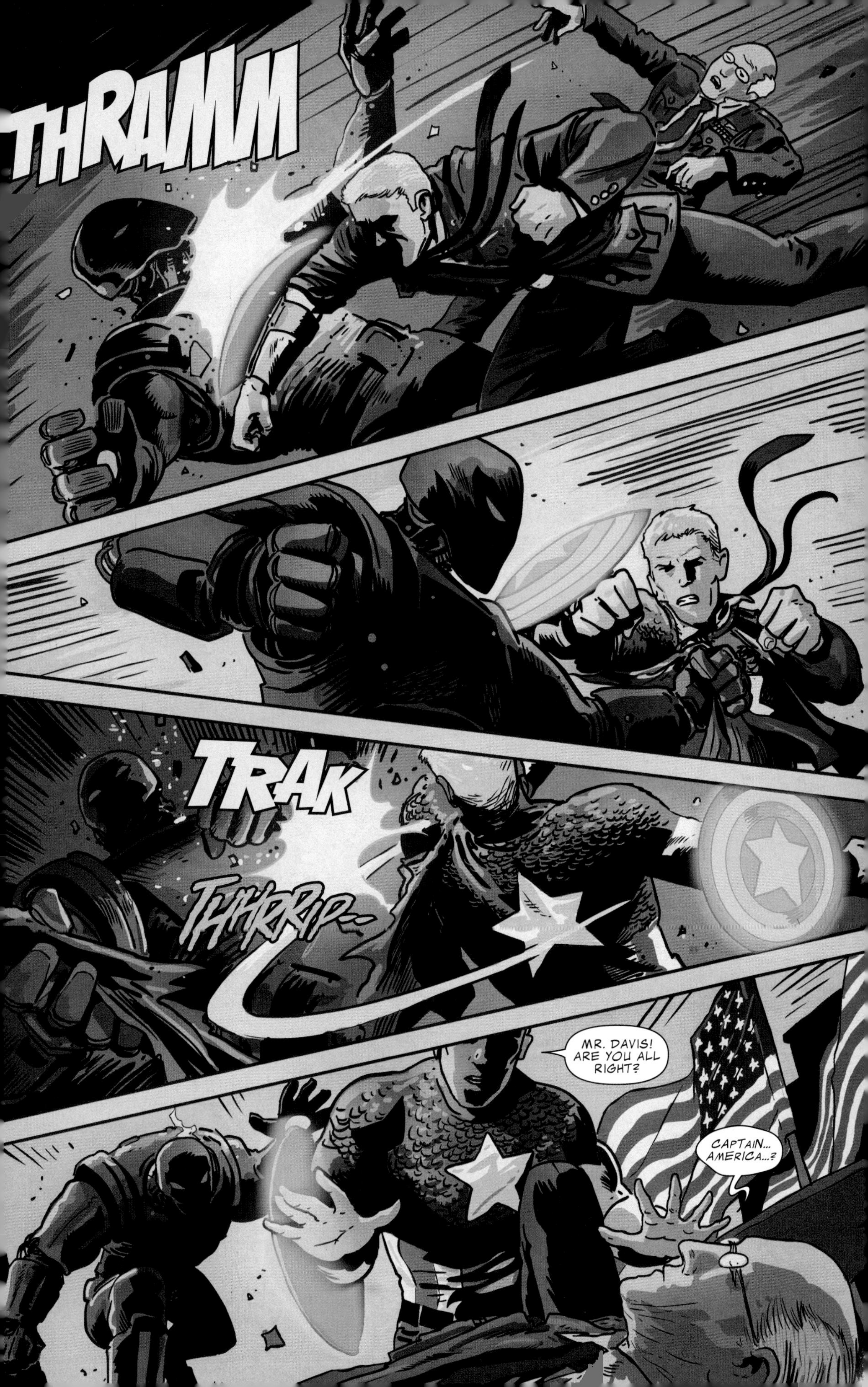
THRAMM
TRAK
THHRRIP--
MR. DAVIS! ARE YOU ALL RIGHT?
CAPTAIN... AMERICA...?

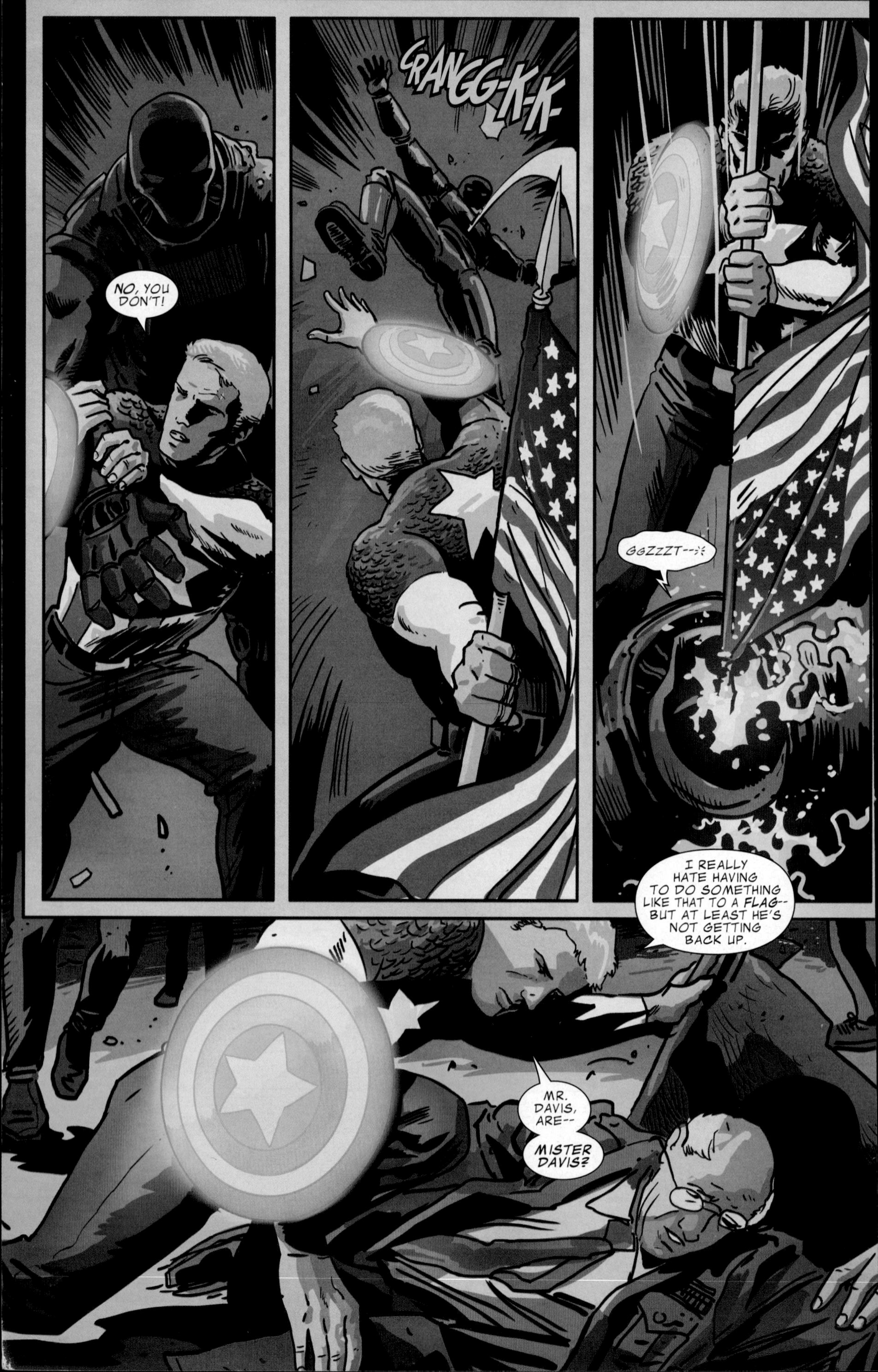
NO, YOU DON'T!
CRANGG-K-K-
GGZZZT--
I REALLY HATE HAVING TO DO SOMETHING LIKE THAT TO A FLAG-- BUT AT LEAST HE'S NOT GETTING BACK UP.
MR. DAVIS, ARE--
MISTER DAVIS?

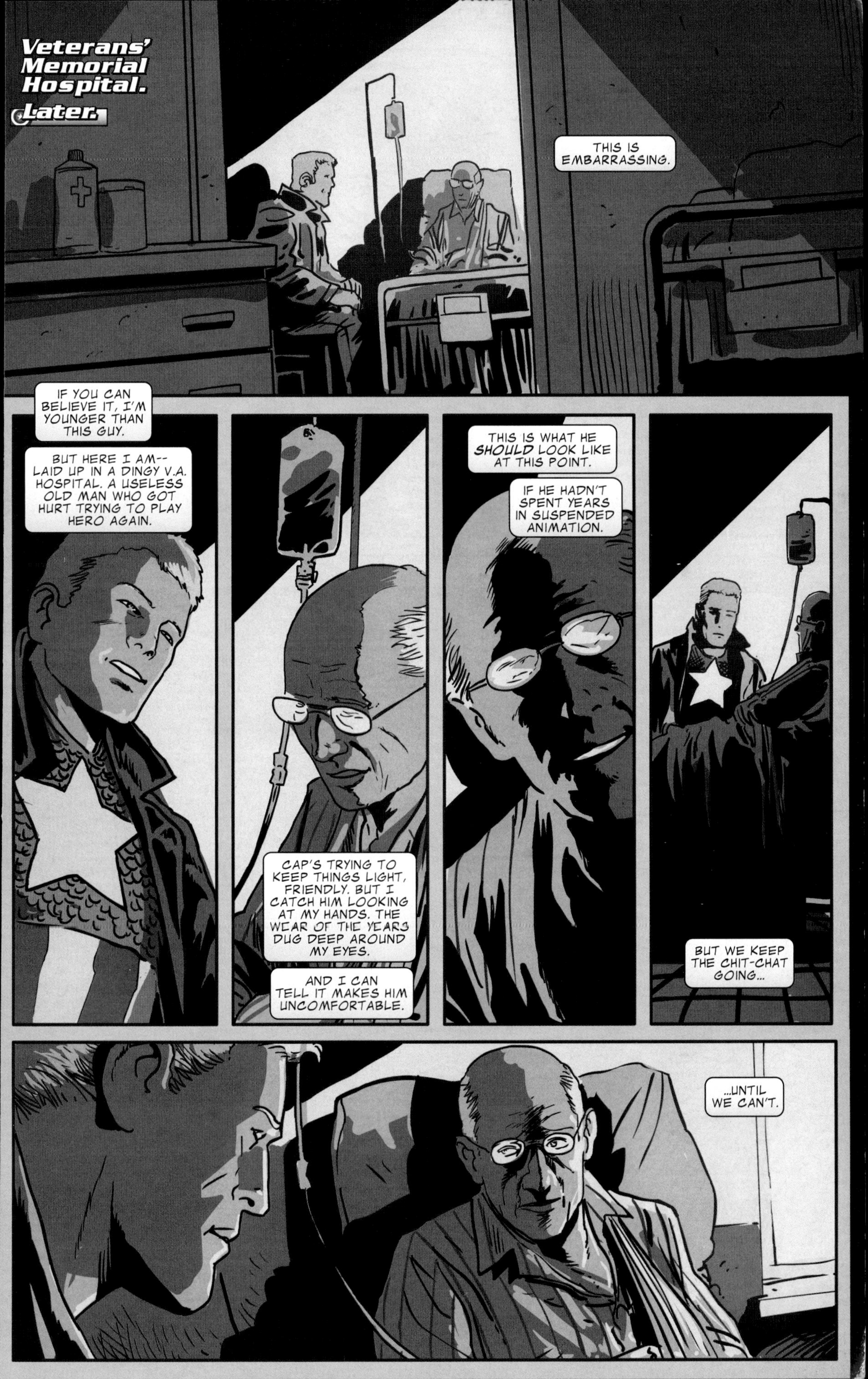
Veterans' Memorial Hospital.
Later.
THIS IS EMBARRASSING.
IF YOU CAN BELIEVE IT, I'M YOUNGER THAN THIS GUY.
BUT HERE I AM-- LAID UP IN A DINGY V.A. HOSPITAL. A USELESS OLD MAN WHO GOT HURT TRYING TO PLAY HERO AGAIN.
CAP'S TRYING TO KEEP THINGS LIGHT, FRIENDLY. BUT I CATCH HIM LOOKING AT MY HANDS. THE WEAR OF THE YEARS DUG DEEP AROUND MY EYES.
AND I CAN TELL IT MAKES HIM UNCOMFORTABLE.
THIS IS WHAT HE SHOULD LOOK LIKE AT THIS POINT.
IF HE HADN'T SPENT YEARS IN SUSPENDED ANIMATION.
BUT WE KEEP THE CHIT-CHAT GOING...
...UNTIL WE CAN'T.

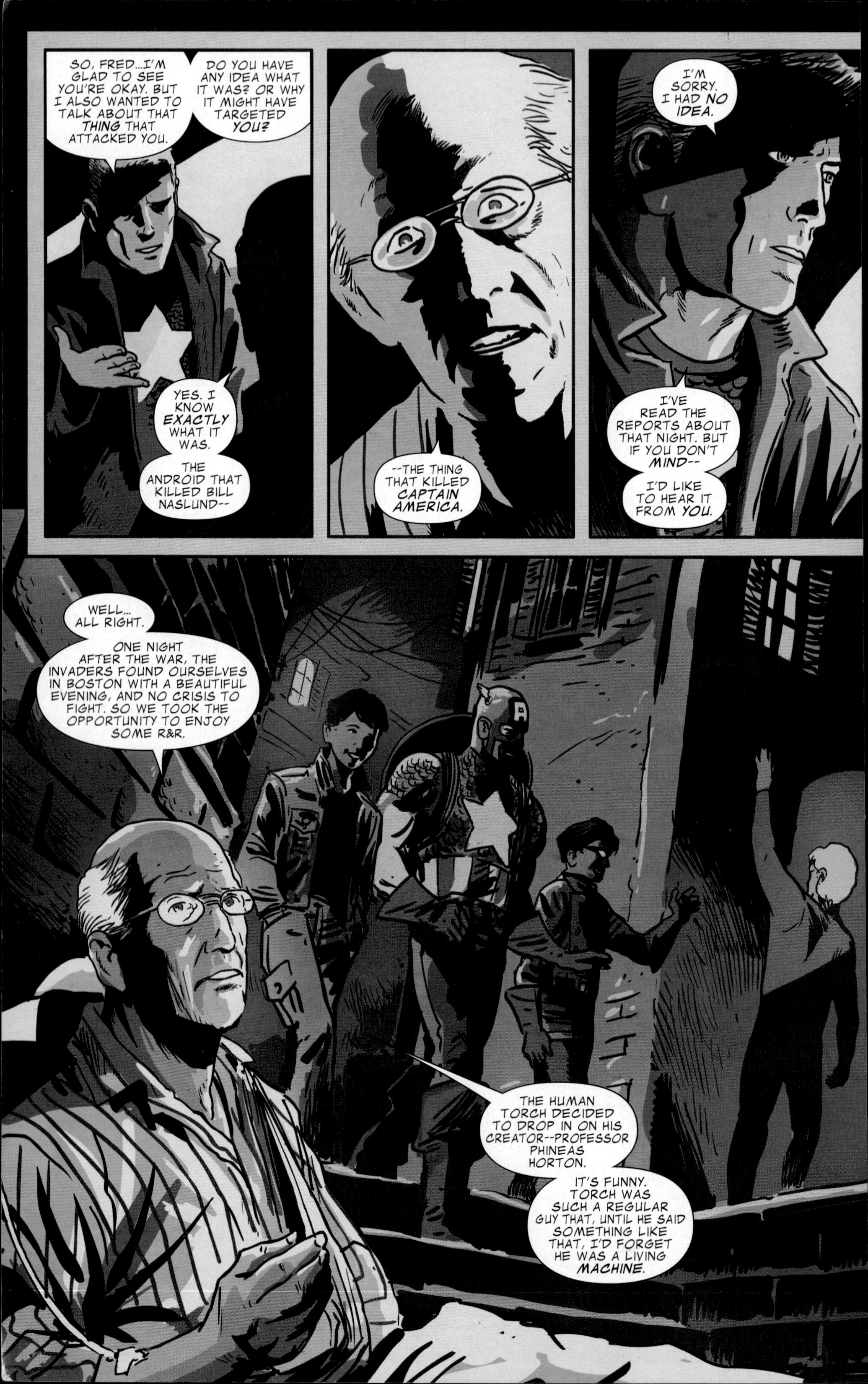
SO, FRED...I'M GLAD TO SEE YOU'RE OKAY. BUT I ALSO WANTED TO TALK ABOUT THAT THING THAT ATTACKED YOU.
DO YOU HAVE ANY IDEA WHAT IT WAS? OR WHY IT MIGHT HAVE TARGETED YOU?
YES. I KNOW EXACTLY WHAT IT WAS.
THE ANDROID THAT KILLED BILL NASLUND--
--THE THING THAT KILLED CAPTAIN AMERICA.
I'M SORRY. I HAD NO IDEA.
I'VE READ THE REPORTS ABOUT THAT NIGHT. BUT IF YOU DON'T MIND--
I'D LIKE TO HEAR IT FROM YOU.
WELL... ALL RIGHT.
ONE NIGHT AFTER THE WAR, THE INVADERS FOUND OURSELVES IN BOSTON WITH A BEAUTIFUL EVENING, AND NO CRISIS TO FIGHT. SO WE TOOK THE OPPORTUNITY TO ENJOY SOME R&R.
THE HUMAN TORCH DECIDED TO DROP IN ON HIS CREATOR--PROFESSOR PHINEAS HORTON.
IT'S FUNNY. TORCH WAS SUCH A REGULAR GUY THAT, UNTIL HE SAID SOMETHING LIKE THAT, I'D FORGET HE WAS A LIVING MACHINE.

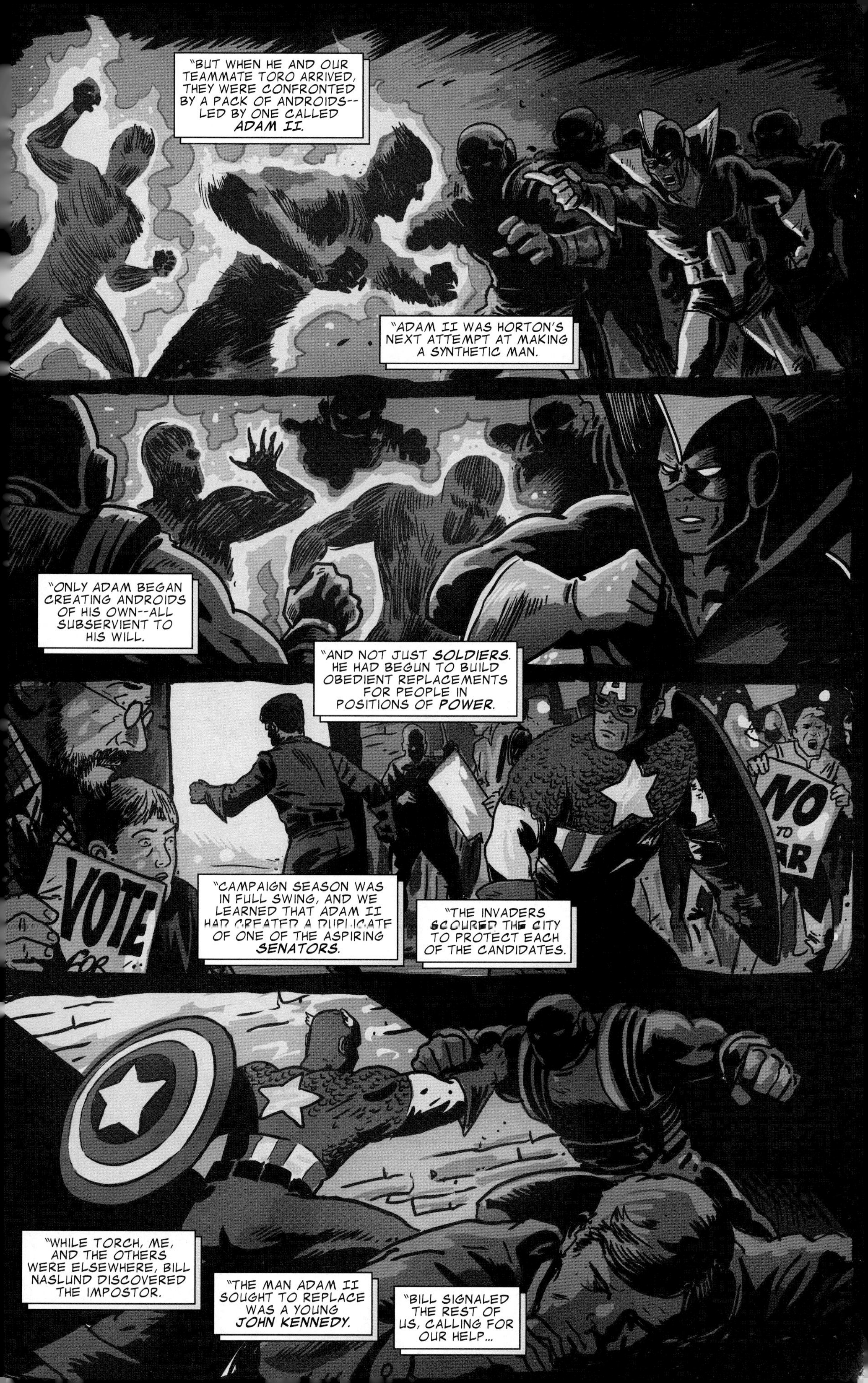
"BUT WHEN HE AND OUR TEAMMATE TORO ARRIVED, THEY WERE CONFRONTED BY A PACK OF ANDROIDS--LED BY ONE CALLED ADAM II.
"ADAM II WAS HORTON'S NEXT ATTEMPT AT MAKING A SYNTHETIC MAN.
"ONLY ADAM BEGAN CREATING ANDROIDS OF HIS OWN--ALL SUBSERVIENT TO HIS WILL.
"AND NOT JUST SOLDIERS. HE HAD BEGUN TO BUILD OBEDIENT REPLACEMENTS FOR PEOPLE IN POSITIONS OF POWER.
NO TO WAR
VOTE FOR
"CAMPAIGN SEASON WAS IN FULL SWING, AND WE LEARNED THAT ADAM II HAD CREATED A DUPLICATE OF ONE OF THE ASPIRING SENATORS.
"THE INVADERS SCOURED THE CITY TO PROTECT EACH OF THE CANDIDATES.
"WHILE TORCH, ME, AND THE OTHERS WERE ELSEWHERE, BILL NASLUND DISCOVERED THE IMPOSTOR.
"THE MAN ADAM II SOUGHT TO REPLACE WAS A YOUNG JOHN KENNEDY.
"BILL SIGNALED THE REST OF US, CALLING FOR OUR HELP...

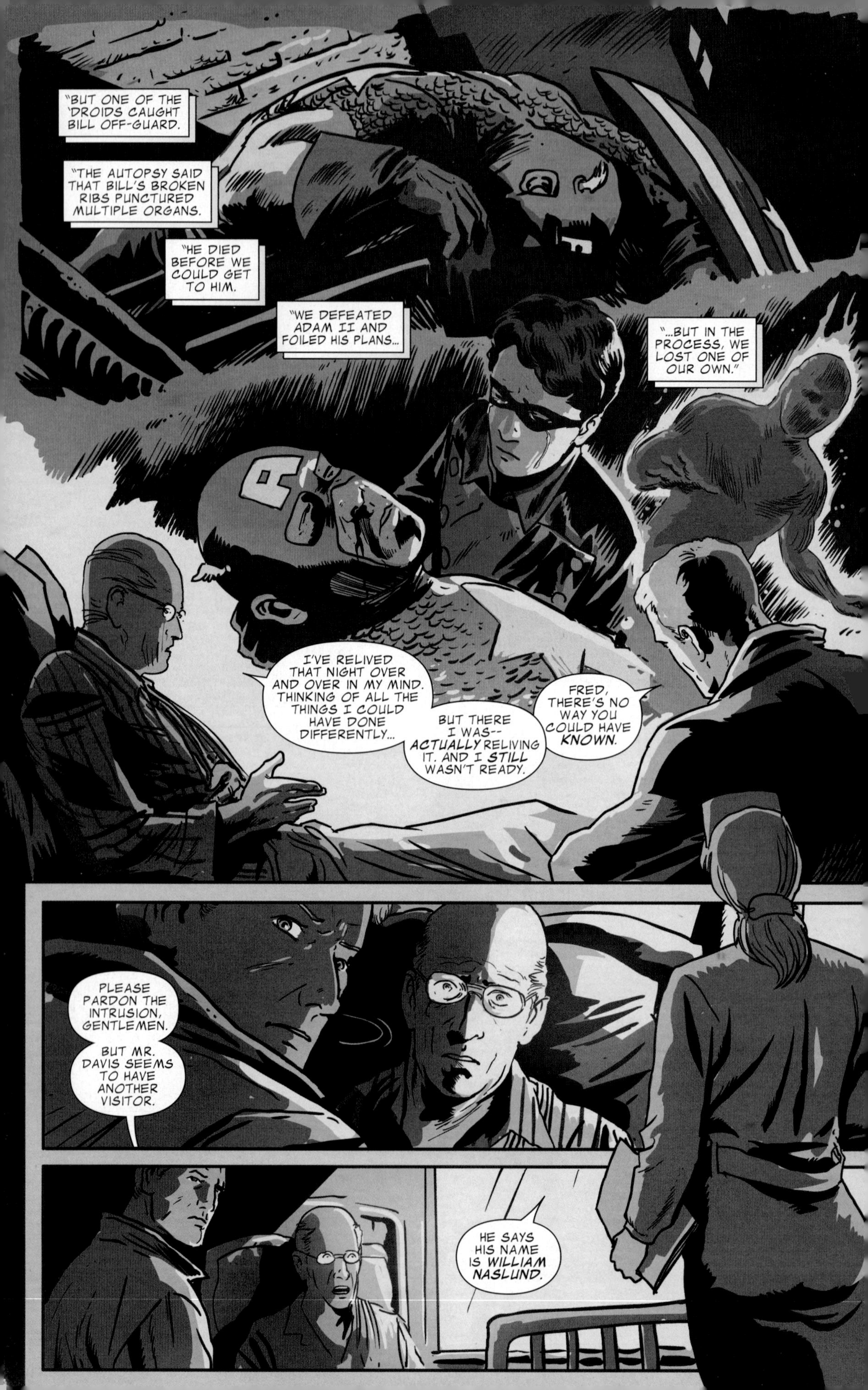
"BUT ONE OF THE 'DROIDS CAUGHT BILL OFF-GUARD.
"THE AUTOPSY SAID THAT BILL'S BROKEN RIBS PUNCTURED MULTIPLE ORGANS.
"HE DIED BEFORE WE COULD GET TO HIM.
"WE DEFEATED ADAM II AND FOILED HIS PLANS...
"...BUT IN THE PROCESS, WE LOST ONE OF OUR OWN."
I'VE RELIVED THAT NIGHT OVER AND OVER IN MY MIND. THINKING OF ALL THE THINGS I COULD HAVE DONE DIFFERENTLY...
BUT THERE I WAS-- ACTUALLY RELIVING IT. AND I STILL WASN'T READY.
FRED, THERE'S NO WAY YOU COULD HAVE KNOWN.
PLEASE PARDON THE INTRUSION, GENTLEMEN.
BUT MR. DAVIS SEEMS TO HAVE ANOTHER VISITOR.
HE SAYS HIS NAME IS WILLIAM NASLUND.

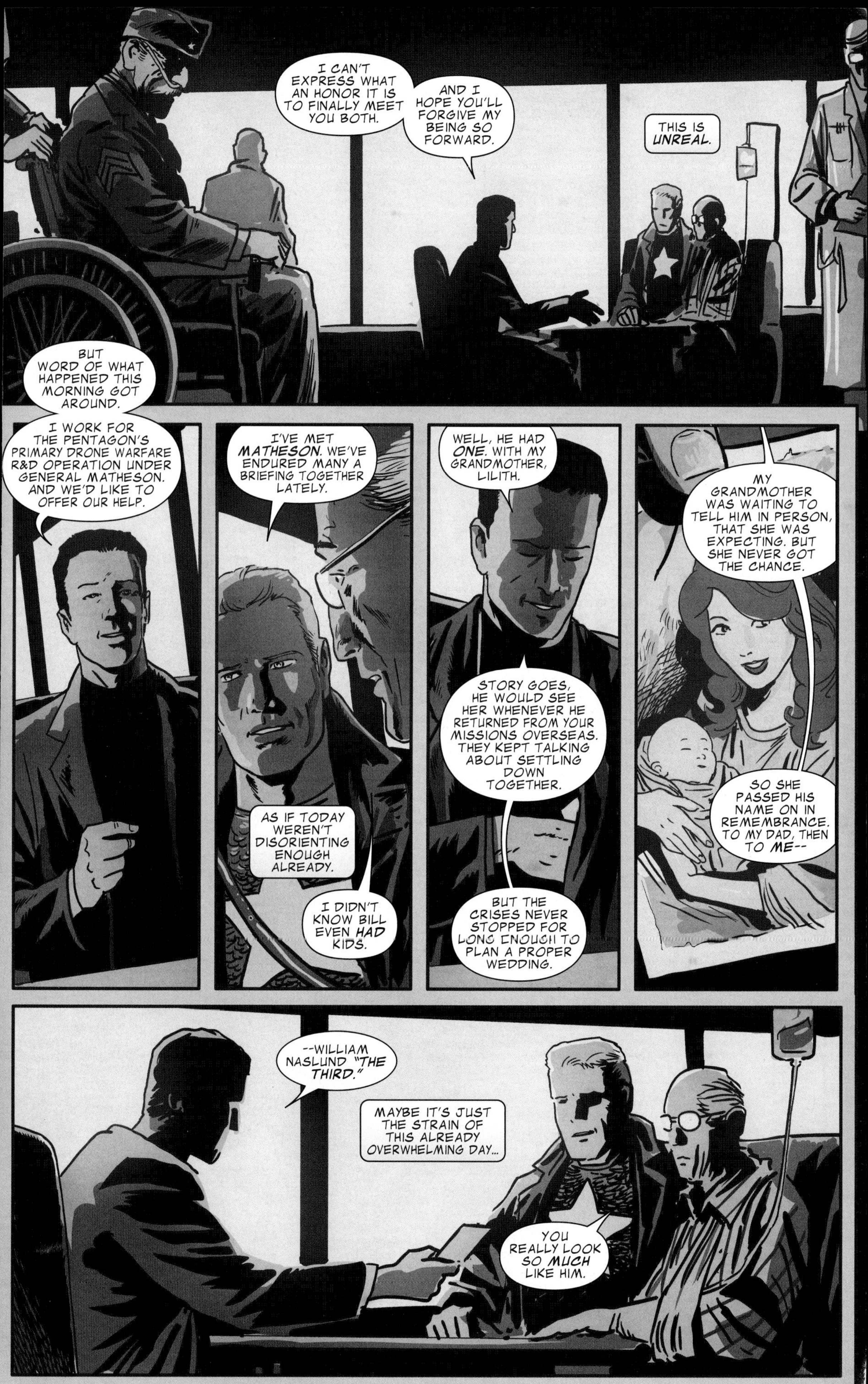
I CAN'T EXPRESS WHAT AN HONOR IT IS TO FINALLY MEET YOU BOTH.
AND I HOPE YOU'LL FORGIVE MY BEING SO FORWARD.
THIS IS UNREAL.
BUT WORD OF WHAT HAPPENED THIS MORNING GOT AROUND.
I WORK FOR THE PENTAGON'S PRIMARY DRONE WARFARE R&D OPERATION UNDER GENERAL MATHESON. AND WE'D LIKE TO OFFER OUR HELP.
I'VE MET MATHESON. WE'VE ENDURED MANY A BRIEFING TOGETHER LATELY.
AS IF TODAY WEREN'T DISORIENTING ENOUGH ALREADY.
I DIDN'T KNOW BILL EVEN HAD KIDS.
WELL, HE HAD ONE. WITH MY GRANDMOTHER, LILITH.
STORY GOES, HE WOULD SEE HER WHENEVER HE RETURNED FROM YOUR MISSIONS OVERSEAS. THEY KEPT TALKING ABOUT SETTLING DOWN TOGETHER.
BUT THE CRISES NEVER STOPPED FOR LONG ENOUGH TO PLAN A PROPER WEDDING.
MY GRANDMOTHER WAS WAITING TO TELL HIM IN PERSON, THAT SHE WAS EXPECTING. BUT SHE NEVER GOT THE CHANCE.
SO SHE PASSED HIS NAME ON IN REMEMBRANCE. TO MY DAD, THEN TO ME--
--WILLIAM NASLUND "THE THIRD."
MAYBE IT'S JUST THE STRAIN OF THIS ALREADY OVERWHELMING DAY...
YOU REALLY LOOK SO MUCH LIKE HIM.

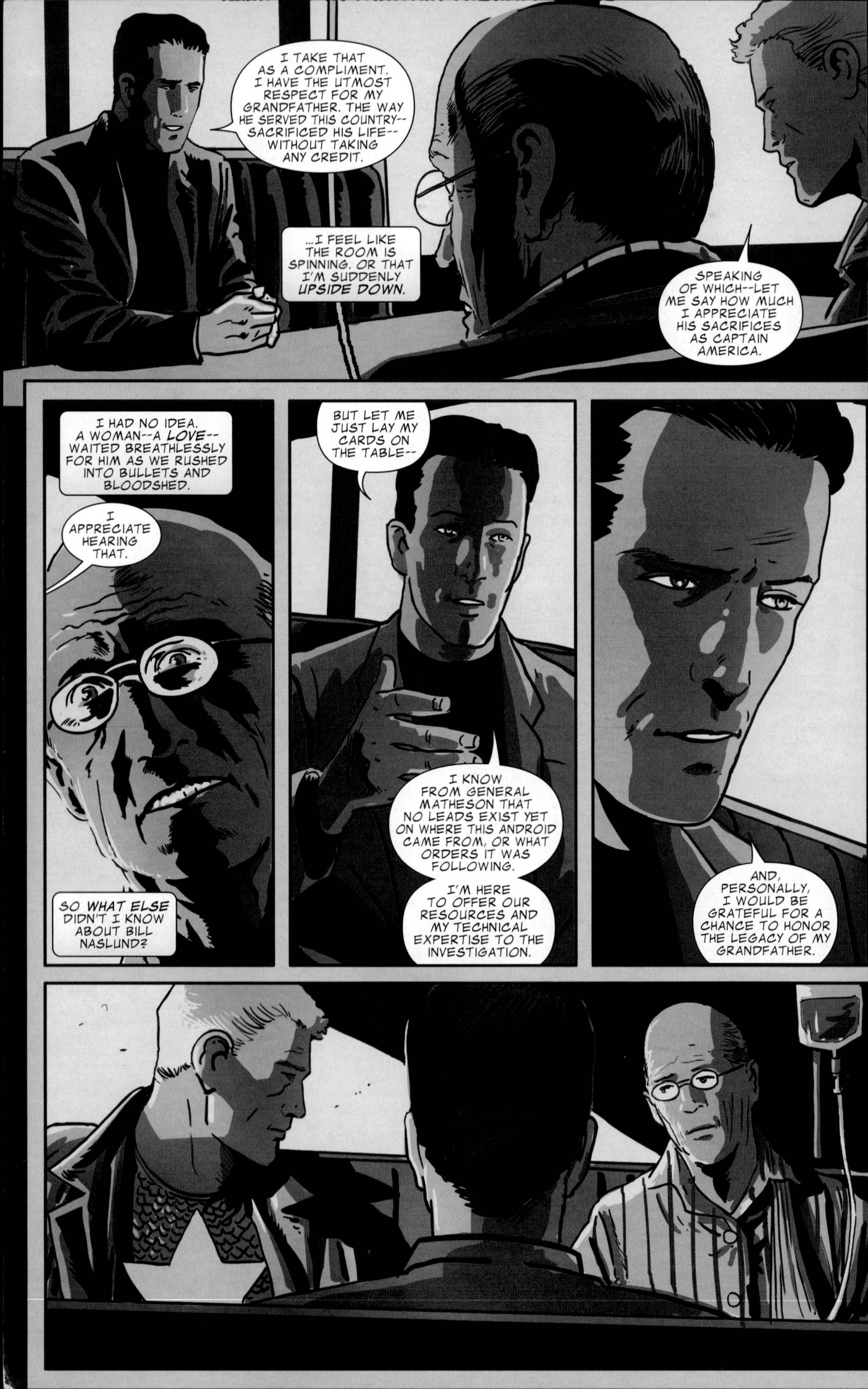

I TAKE THAT AS A COMPLIMENT. I HAVE THE UTMOST RESPECT FOR MY GRANDFATHER. THE WAY HE SERVED THIS COUNTRY--SACRIFICED HIS LIFE--WITHOUT TAKING ANY CREDIT.
...I FEEL LIKE THE ROOM IS SPINNING. OR THAT I'M SUDDENLY *UPSIDE DOWN.*
SPEAKING OF WHICH--LET ME SAY HOW MUCH I APPRECIATE HIS SACRIFICES AS CAPTAIN AMERICA.
I HAD NO IDEA. A WOMAN--A *LOVE*--WAITED BREATHLESSLY FOR HIM AS WE RUSHED INTO BULLETS AND BLOODSHED.
I APPRECIATE HEARING THAT.
SO *WHAT ELSE* DIDN'T I KNOW ABOUT BILL NASLUND?
BUT LET ME JUST LAY MY CARDS ON THE TABLE--
I KNOW FROM GENERAL MATHESON THAT NO LEADS EXIST YET ON WHERE THIS ANDROID CAME FROM, OR WHAT ORDERS IT WAS FOLLOWING.
I'M HERE TO OFFER OUR RESOURCES AND MY TECHNICAL EXPERTISE TO THE INVESTIGATION.
AND, PERSONALLY, I WOULD BE GRATEFUL FOR A CHANCE TO HONOR THE LEGACY OF MY GRANDFATHER.

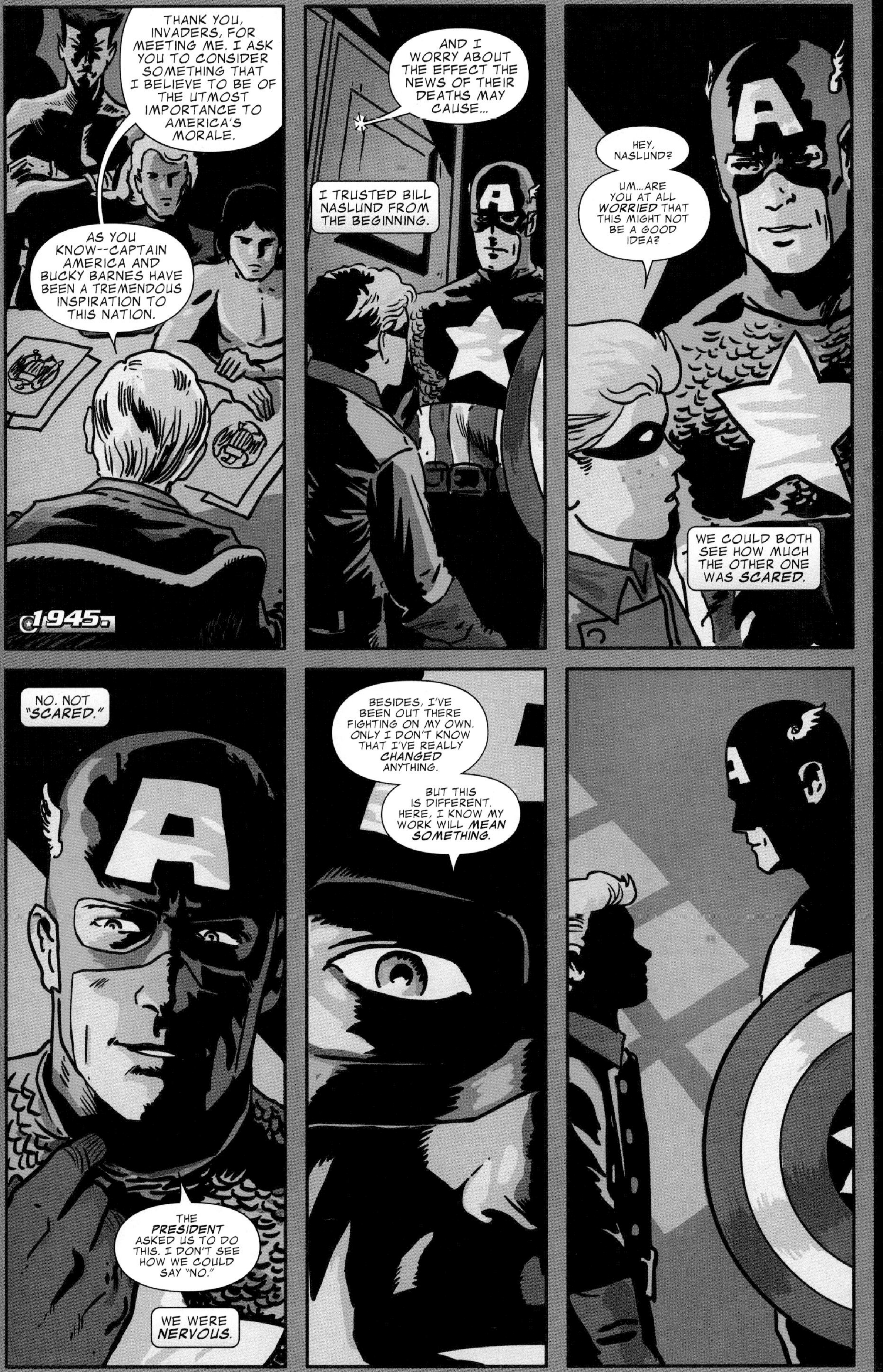
1945.
THANK YOU, INVADERS, FOR MEETING ME. I ASK YOU TO CONSIDER SOMETHING THAT I BELIEVE TO BE OF THE UTMOST IMPORTANCE TO AMERICA'S MORALE.
AS YOU KNOW--CAPTAIN AMERICA AND BUCKY BARNES HAVE BEEN A TREMENDOUS INSPIRATION TO THIS NATION.
AND I WORRY ABOUT THE EFFECT THE NEWS OF THEIR DEATHS MAY CAUSE...
I TRUSTED BILL NASLUND FROM THE BEGINNING.
HEY, NASLUND?
UM...ARE YOU AT ALL WORRIED THAT THIS MIGHT NOT BE A GOOD IDEA?
WE COULD BOTH SEE HOW MUCH THE OTHER ONE WAS SCARED.
NO. NOT "SCARED."
THE PRESIDENT ASKED US TO DO THIS. I DON'T SEE HOW WE COULD SAY "NO."
WE WERE NERVOUS.
BESIDES, I'VE BEEN OUT THERE FIGHTING ON MY OWN. ONLY I DON'T KNOW THAT I'VE REALLY CHANGED ANYTHING.
BUT THIS IS DIFFERENT. HERE, I KNOW MY WORK WILL MEAN SOMETHING.

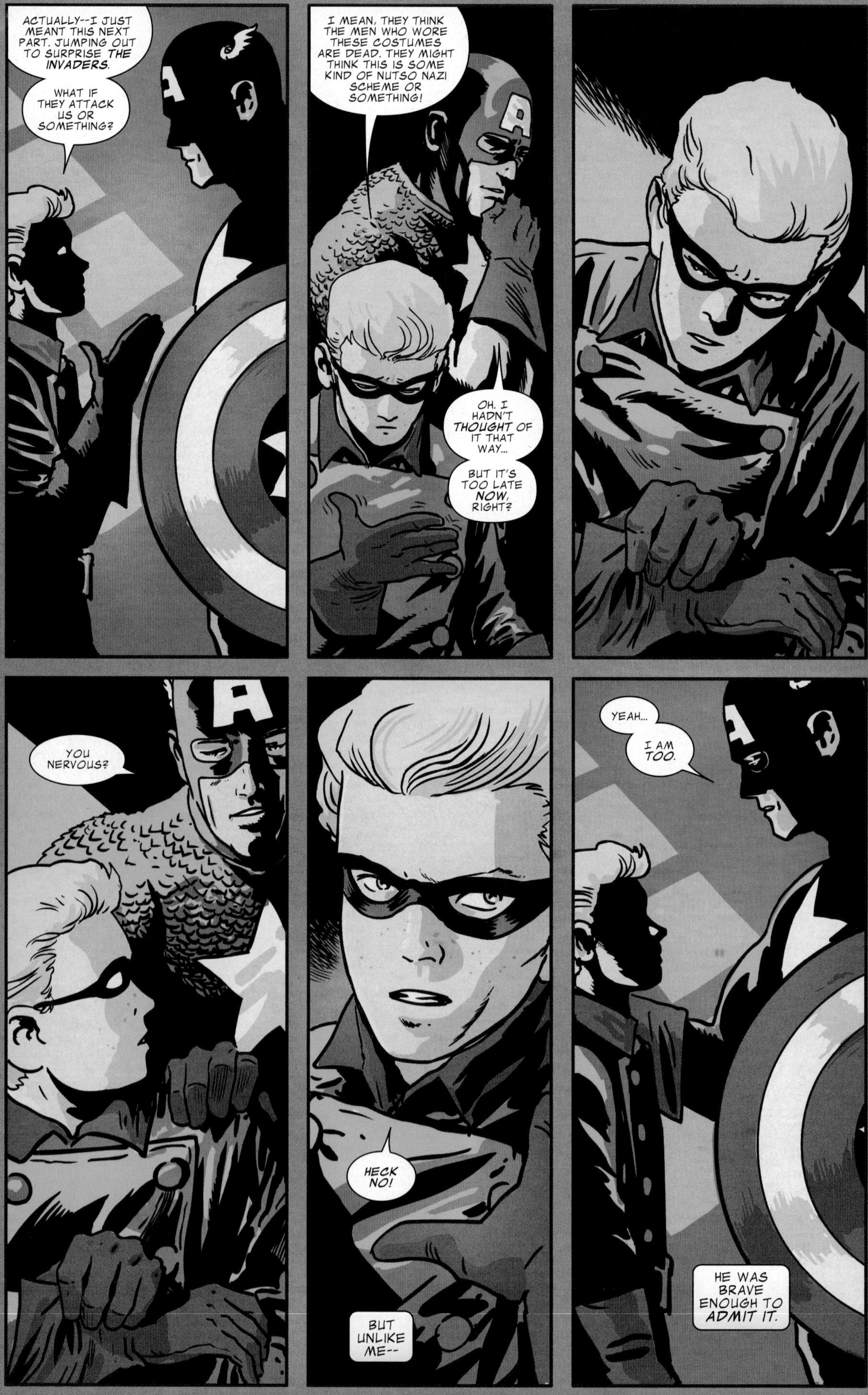
ACTUALLY--I JUST MEANT THIS NEXT PART. JUMPING OUT TO SURPRISE **THE INVADERS**.
WHAT IF THEY ATTACK US OR SOMETHING?
I MEAN, THEY THINK THE MEN WHO WORE THESE COSTUMES ARE DEAD. THEY MIGHT THINK THIS IS SOME KIND OF NUTSO NAZI SCHEME OR SOMETHING!
OH. I HADN'T *THOUGHT* OF IT THAT WAY...
BUT IT'S TOO LATE *NOW*, RIGHT?
YOU NERVOUS?
HECK NO!
BUT UNLIKE ME--
YEAH...
I AM *TOO*.
HE WAS BRAVE ENOUGH TO *ADMIT IT*.

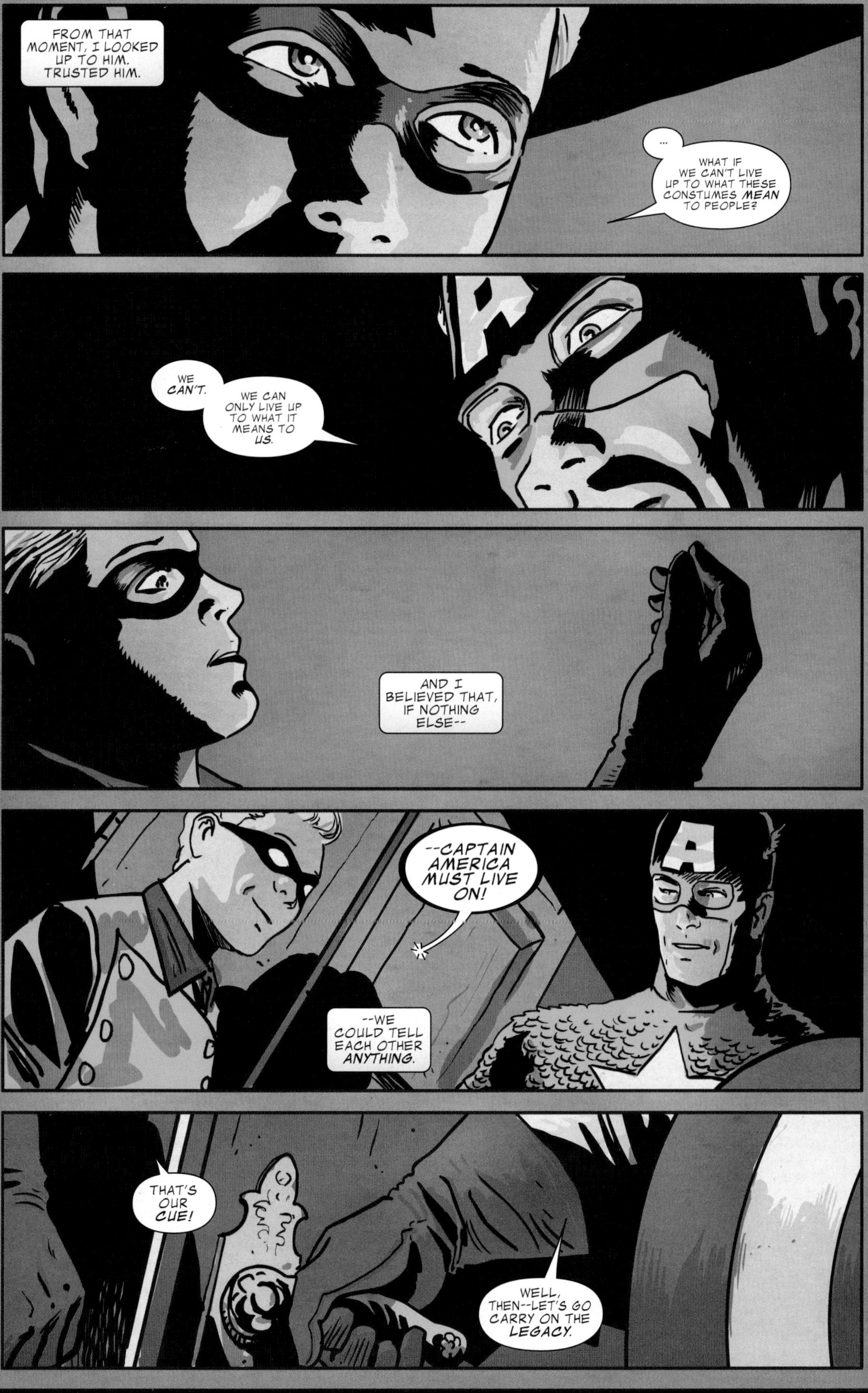
FROM THAT MOMENT, I LOOKED UP TO HIM. TRUSTED HIM.
...
WHAT IF WE CAN'T LIVE UP TO WHAT THESE CONSTUMES MEAN TO PEOPLE?
WE CAN'T.
WE CAN ONLY LIVE UP TO WHAT IT MEANS TO US.
AND I BELIEVED THAT, IF NOTHING ELSE--
--CAPTAIN AMERICA MUST LIVE ON!
--WE COULD TELL EACH OTHER ANYTHING.
THAT'S OUR CUE!
WELL, THEN--LET'S GO CARRY ON THE LEGACY.

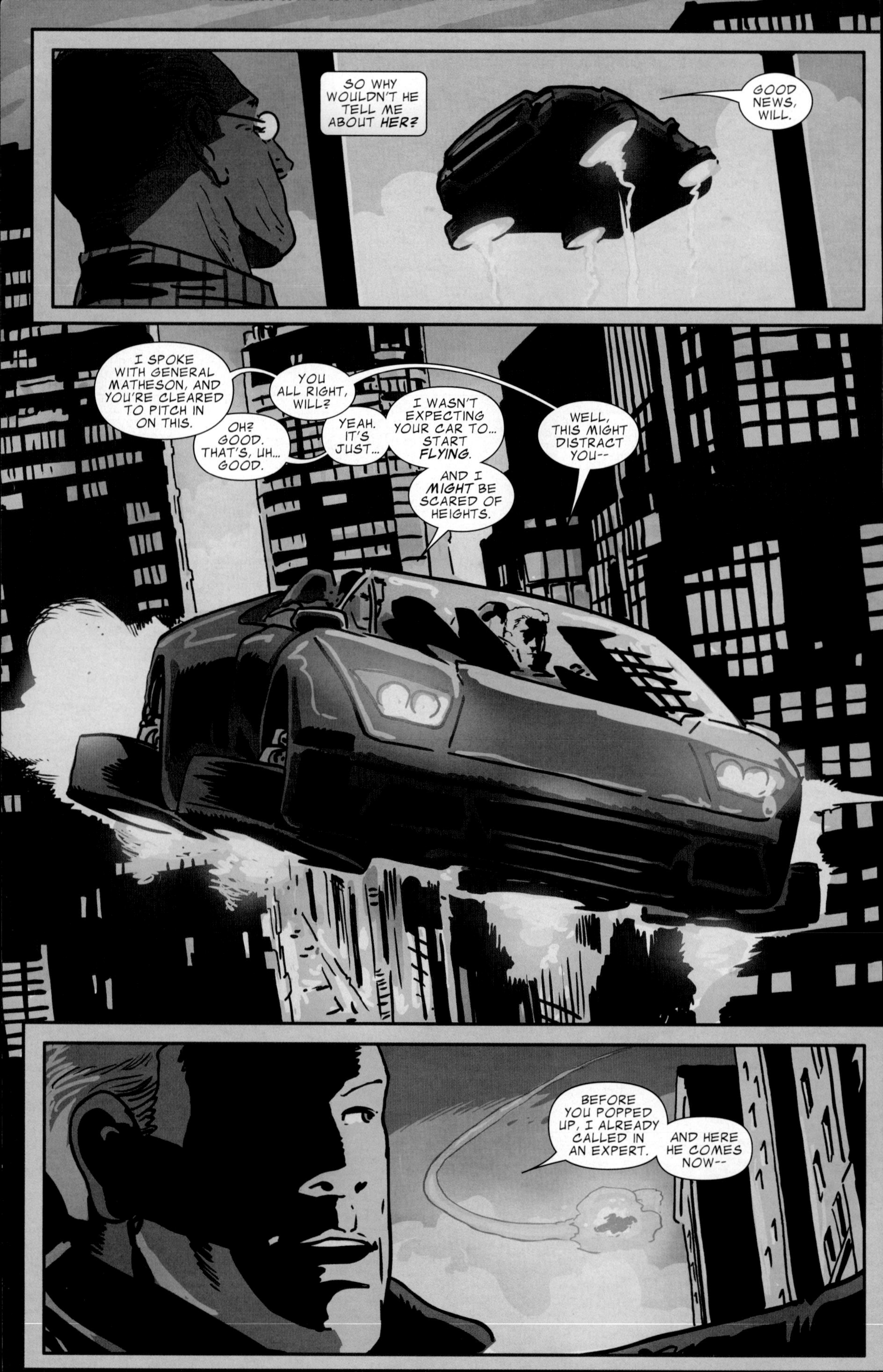
SO WHY WOULDN'T HE TELL ME ABOUT HER?
GOOD NEWS, WILL.
I SPOKE WITH GENERAL MATHESON, AND YOU'RE CLEARED TO PITCH IN ON THIS.
OH? GOOD. THAT'S, UH... GOOD.
YOU ALL RIGHT, WILL?
YEAH. IT'S JUST...
I WASN'T EXPECTING YOUR CAR TO... START FLYING.
AND I MIGHT BE SCARED OF HEIGHTS.
WELL, THIS MIGHT DISTRACT YOU--
BEFORE YOU POPPED UP, I ALREADY CALLED IN AN EXPERT.
AND HERE HE COMES NOW--

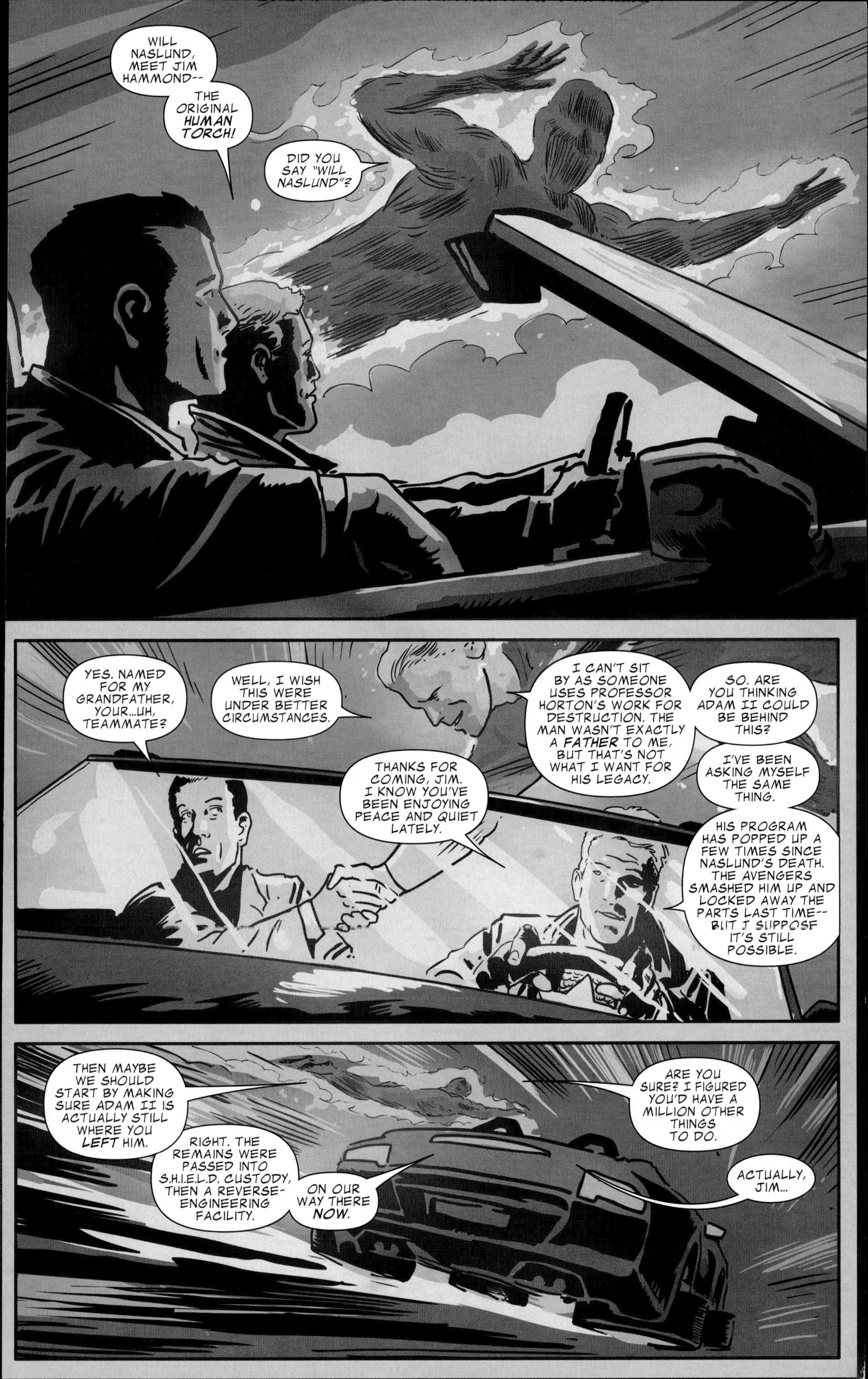
WILL NASLUND, MEET JIM HAMMOND--
THE ORIGINAL HUMAN TORCH!
DID YOU SAY "WILL NASLUND"?
YES. NAMED FOR MY GRANDFATHER, YOUR...UH, TEAMMATE?
WELL, I WISH THIS WERE UNDER BETTER CIRCUMSTANCES.
I CAN'T SIT BY AS SOMEONE USES PROFESSOR HORTON'S WORK FOR DESTRUCTION. THE MAN WASN'T EXACTLY A FATHER TO ME, BUT THAT'S NOT WHAT I WANT FOR HIS LEGACY.
THANKS FOR COMING, JIM. I KNOW YOU'VE BEEN ENJOYING PEACE AND QUIET LATELY.
SO. ARE YOU THINKING ADAM II COULD BE BEHIND THIS?
I'VE BEEN ASKING MYSELF THE SAME THING.
HIS PROGRAM HAS POPPED UP A FEW TIMES SINCE NASLUND'S DEATH. THE AVENGERS SMASHED HIM UP AND LOCKED AWAY THE PARTS LAST TIME-- BUT I SUPPOSE IT'S STILL POSSIBLE.
THEN MAYBE WE SHOULD START BY MAKING SURE ADAM II IS ACTUALLY STILL WHERE YOU LEFT HIM.
RIGHT. THE REMAINS WERE PASSED INTO S.H.I.E.L.D. CUSTODY, THEN A REVERSE-ENGINEERING FACILITY.
ON OUR WAY THERE NOW.
ARE YOU SURE? I FIGURED YOU'D HAVE A MILLION OTHER THINGS TO DO.
ACTUALLY, JIM...

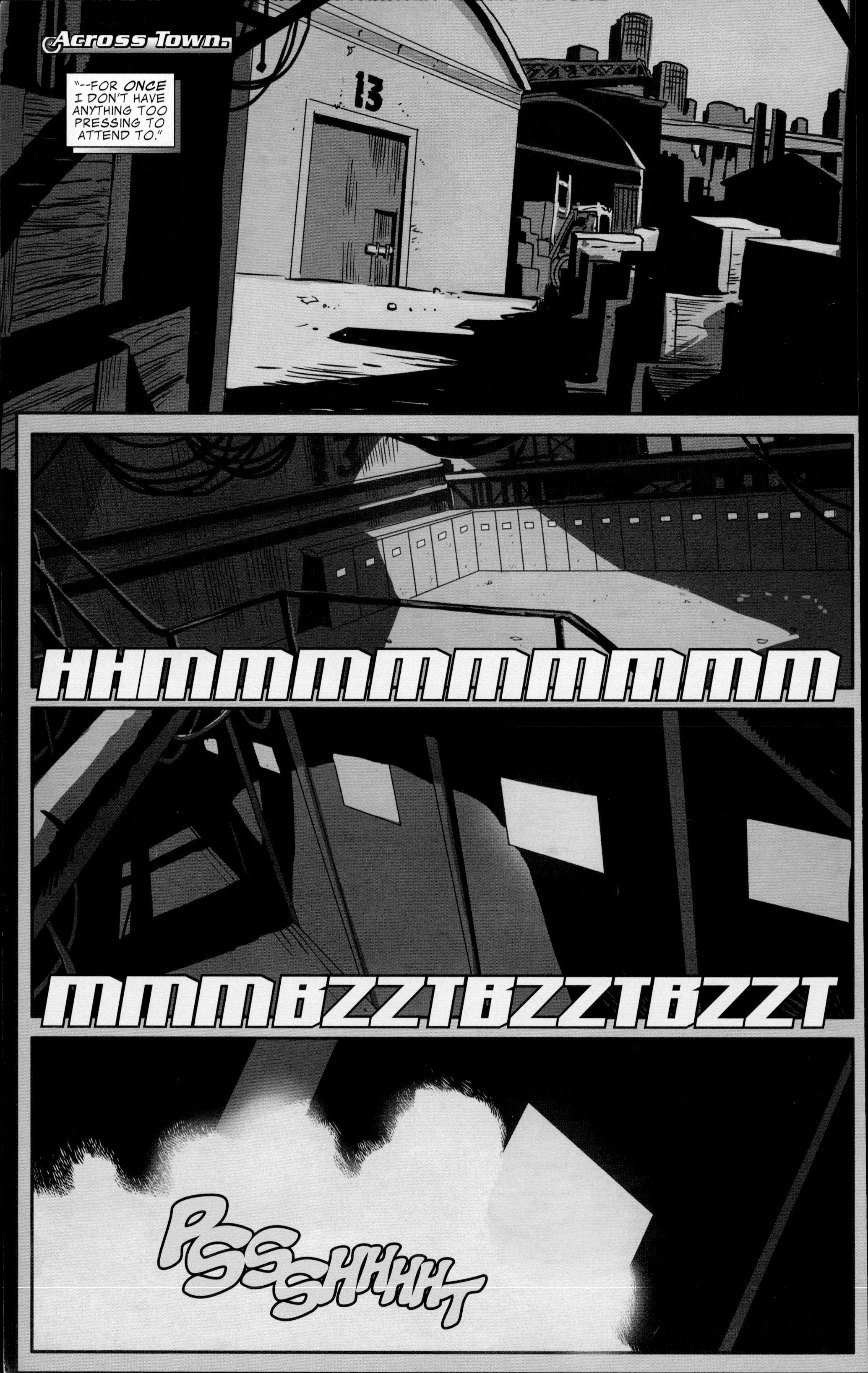
Across Town.
"--FOR ONCE I DON'T HAVE ANYTHING TOO PRESSING TO ATTEND TO."
13
HHMMMMMMMMMMM
MMMMBZZTBZZTBZZT
PSSSHHHHT

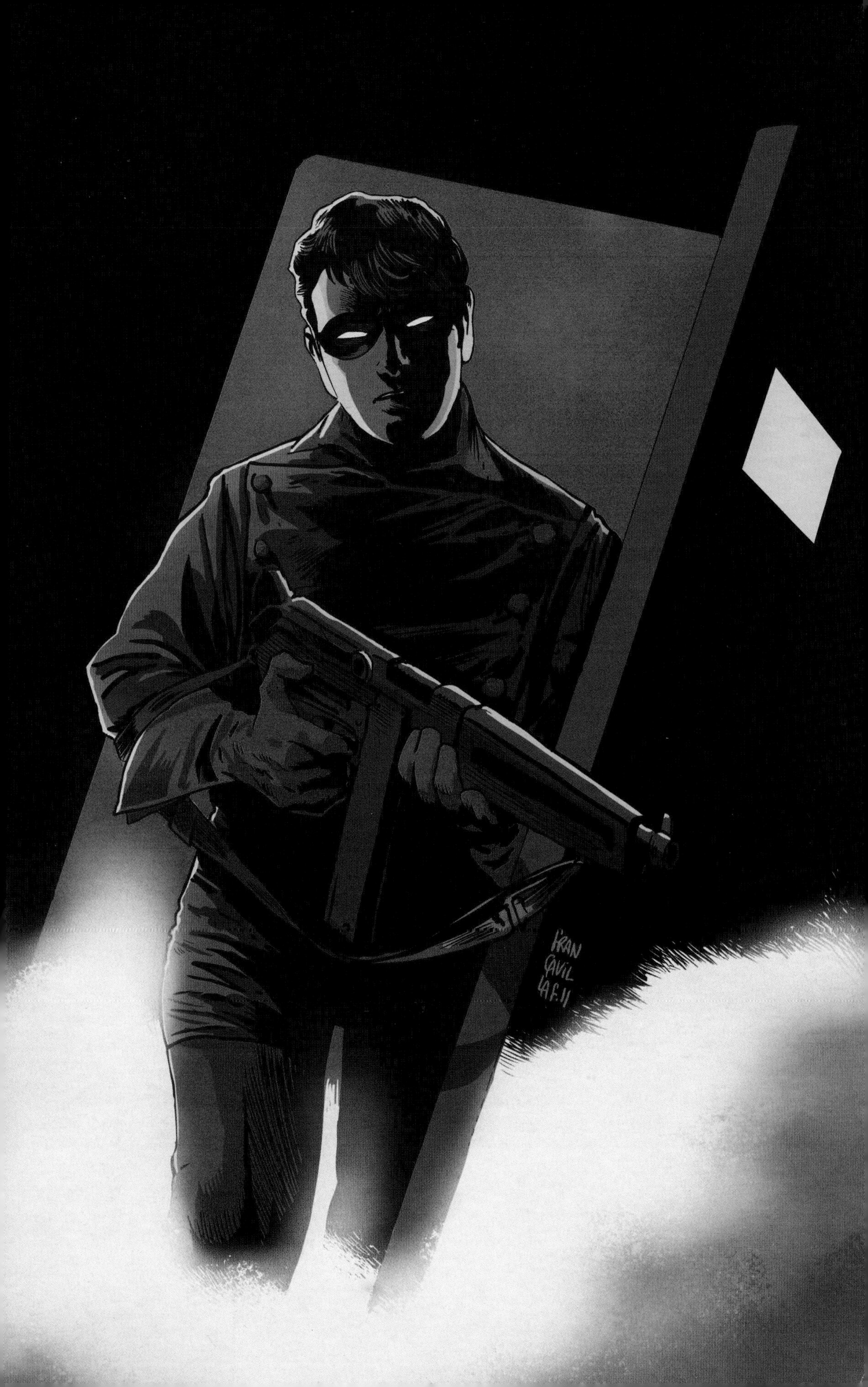

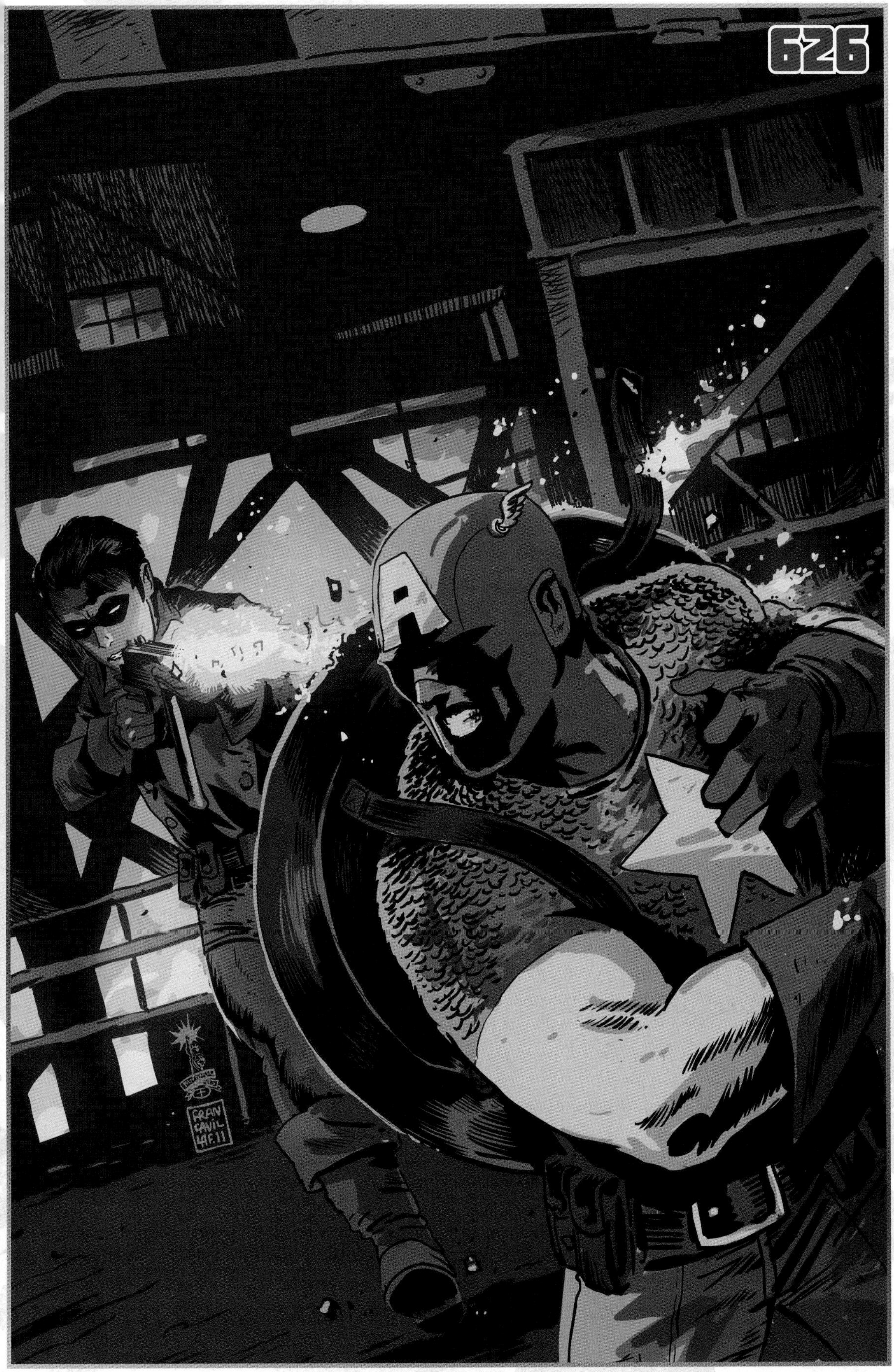
626

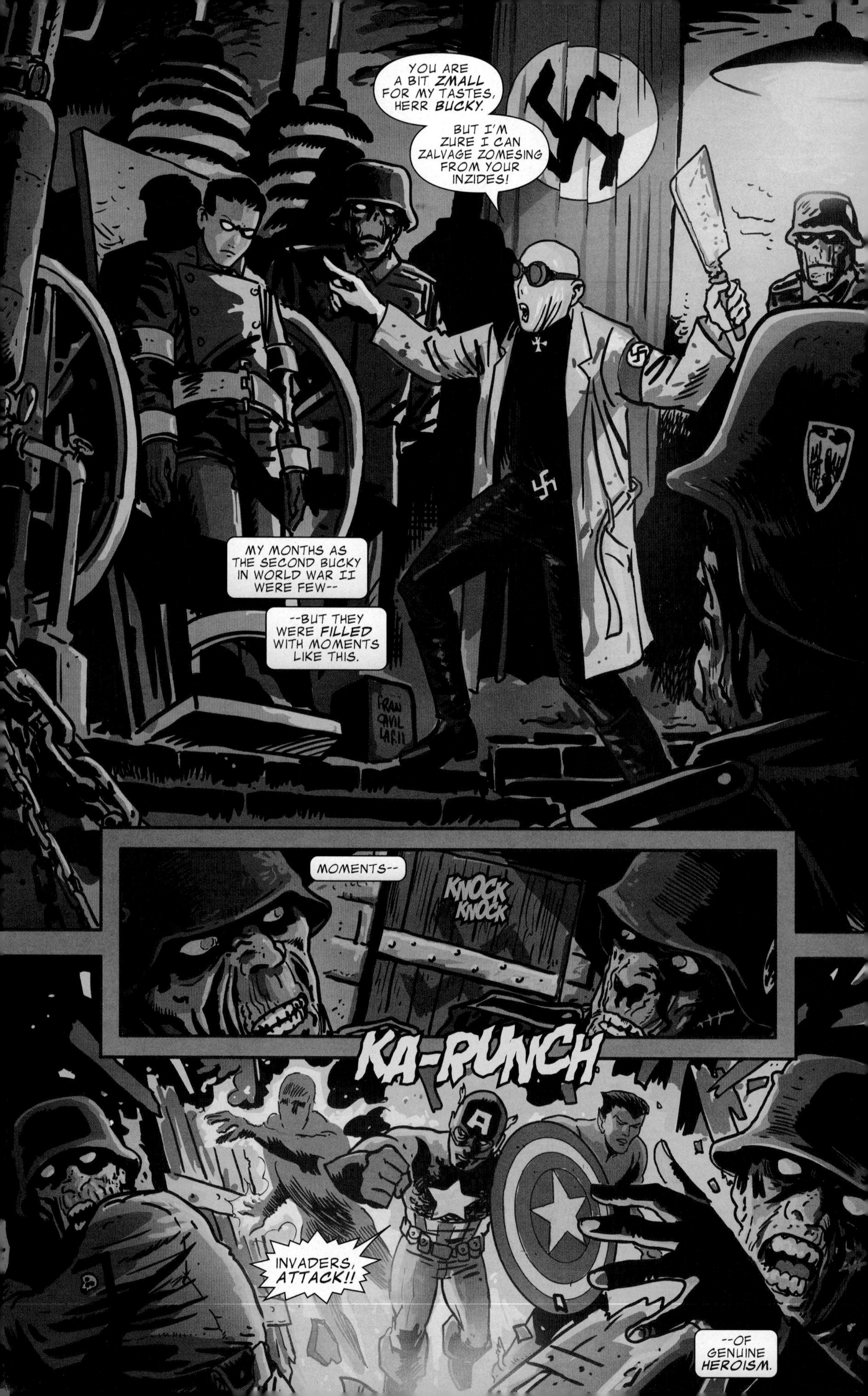
YOU ARE A BIT ZMALL FOR MY TASTES, HERR BUCKY.
BUT I'M ZURE I CAN ZALVAGE ZOMESING FROM YOUR INZIDES!
MY MONTHS AS THE SECOND BUCKY IN WORLD WAR II WERE FEW--
--BUT THEY WERE FILLED WITH MOMENTS LIKE THIS.
MOMENTS--
KNOCK KNOCK
KA-RUNCH
INVADERS, ATTACK!!
--OF GENUINE HEROISM.

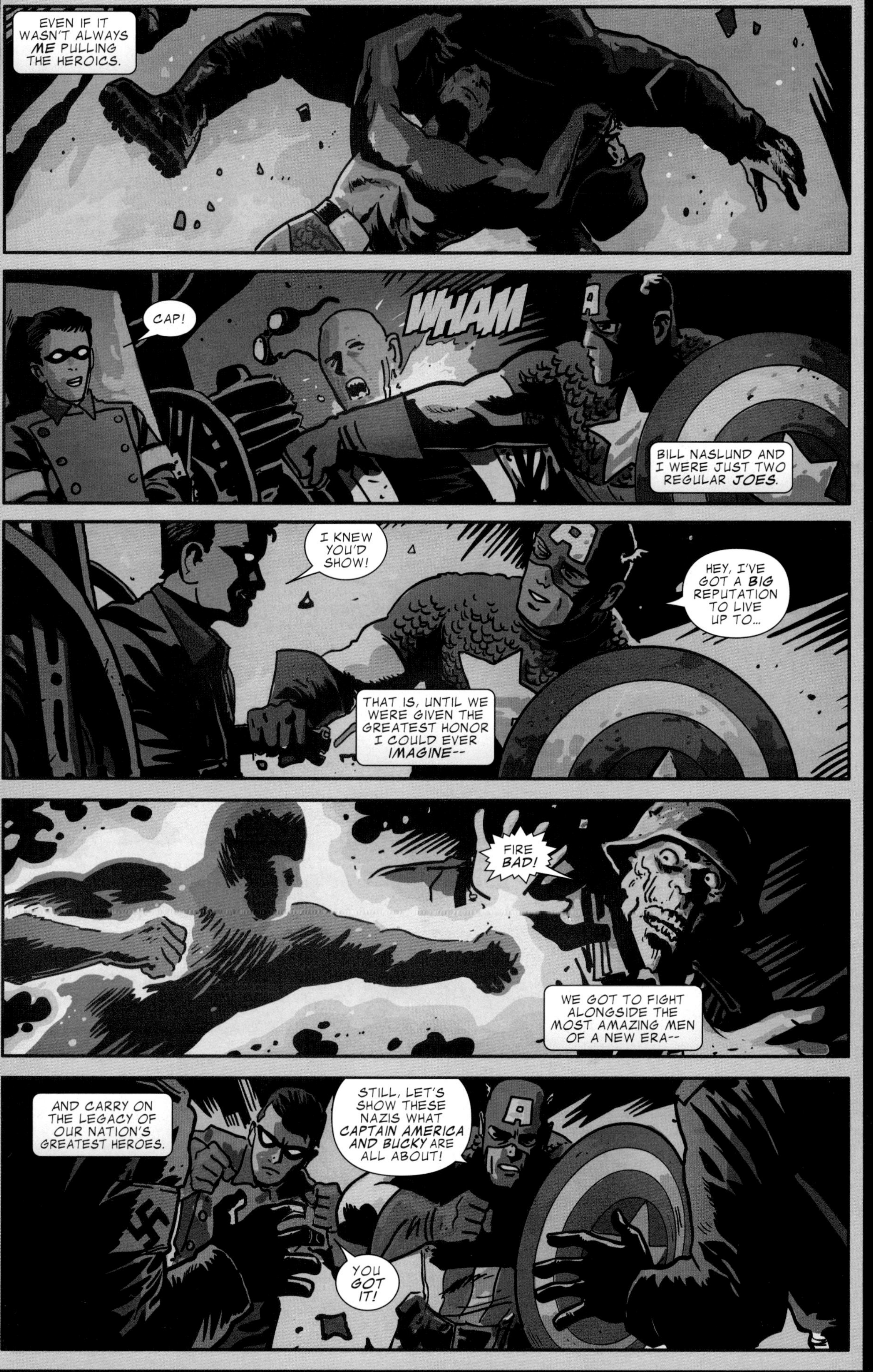

EVEN IF IT WASN'T ALWAYS ME PULLING THE HEROICS.
CAP!
WHAM
BILL NASLUND AND I WERE JUST TWO REGULAR JOES.
I KNEW YOU'D SHOW!
HEY, I'VE GOT A BIG REPUTATION TO LIVE UP TO...
THAT IS, UNTIL WE WERE GIVEN THE GREATEST HONOR I COULD EVER IMAGINE--
FIRE BAD!
WE GOT TO FIGHT ALONGSIDE THE MOST AMAZING MEN OF A NEW ERA--
AND CARRY ON THE LEGACY OF OUR NATION'S GREATEST HEROES.
STILL, LET'S SHOW THESE NAZIS WHAT CAPTAIN AMERICA AND BUCKY ARE ALL ABOUT!
YOU GOT IT!

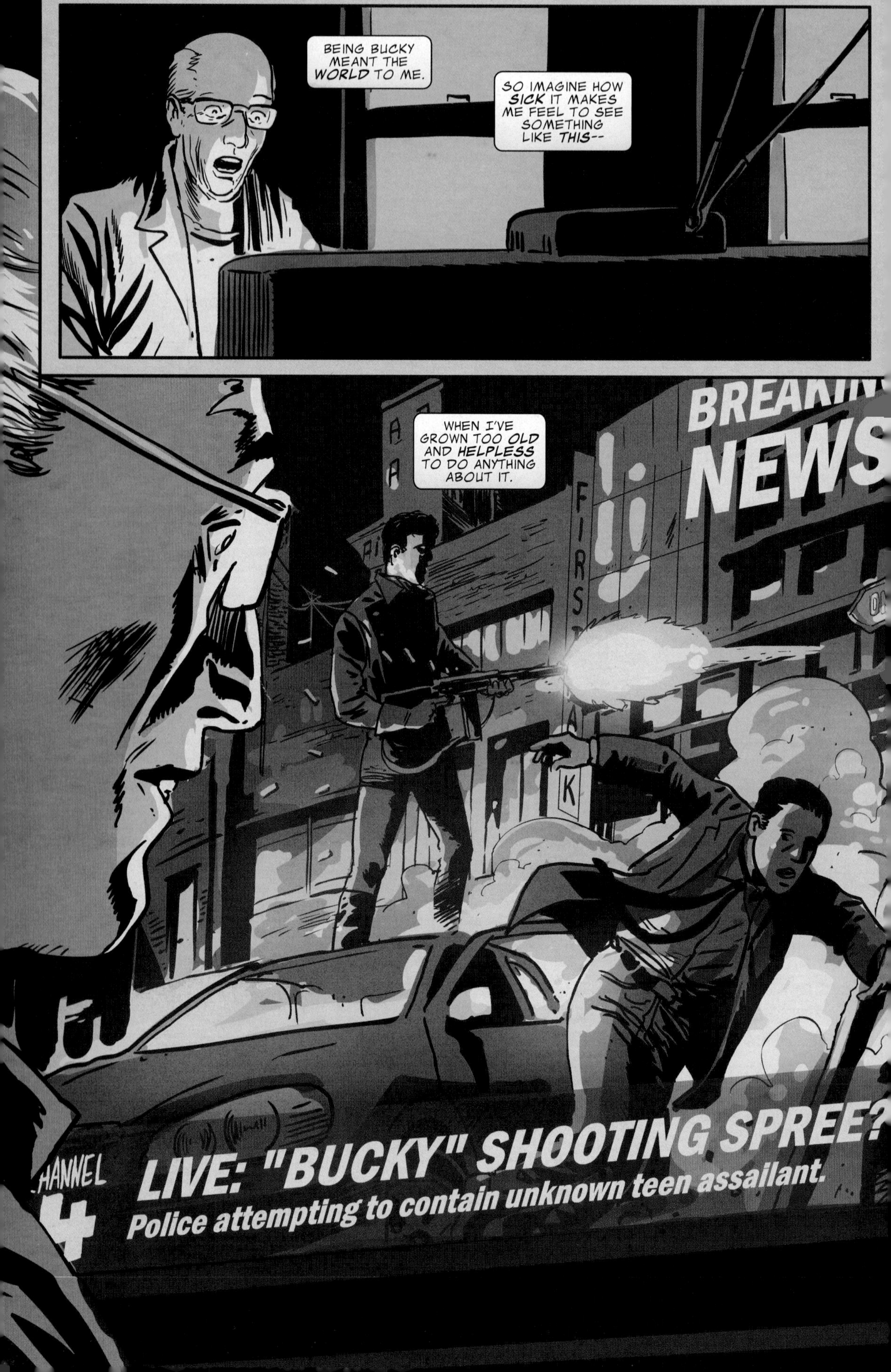
BEING BUCKY MEANT THE WORLD TO ME.
SO IMAGINE HOW SICK IT MAKES ME FEEL TO SEE SOMETHING LIKE THIS--
WHEN I'VE GROWN TOO OLD AND HELPLESS TO DO ANYTHING ABOUT IT.
BREAKIN
NEWS
CHANNEL 4
LIVE: "BUCKY" SHOOTING SPREE?
Police attempting to contain unknown teen assailant.

Pentagon-Operated Advanced and Alien Technologies Reverse-Engineering Facility.

Hoboken, New Jersey.

CAPTAIN AMERICA, SIR! I APOLOGIZE FOR THE DELAY.

BUT HERE ARE THE ADAM II ANDROID REMAINS. THEY WERE STORED PRETTY **DEEP.**

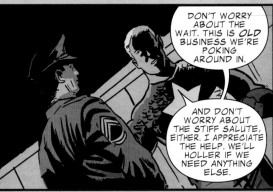

DON'T WORRY ABOUT THE WAIT. THIS IS **OLD** BUSINESS WE'RE POKING AROUND IN.

AND DON'T WORRY ABOUT THE STIFF SALUTE, EITHER. I APPRECIATE THE HELP. WE'LL HOLLER IF WE NEED ANYTHING ELSE.

IF YOU DIDN'T WANT TO BE SALUTED, WHY DID YOU CHANGE INTO THE UNIFORM?

SAME REASON I HAD YOU MAKE A FLYING, BURNING ENTRANCE AS **THE TORCH,** JIM.

IT'S THE KIND OF **SHOCK AND AWE** THAT BYPASSES A LOT OF BUREAUCRATIC PAPERWORK--

SO WE CAN FIGURE OUT IF THIS THING WAS SOMEHOW BEHIND THE ANDROID ATTACK ON FRED DAVIS.

BZZT BZZT

THAT NOISE--?

OH, GOD! IT'S **ALIVE!**

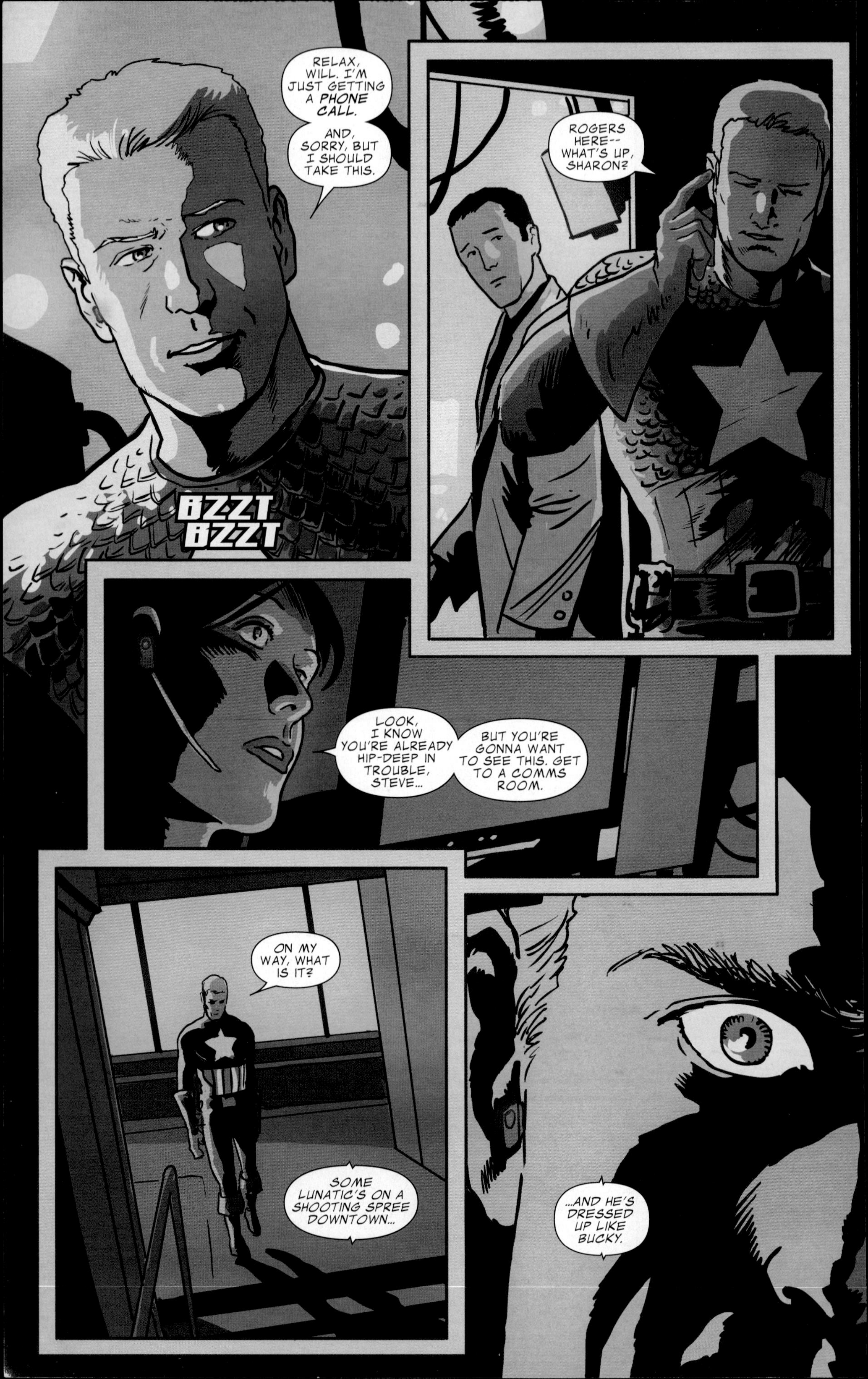
RELAX, WILL. I'M JUST GETTING A PHONE CALL.
AND, SORRY, BUT I SHOULD TAKE THIS.
BZZT BZZT
ROGERS HERE-- WHAT'S UP, SHARON?
LOOK, I KNOW YOU'RE ALREADY HIP-DEEP IN TROUBLE, STEVE...
BUT YOU'RE GONNA WANT TO SEE THIS. GET TO A COMMS ROOM.
ON MY WAY, WHAT IS IT?
SOME LUNATIC'S ON A SHOOTING SPREE DOWNTOWN...
...AND HE'S DRESSED UP LIKE BUCKY.

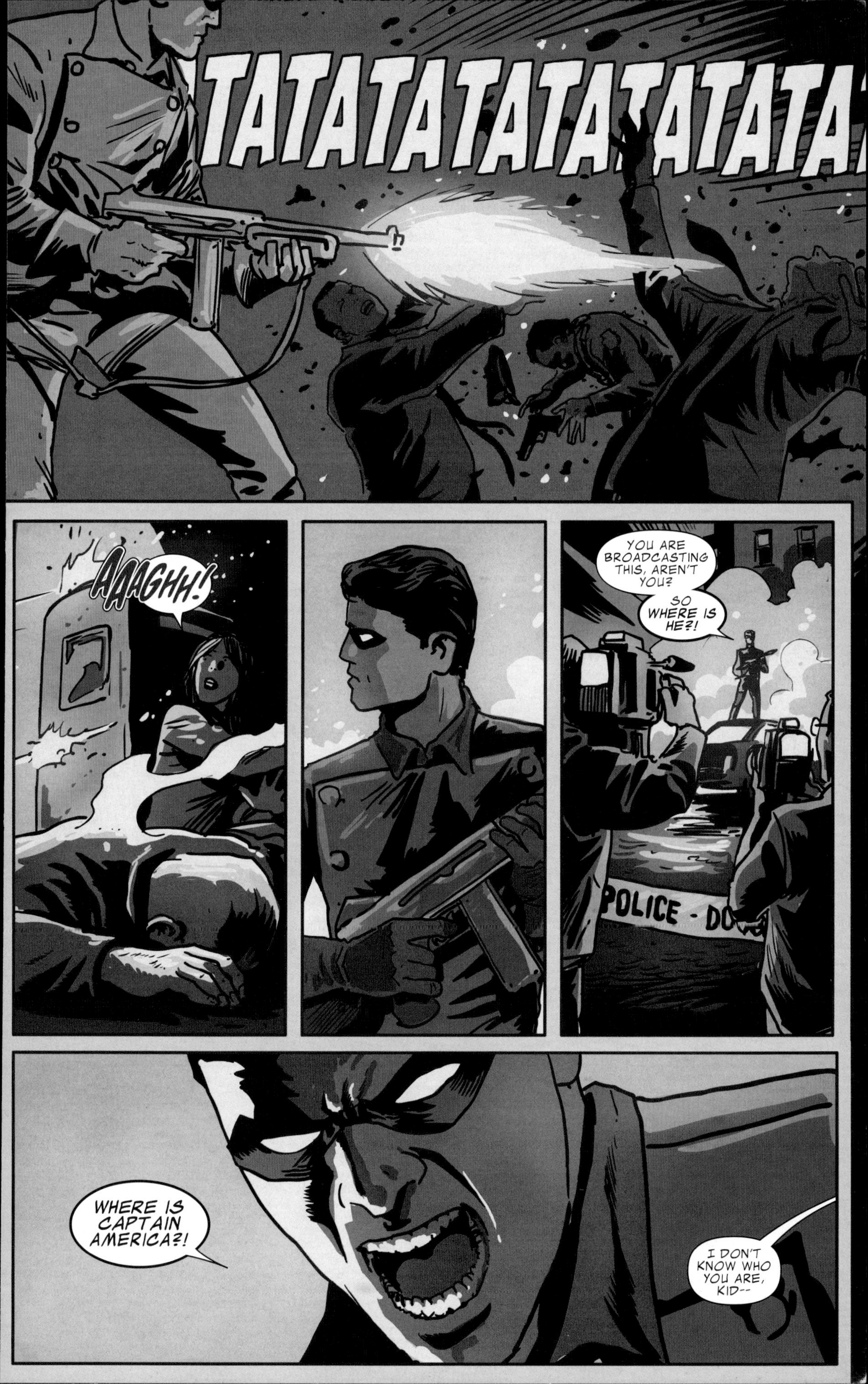
TATATATATATATATATA
AAAGHH!
YOU ARE BROADCASTING THIS, AREN'T YOU?
SO WHERE IS HE?!
POLICE - DO
WHERE IS CAPTAIN AMERICA?!
I DON'T KNOW WHO YOU ARE, KID--

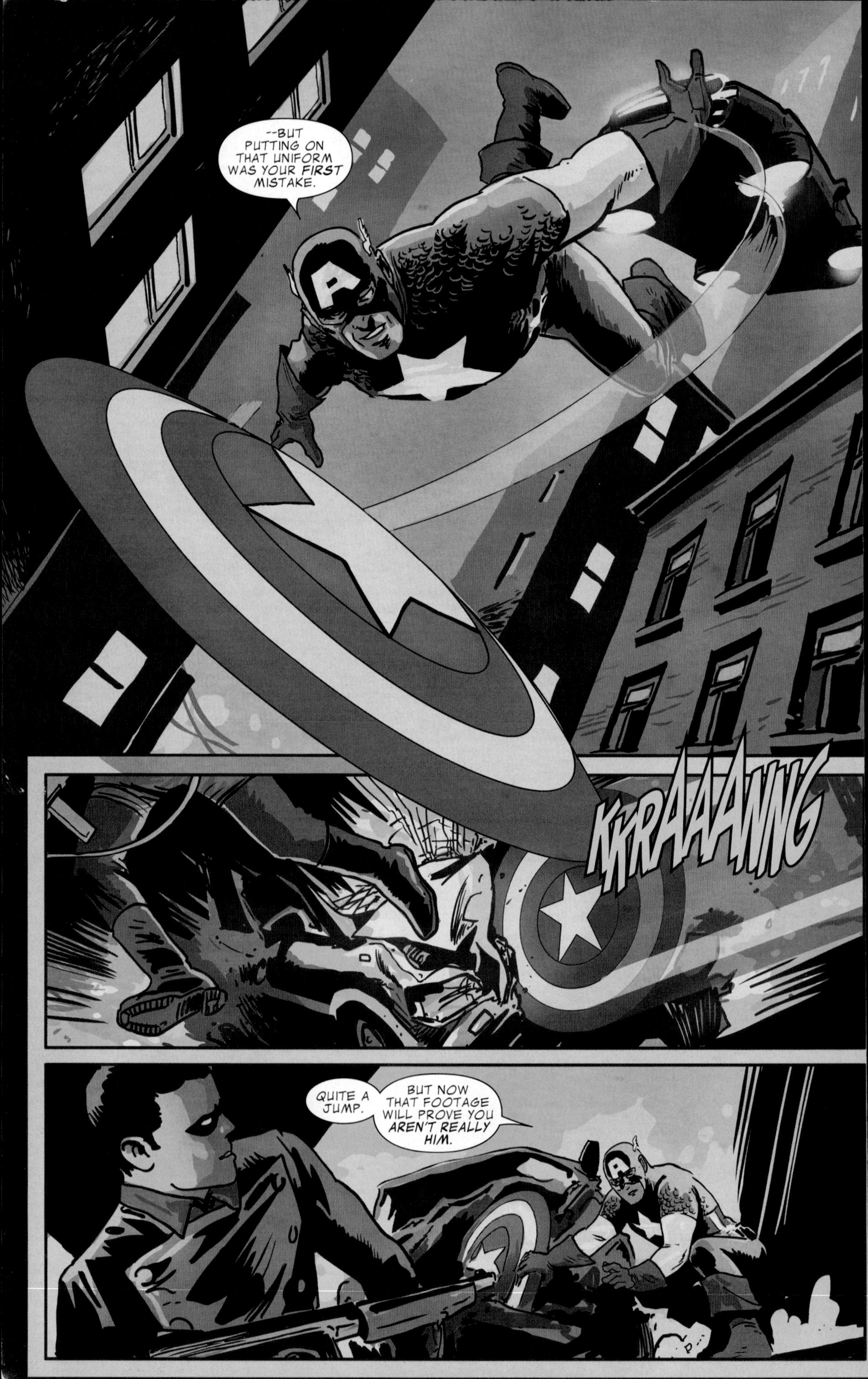

--BUT PUTTING ON THAT UNIFORM WAS YOUR FIRST MISTAKE.
KKRAAAANNG
QUITE A JUMP.
BUT NOW THAT FOOTAGE WILL PROVE YOU AREN'T REALLY HIM.

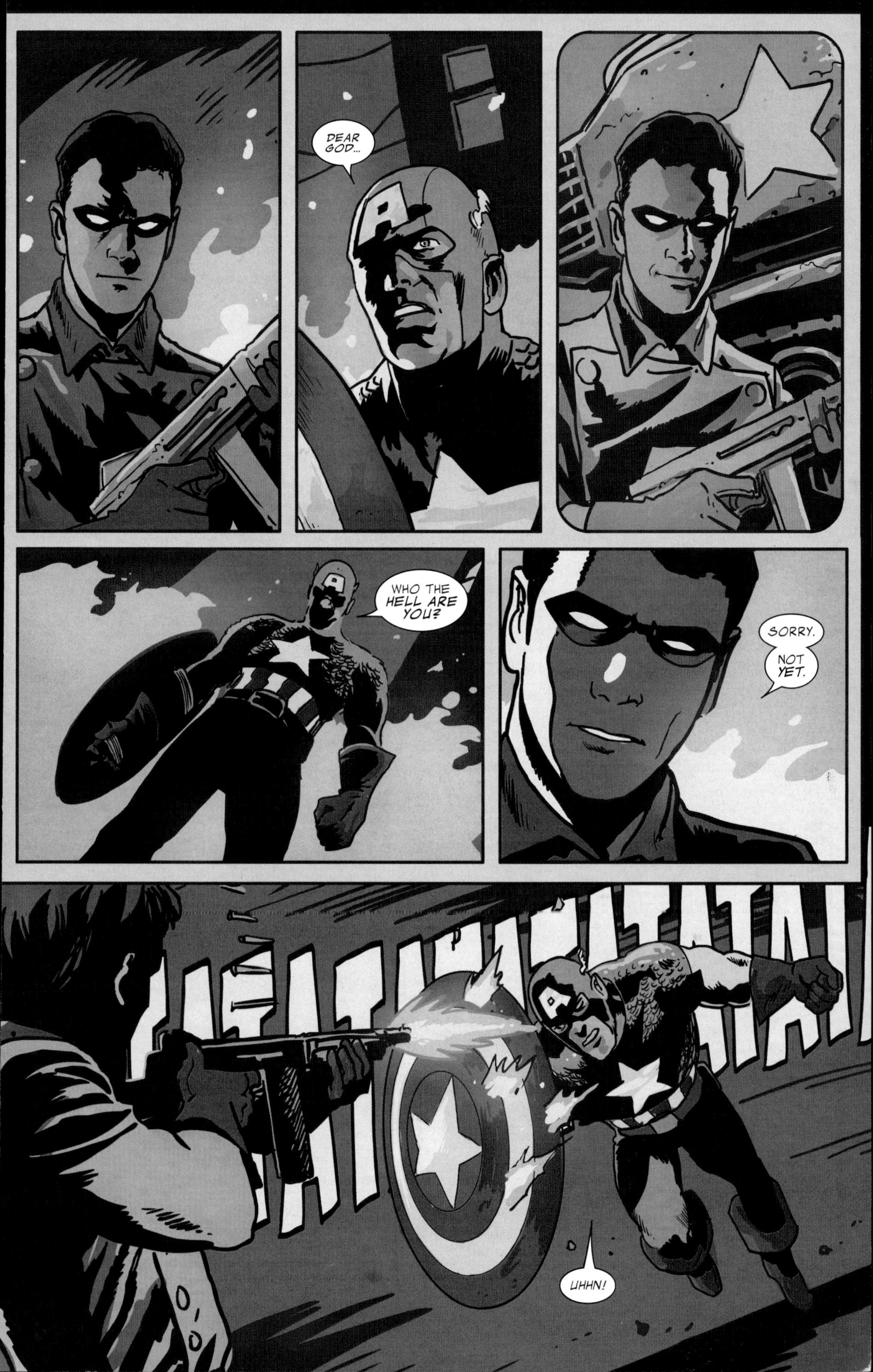
DEAR GOD...
WHO THE HELL ARE YOU?
SORRY.
NOT YET.
UHHN!

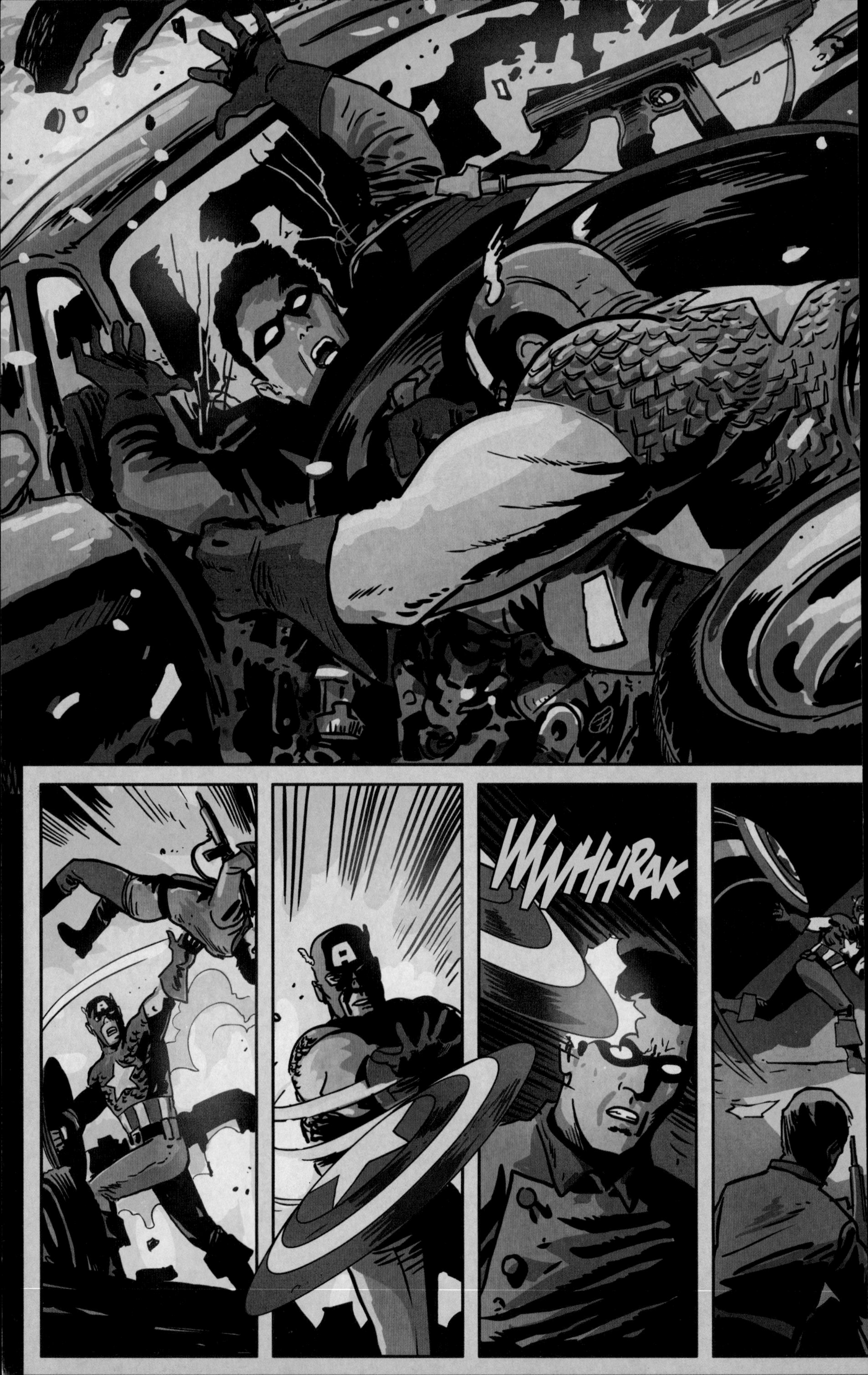
WWHHRAK

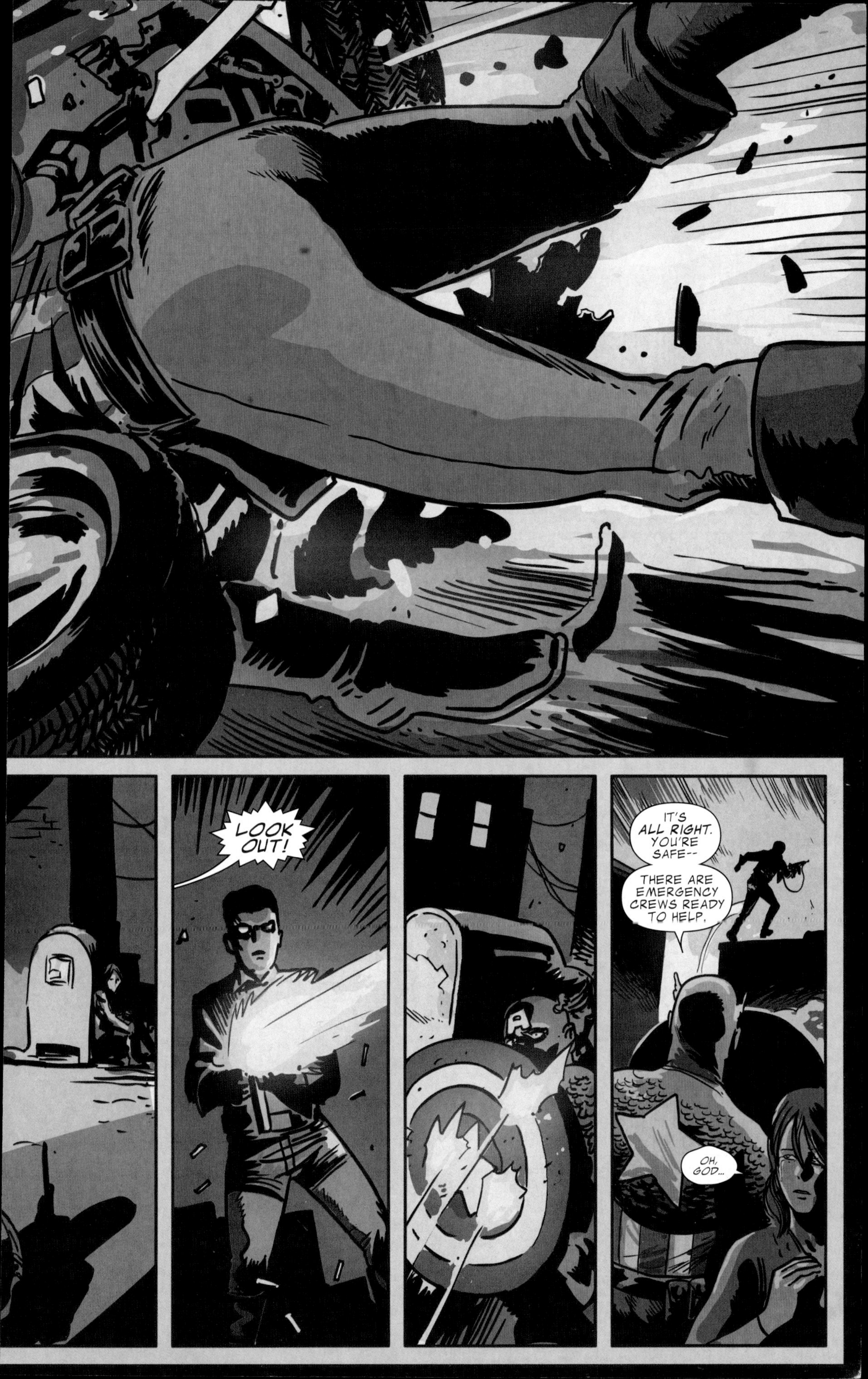
LOOK OUT!
IT'S ALL RIGHT. YOU'RE SAFE--
THERE ARE EMERGENCY CREWS READY TO HELP.
OH, GOD...

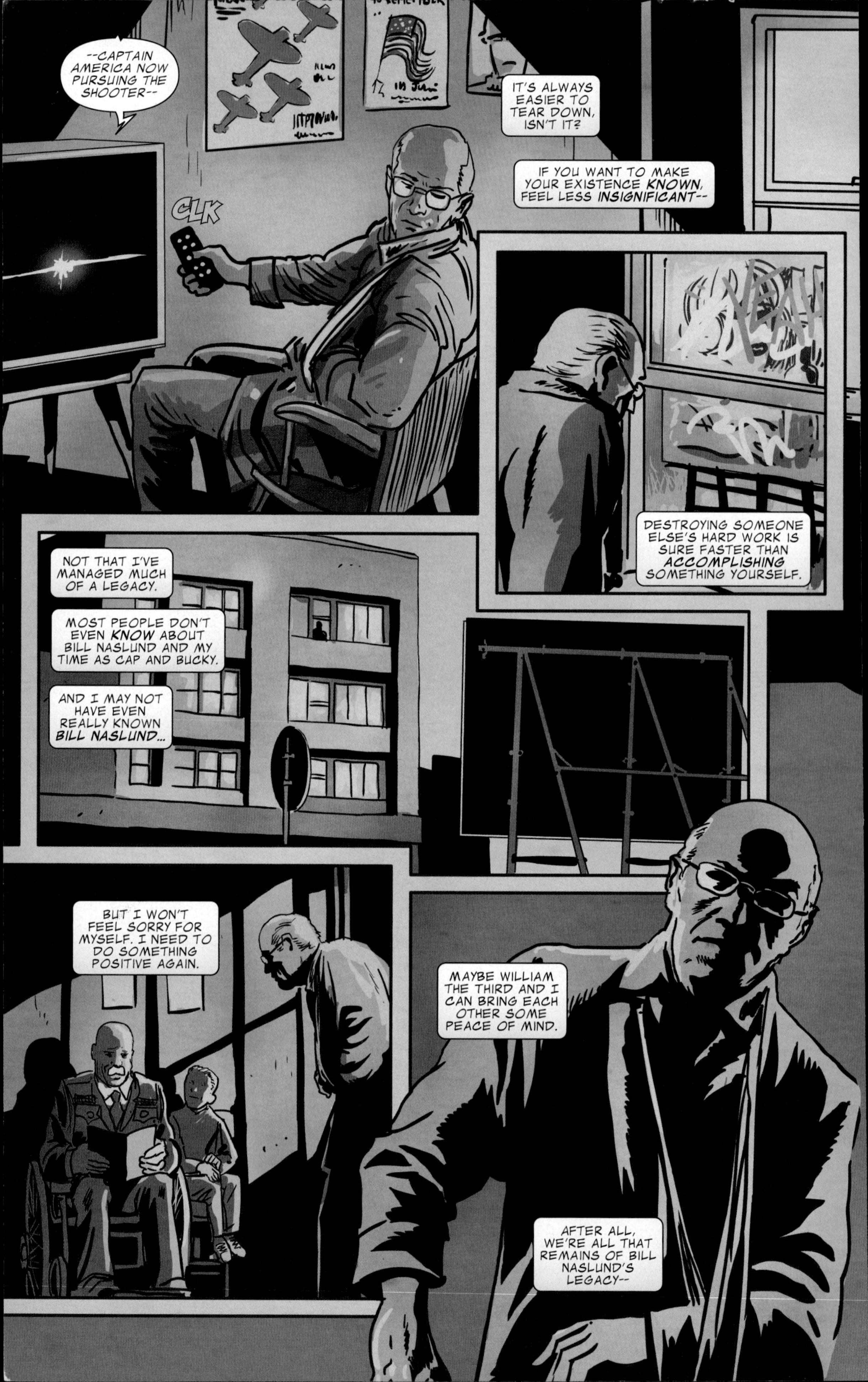
--CAPTAIN AMERICA NOW PURSUING THE SHOOTER--
CLK
IT'S ALWAYS EASIER TO TEAR DOWN, ISN'T IT?
IF YOU WANT TO MAKE YOUR EXISTENCE KNOWN, FEEL LESS INSIGNIFICANT--
DESTROYING SOMEONE ELSE'S HARD WORK IS SURE FASTER THAN ACCOMPLISHING SOMETHING YOURSELF.
NOT THAT I'VE MANAGED MUCH OF A LEGACY.
MOST PEOPLE DON'T EVEN KNOW ABOUT BILL NASLUND AND MY TIME AS CAP AND BUCKY.
AND I MAY NOT HAVE EVEN REALLY KNOWN BILL NASLUND...
BUT I WON'T FEEL SORRY FOR MYSELF. I NEED TO DO SOMETHING POSITIVE AGAIN.
MAYBE WILLIAM THE THIRD AND I CAN BRING EACH OTHER SOME PEACE OF MIND.
AFTER ALL, WE'RE ALL THAT REMAINS OF BILL NASLUND'S LEGACY--

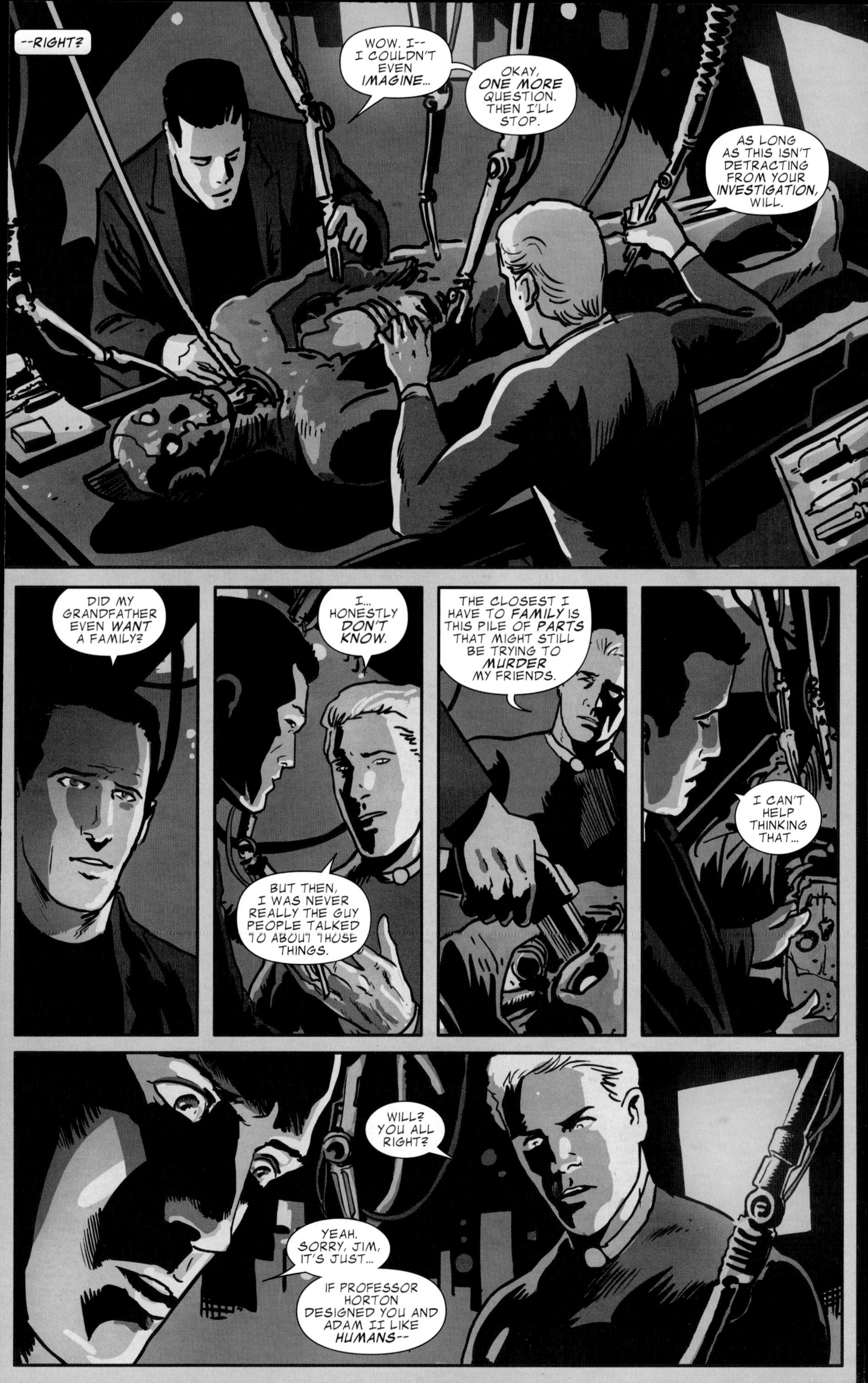
--RIGHT?
WOW. I-- I COULDN'T EVEN IMAGINE...
OKAY, ONE MORE QUESTION. THEN I'LL STOP.
AS LONG AS THIS ISN'T DETRACTING FROM YOUR INVESTIGATION, WILL.
DID MY GRANDFATHER EVEN WANT A FAMILY?
I... HONESTLY DON'T KNOW.
BUT THEN, I WAS NEVER REALLY THE GUY PEOPLE TALKED TO ABOUT THOSE THINGS.
THE CLOSEST I HAVE TO FAMILY IS THIS PILE OF PARTS THAT MIGHT STILL BE TRYING TO MURDER MY FRIENDS.
I CAN'T HELP THINKING THAT...
WILL? YOU ALL RIGHT?
YEAH. SORRY, JIM, IT'S JUST...
IF PROFESSOR HORTON DESIGNED YOU AND ADAM II LIKE HUMANS--

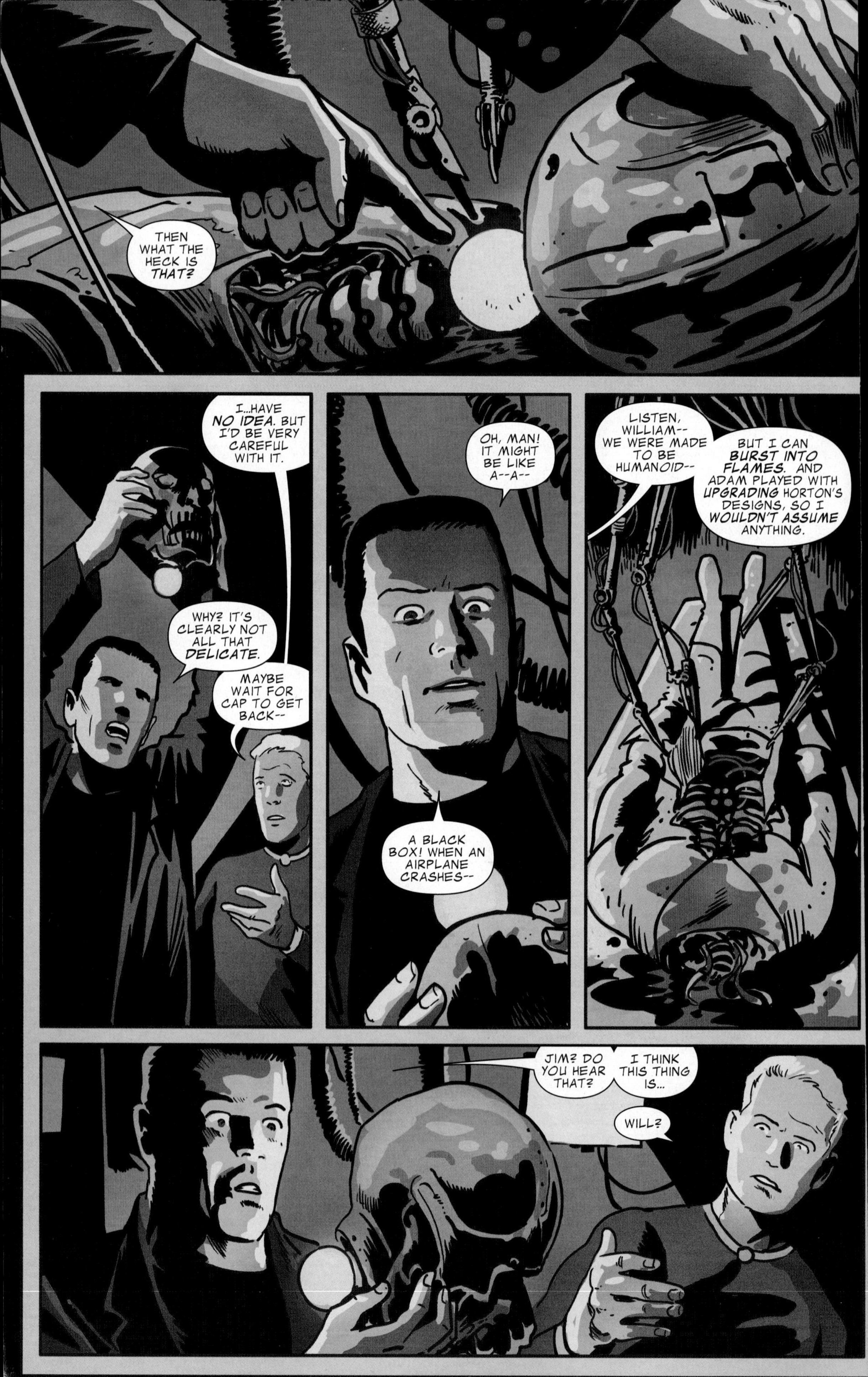
THEN WHAT THE HECK IS THAT?
I...HAVE NO IDEA. BUT I'D BE VERY CAREFUL WITH IT.
WHY? IT'S CLEARLY NOT ALL THAT DELICATE.
MAYBE WAIT FOR CAP TO GET BACK--
OH, MAN! IT MIGHT BE LIKE A--A--
A BLACK BOX! WHEN AN AIRPLANE CRASHES--
LISTEN, WILLIAM-- WE WERE MADE TO BE HUMANOID--
BUT I CAN BURST INTO FLAMES. AND ADAM PLAYED WITH UPGRADING HORTON'S DESIGNS, SO I WOULDN'T ASSUME ANYTHING.
JIM? DO YOU HEAR THAT?
I THINK THIS THING IS...
WILL?

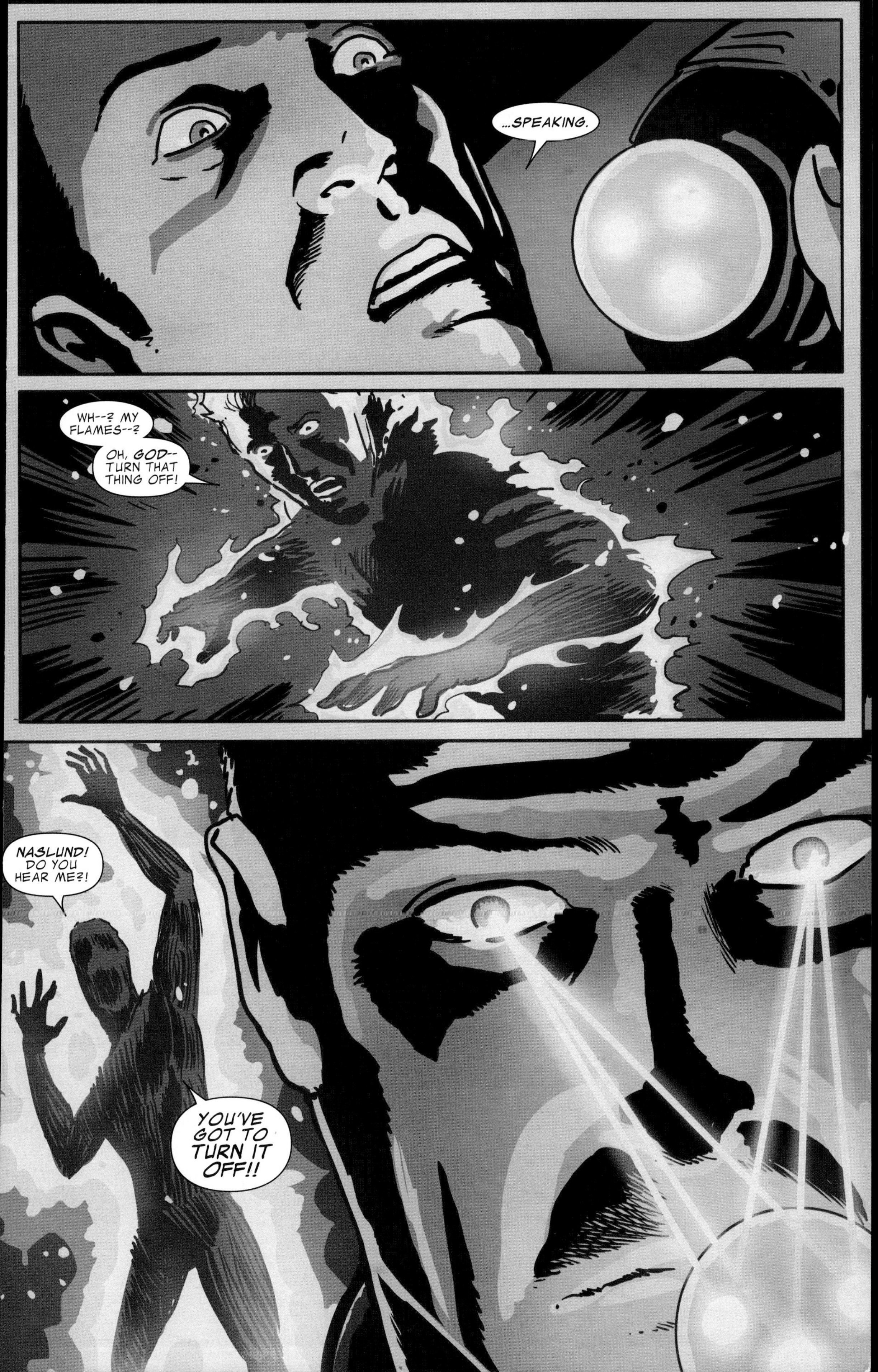
...SPEAKING.
WH--? MY FLAMES--?
OH, GOD-- TURN THAT THING OFF!
NASLUND! DO YOU HEAR ME?!
YOU'VE GOT TO TURN IT OFF!!

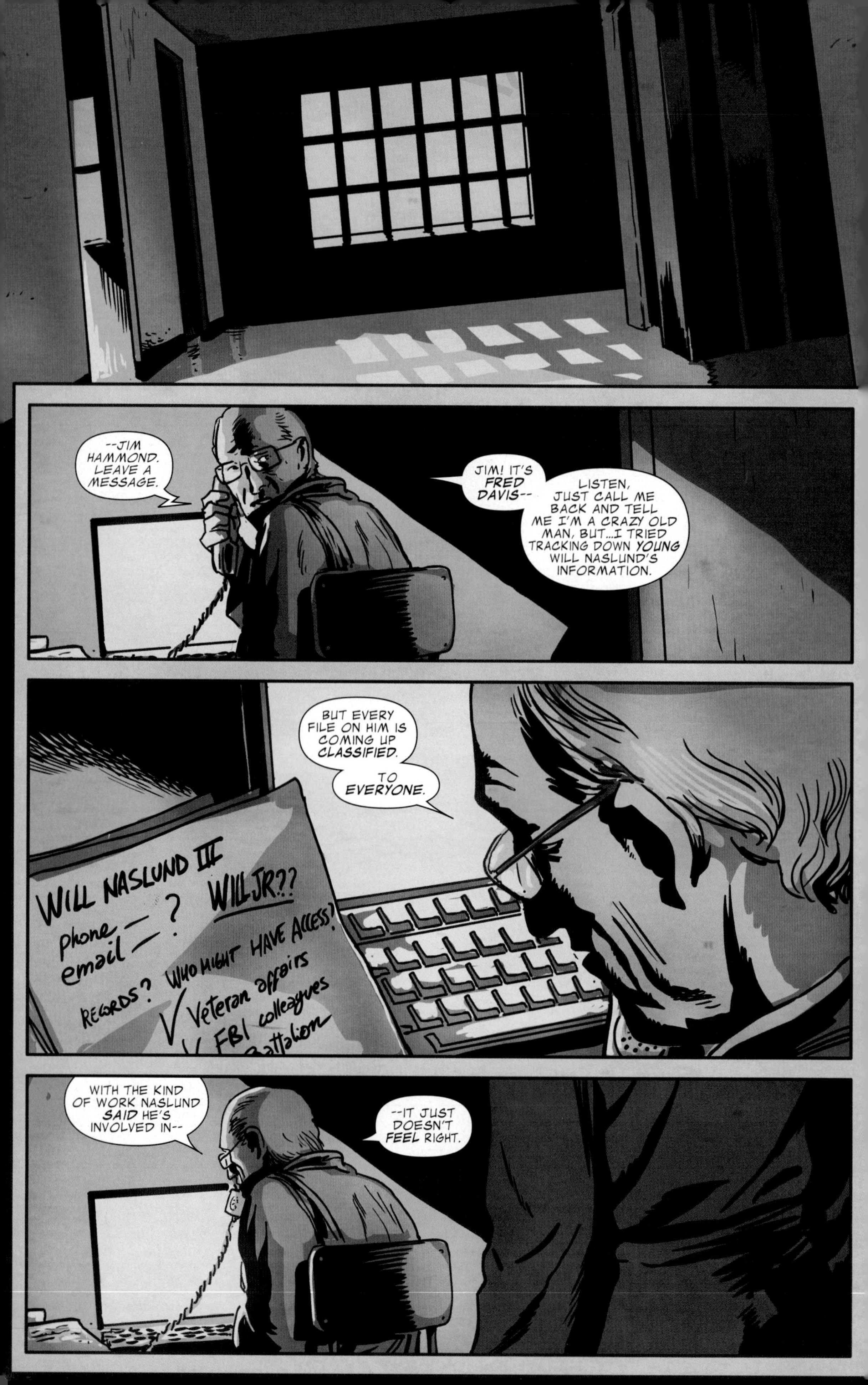
--JIM HAMMOND. LEAVE A MESSAGE.
JIM! IT'S FRED DAVIS--
LISTEN, JUST CALL ME BACK AND TELL ME I'M A CRAZY OLD MAN, BUT...I TRIED TRACKING DOWN YOUNG WILL NASLUND'S INFORMATION.
BUT EVERY FILE ON HIM IS COMING UP CLASSIFIED.
TO EVERYONE.
WILL NASLUND III
WILL JR??
phone — ?
email —
RECORDS? WHO MIGHT HAVE ACCESS?
Veteran affairs
FBI colleagues
WITH THE KIND OF WORK NASLUND SAID HE'S INVOLVED IN--
--IT JUST DOESN'T FEEL RIGHT.

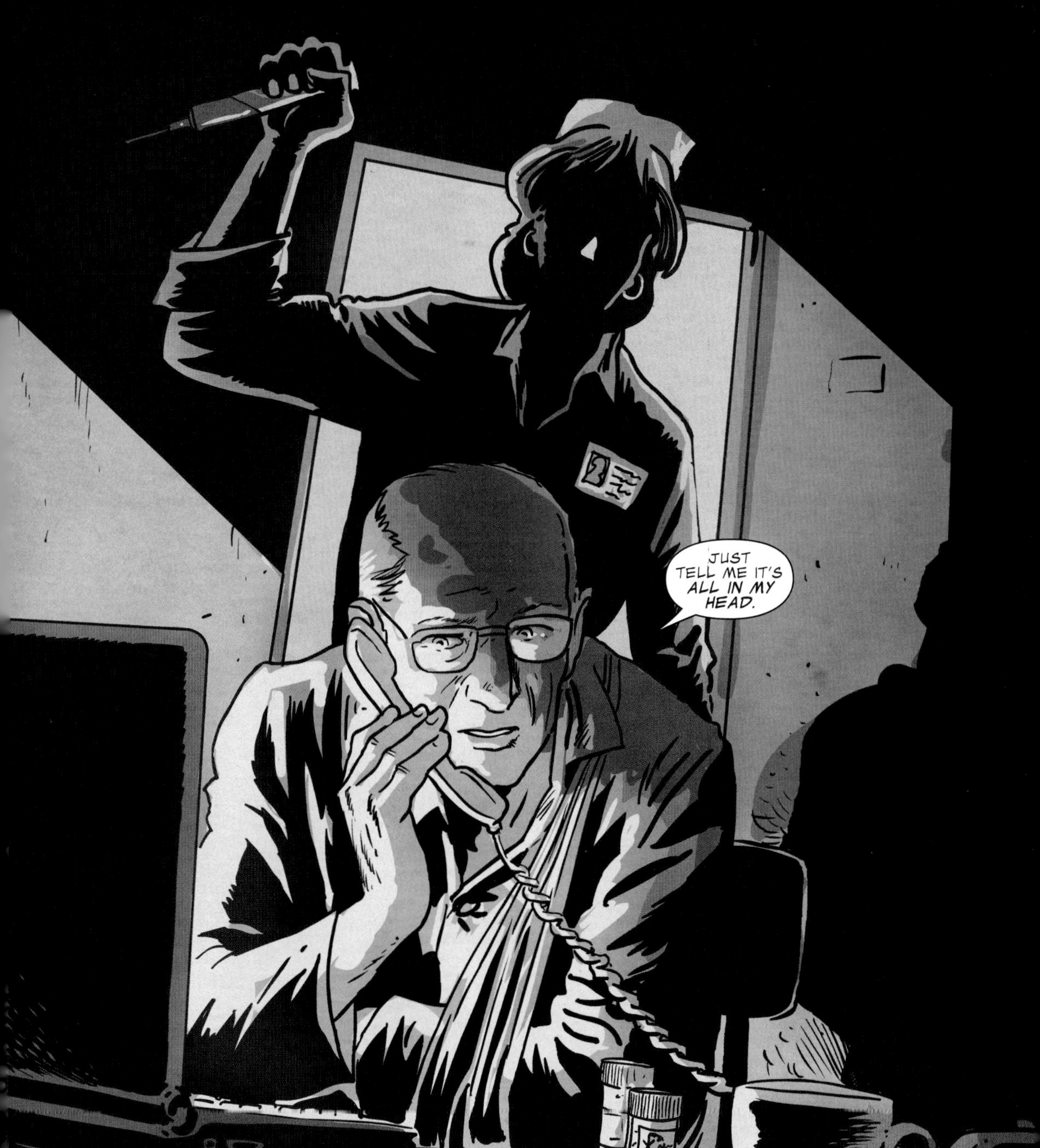
JUST TELL ME IT'S ALL IN MY HEAD.

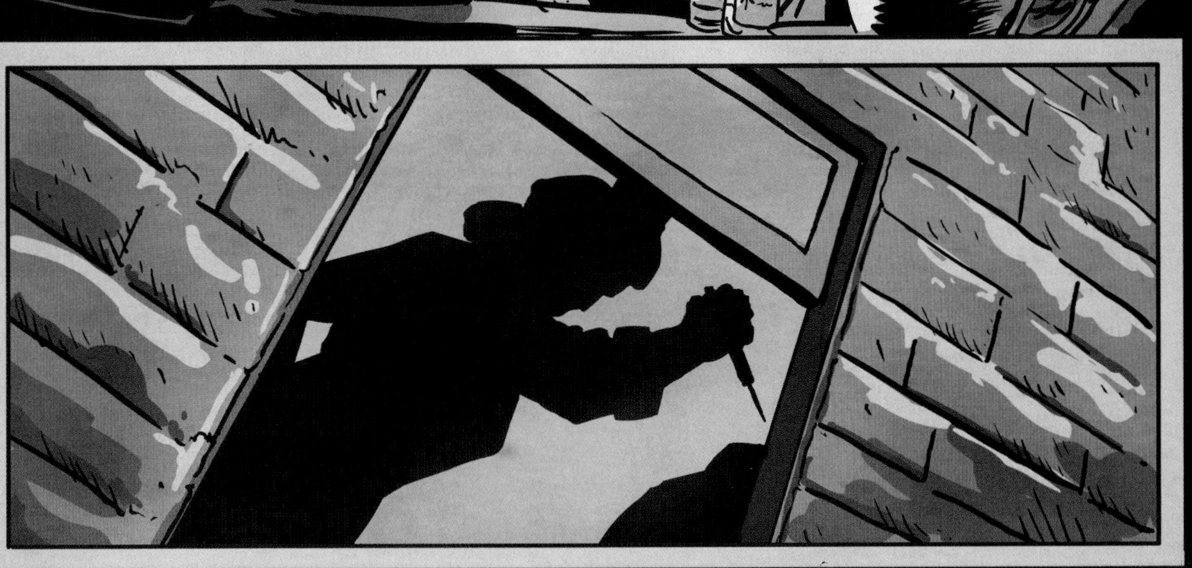

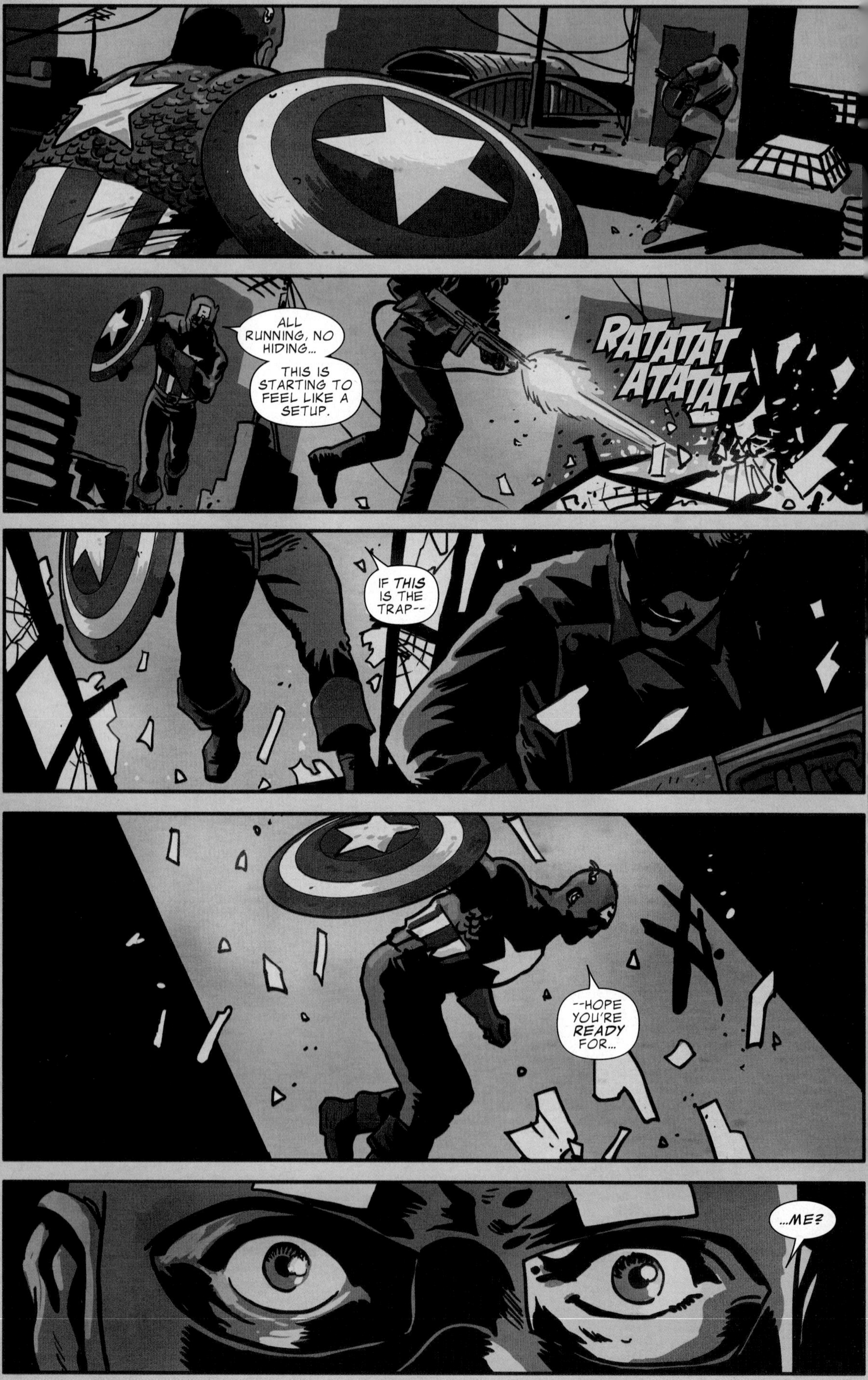
ALL RUNNING, NO HIDING...
THIS IS STARTING TO FEEL LIKE A SETUP.
RATATAT ATATAT
IF THIS IS THE TRAP--
--HOPE YOU'RE READY FOR...
...ME?

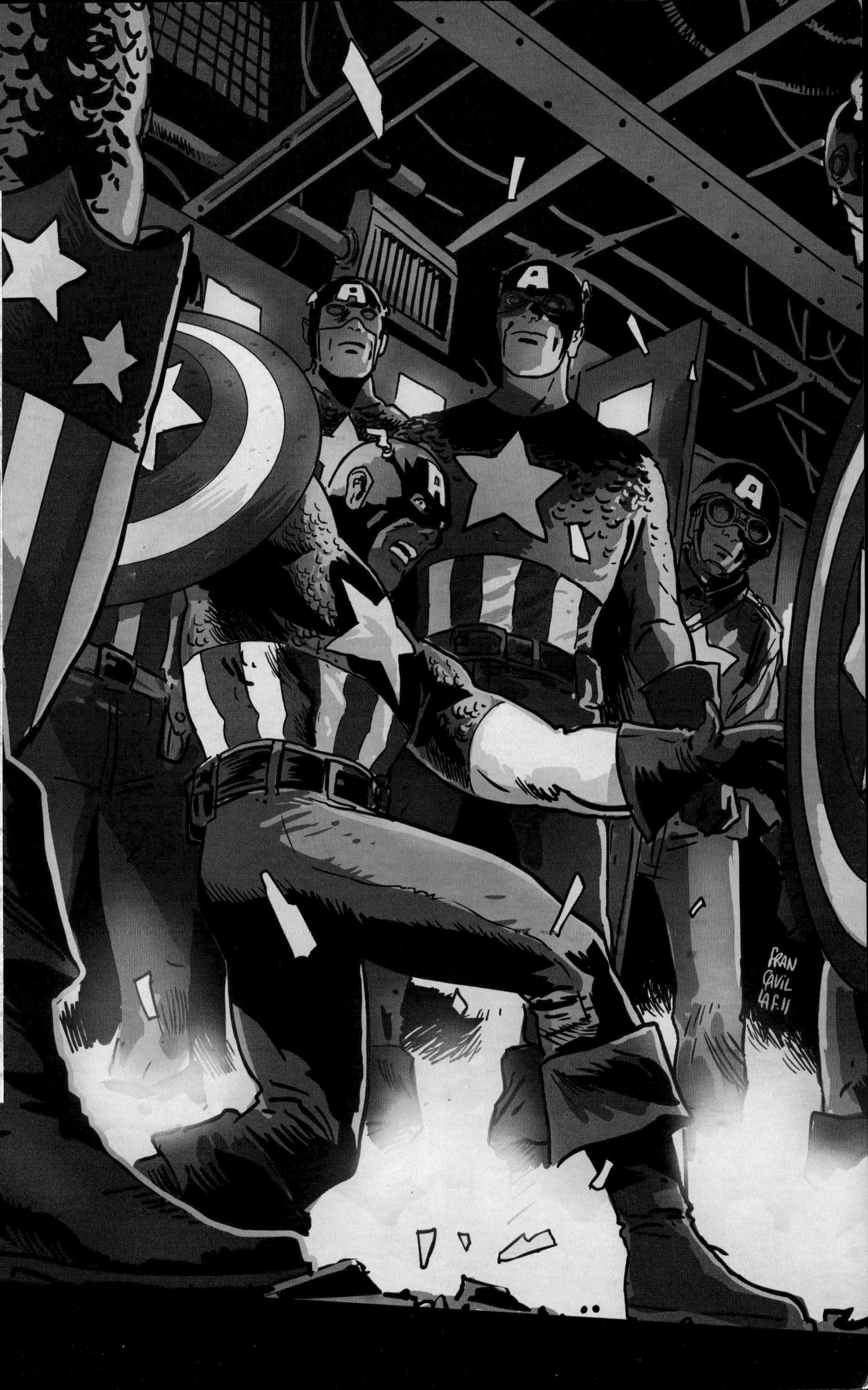
FRAN CAVIL LA F. 11

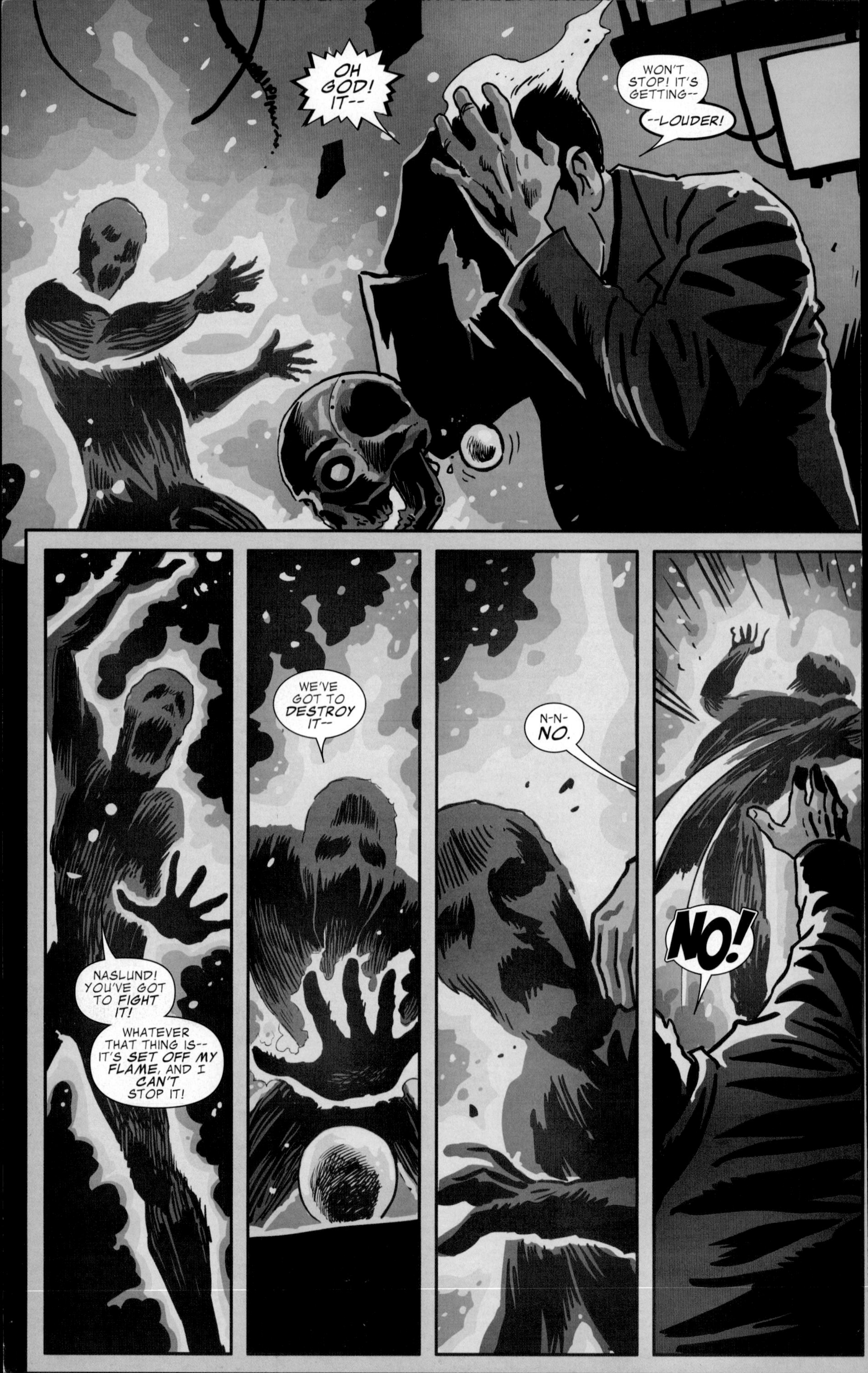
OH GOD! IT--
WON'T STOP! IT'S GETTING--
--LOUDER!
NASLUND! YOU'VE GOT TO FIGHT IT!
WHATEVER THAT THING IS-- IT'S SET OFF MY FLAME, AND I CAN'T STOP IT!
WE'VE GOT TO DESTROY IT--
N-N- NO.
NO!

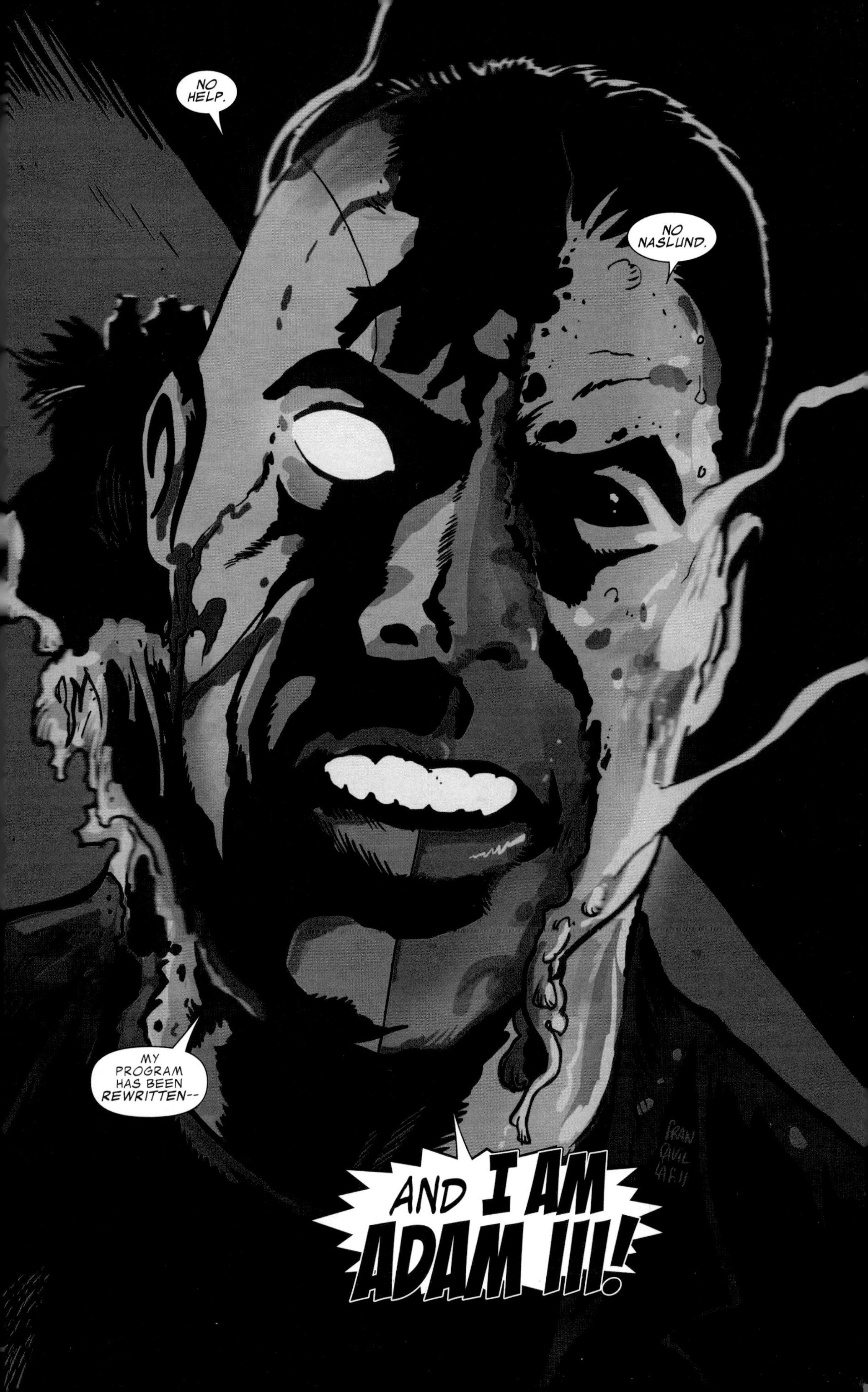
NO HELP.
NO NASLUND.
MY PROGRAM HAS BEEN REWRITTEN--
AND I AM ADAM III!
FRAN CAVIL 4F.11

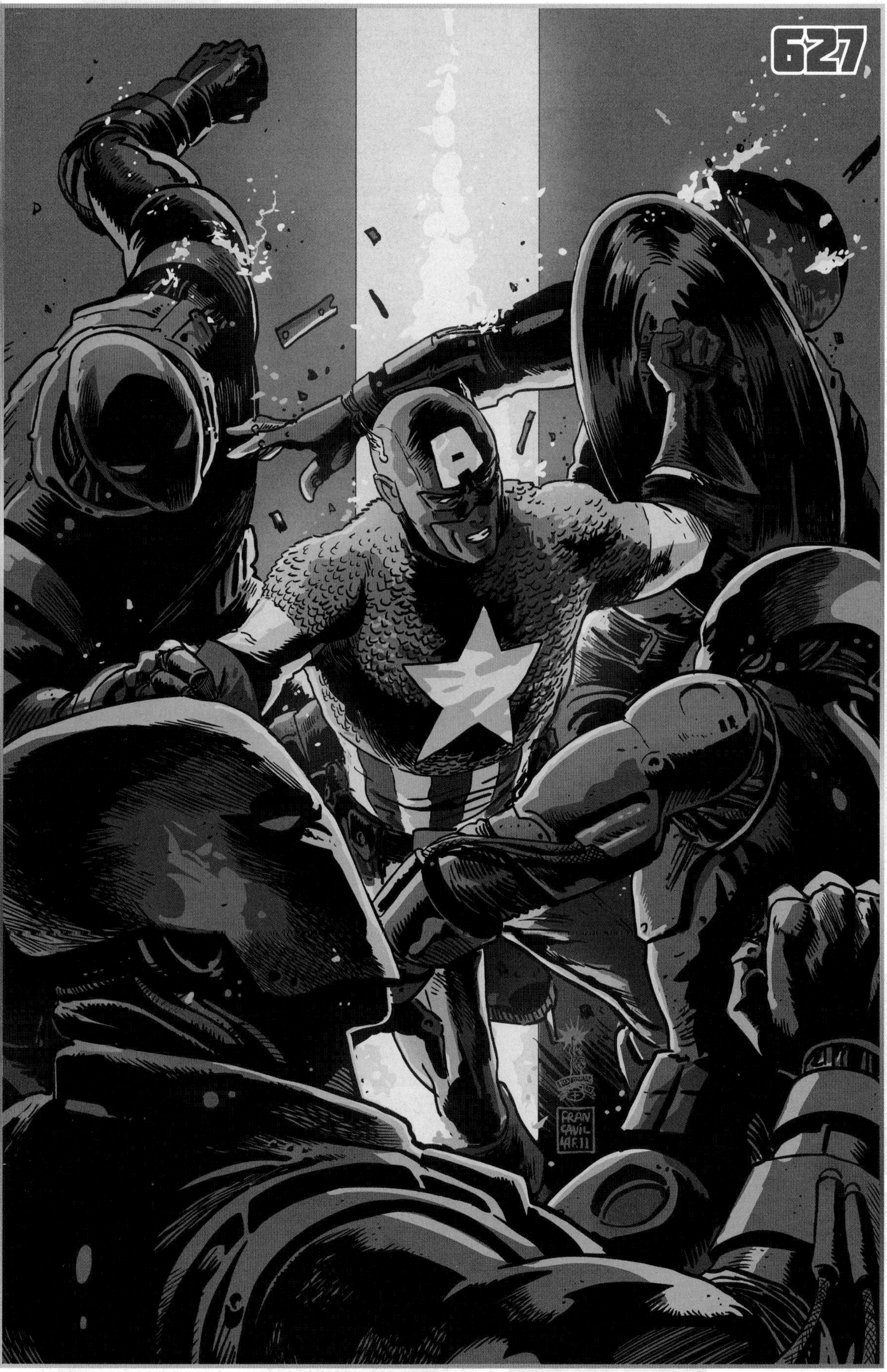
627
FRAN
CAVIL
IAF.11

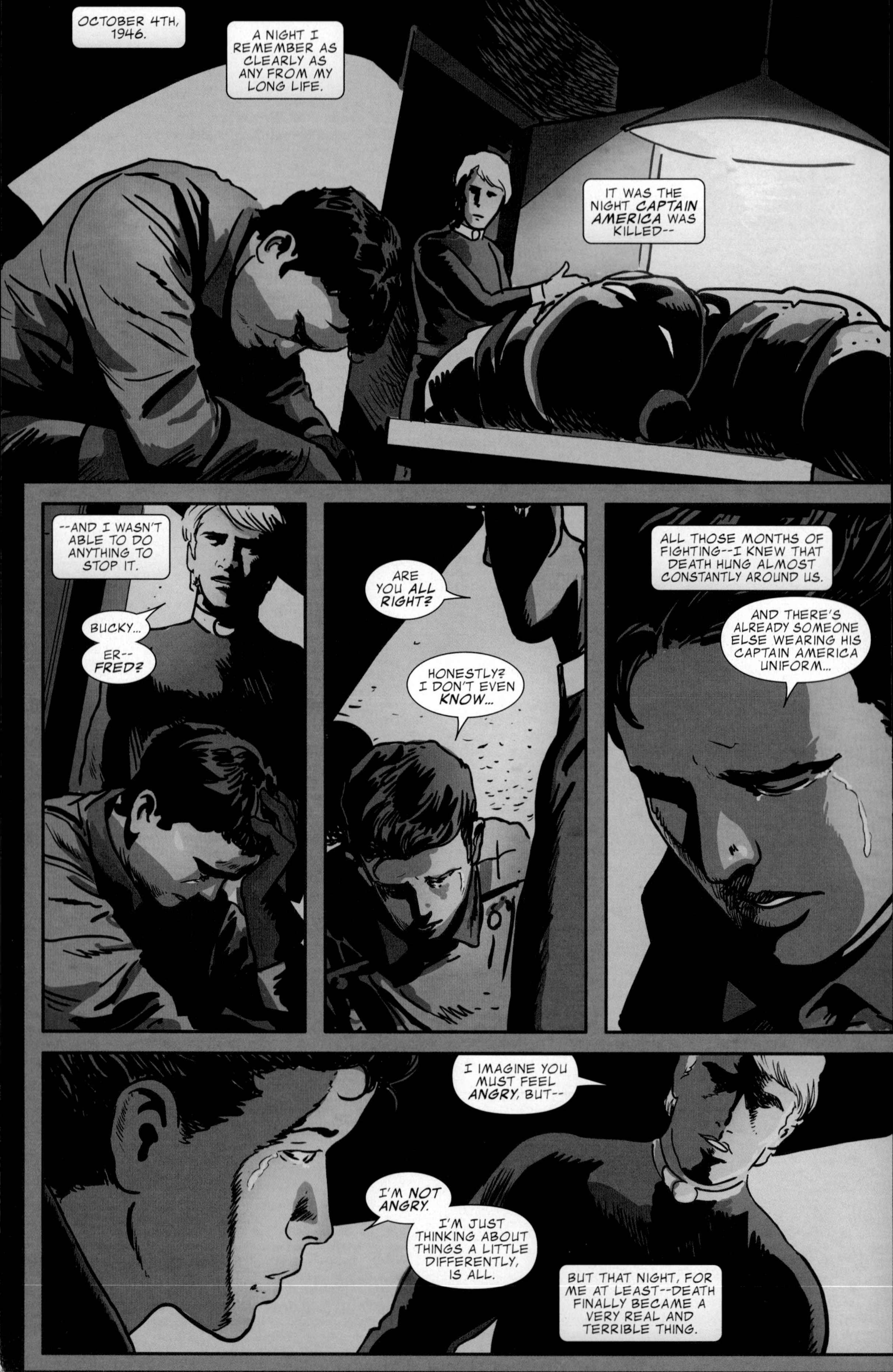
OCTOBER 4TH, 1946.
A NIGHT I REMEMBER AS CLEARLY AS ANY FROM MY LONG LIFE.
IT WAS THE NIGHT CAPTAIN AMERICA WAS KILLED--
--AND I WASN'T ABLE TO DO ANYTHING TO STOP IT.
BUCKY...
ER-- FRED?
ARE YOU ALL RIGHT?
HONESTLY? I DON'T EVEN KNOW...
ALL THOSE MONTHS OF FIGHTING--I KNEW THAT DEATH HUNG ALMOST CONSTANTLY AROUND US.
AND THERE'S ALREADY SOMEONE ELSE WEARING HIS CAPTAIN AMERICA UNIFORM...
I IMAGINE YOU MUST FEEL ANGRY, BUT--
I'M NOT ANGRY.
I'M JUST THINKING ABOUT THINGS A LITTLE DIFFERENTLY, IS ALL.
BUT THAT NIGHT, FOR ME AT LEAST--DEATH FINALLY BECAME A VERY REAL AND TERRIBLE THING.

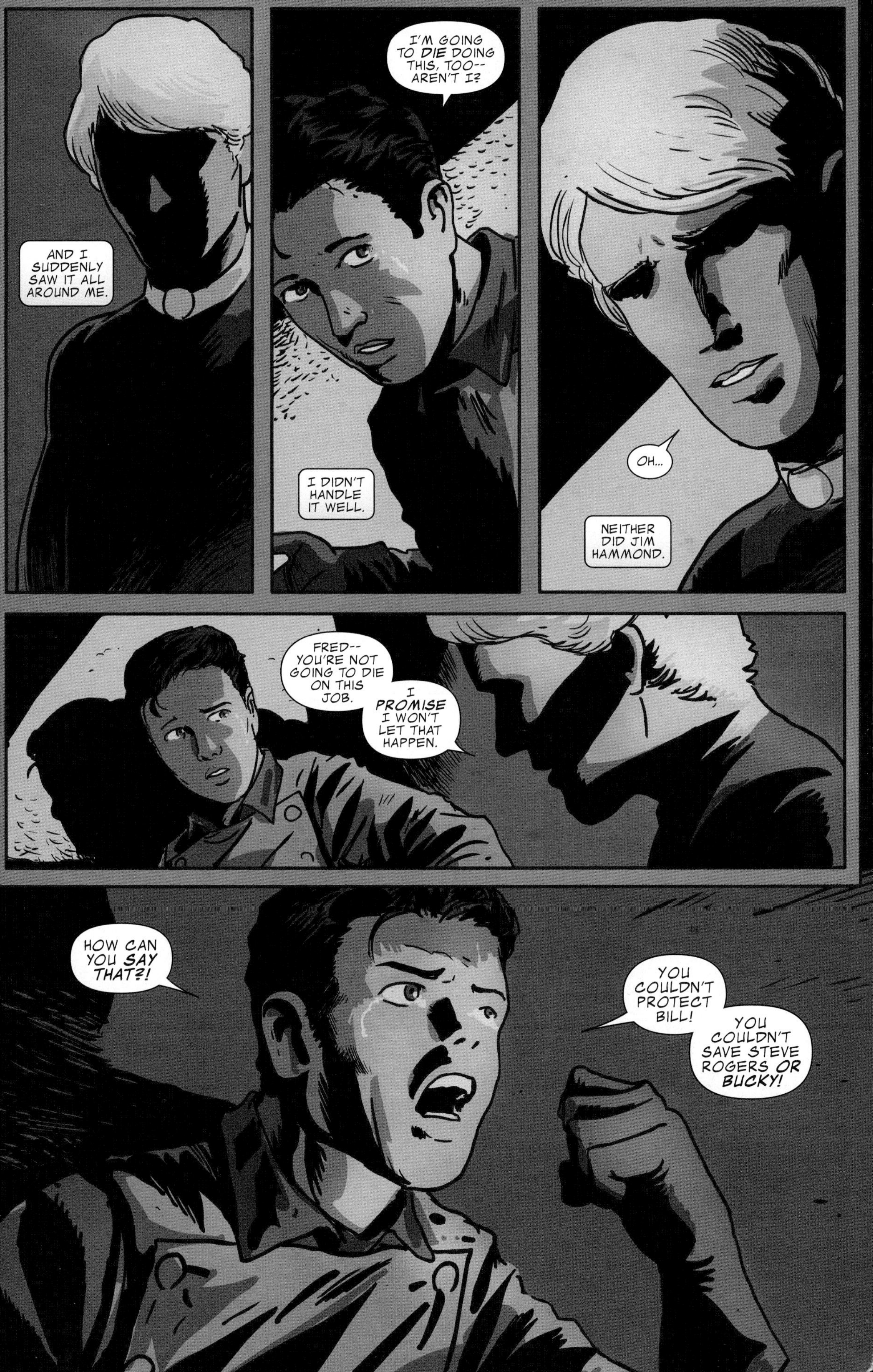
AND I SUDDENLY SAW IT ALL AROUND ME.
I'M GOING TO DIE DOING THIS, TOO-- AREN'T I?
I DIDN'T HANDLE IT WELL.
OH...
NEITHER DID JIM HAMMOND.
FRED-- YOU'RE NOT GOING TO DIE ON THIS JOB.
I PROMISE I WON'T LET THAT HAPPEN.
HOW CAN YOU SAY THAT?!
YOU COULDN'T PROTECT BILL!
YOU COULDN'T SAVE STEVE ROGERS OR BUCKY!

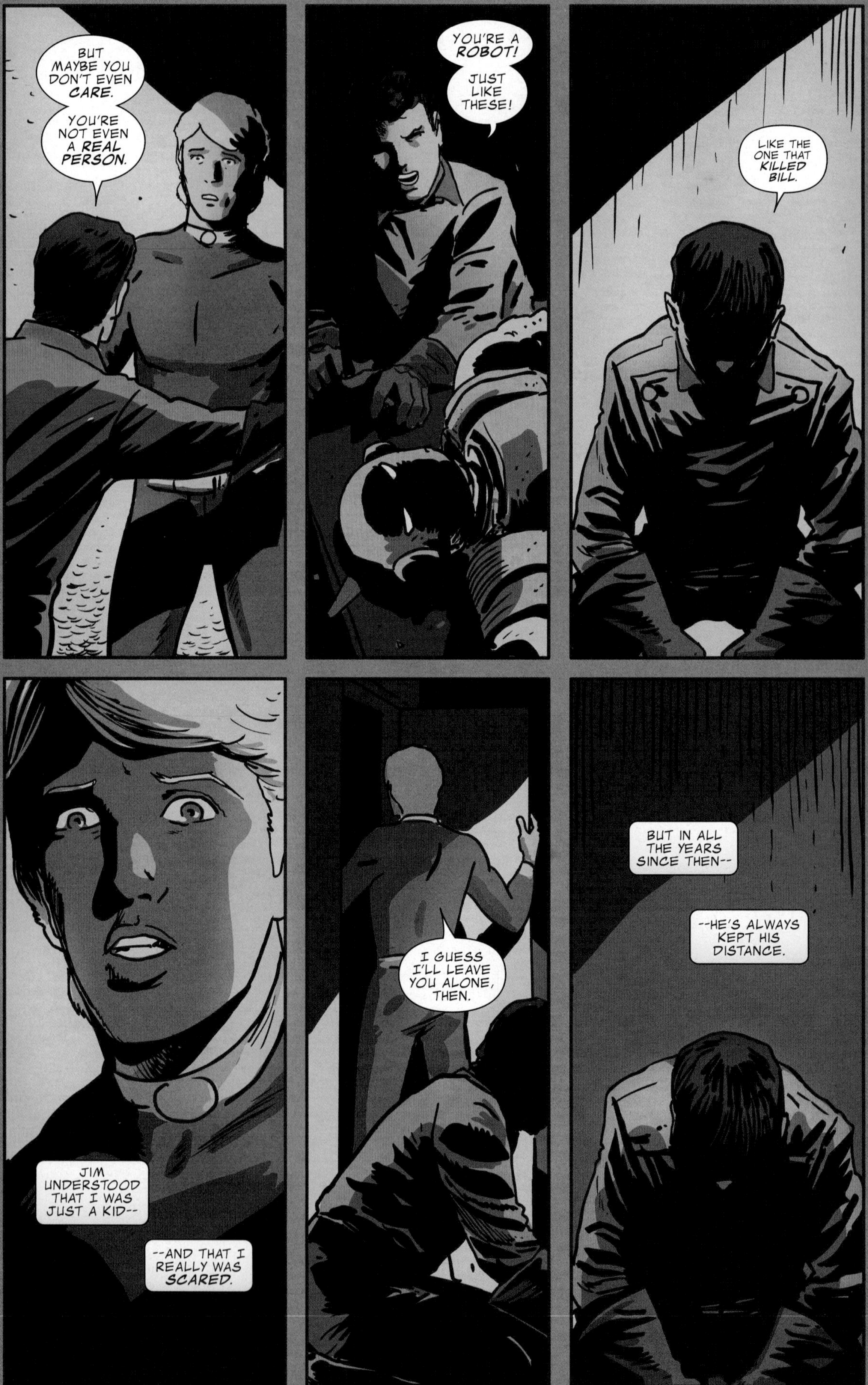
BUT MAYBE YOU DON'T EVEN CARE.
YOU'RE NOT EVEN A REAL PERSON.
YOU'RE A ROBOT!
JUST LIKE THESE!
LIKE THE ONE THAT KILLED BILL.
JIM UNDERSTOOD THAT I WAS JUST A KID--
--AND THAT I REALLY WAS SCARED.
I GUESS I'LL LEAVE YOU ALONE, THEN.
BUT IN ALL THE YEARS SINCE THEN--
--HE'S ALWAYS KEPT HIS DISTANCE.

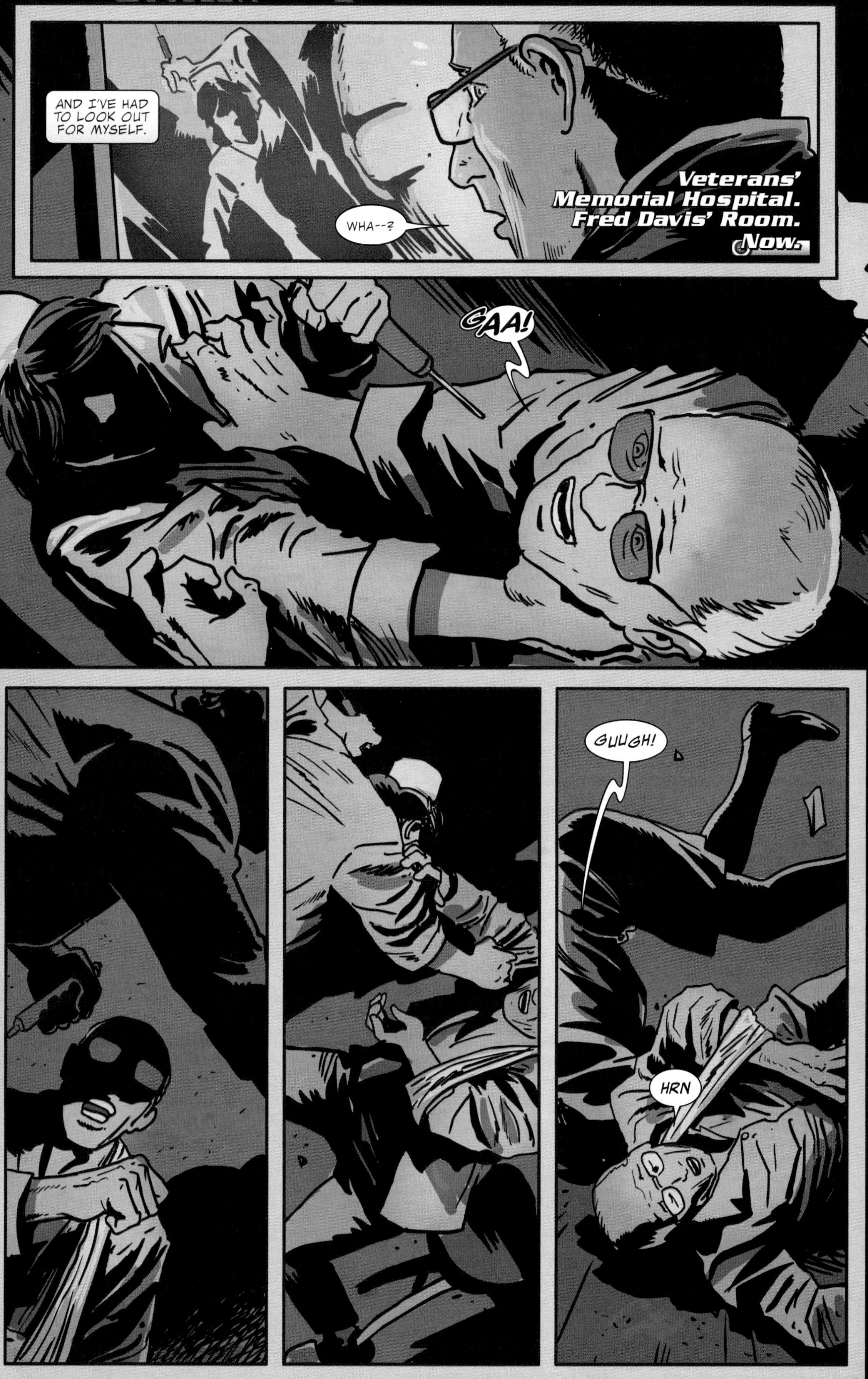
AND I'VE HAD TO LOOK OUT FOR MYSELF.
Veterans' Memorial Hospital. Fred Davis' Room. Now.
WHA--?
GAA!
GUUGH!
HRN

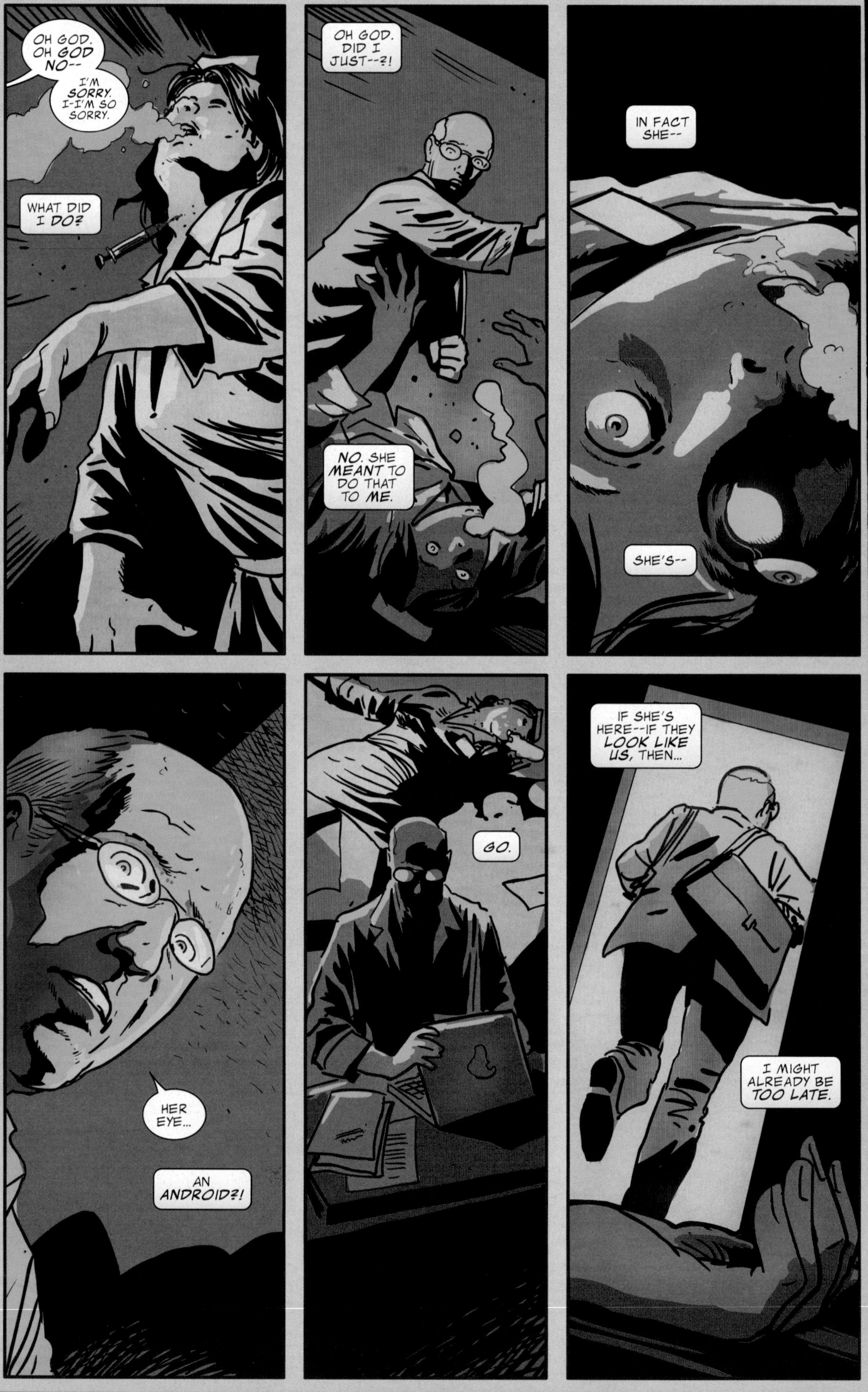
OH GOD. OH GOD NO--
I'M SORRY. I-I'M SO SORRY.
WHAT DID I DO?
OH GOD. DID I JUST--?!
NO. SHE MEANT TO DO THAT TO ME.
IN FACT SHE--
SHE'S--
HER EYE...
AN ANDROID?!
GO.
IF SHE'S HERE--IF THEY LOOK LIKE US, THEN...
I MIGHT ALREADY BE TOO LATE.

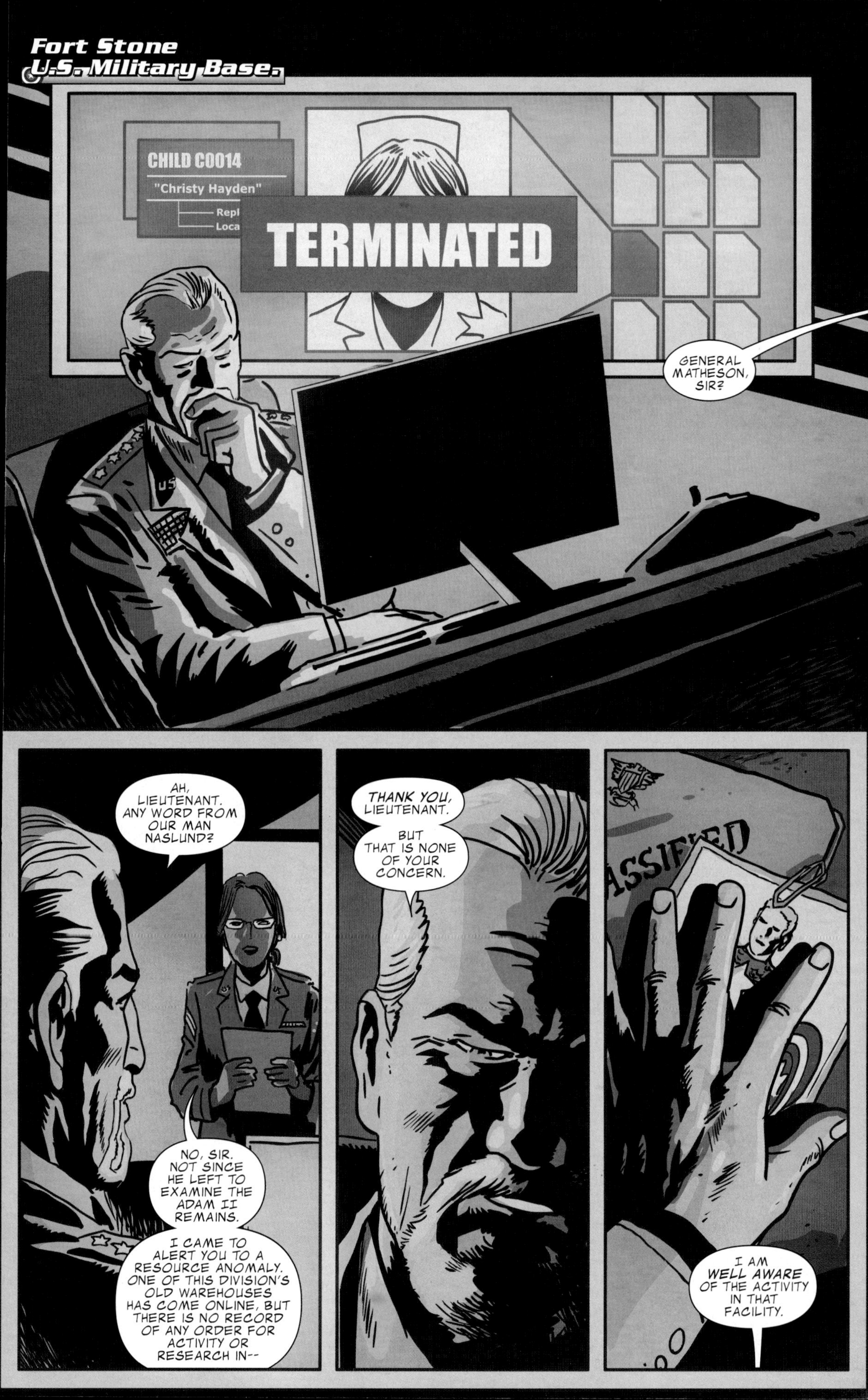
Fort Stone
U.S. Military Base.
CHILD C0014
"Christy Hayden"
TERMINATED
GENERAL MATHESON, SIR?
AH, LIEUTENANT. ANY WORD FROM OUR MAN NASLUND?
NO, SIR. NOT SINCE HE LEFT TO EXAMINE THE ADAM II REMAINS.
I CAME TO ALERT YOU TO A RESOURCE ANOMALY. ONE OF THIS DIVISION'S OLD WAREHOUSES HAS COME ONLINE, BUT THERE IS NO RECORD OF ANY ORDER FOR ACTIVITY OR RESEARCH IN--
THANK YOU, LIEUTENANT.
BUT THAT IS NONE OF YOUR CONCERN.
I AM WELL AWARE OF THE ACTIVITY IN THAT FACILITY.

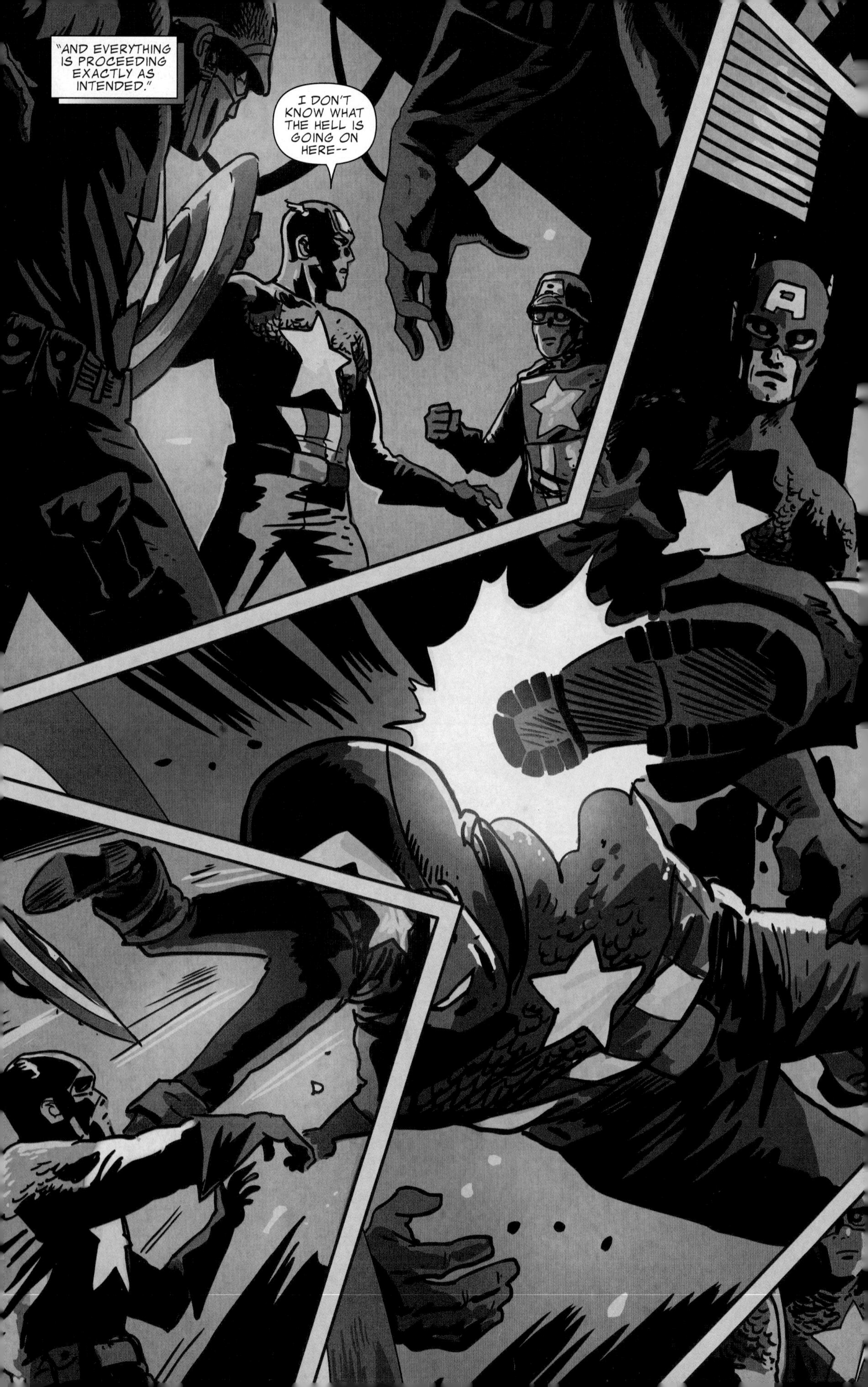
"AND EVERYTHING IS PROCEEDING EXACTLY AS INTENDED."
I DON'T KNOW WHAT THE HELL IS GOING ON HERE--

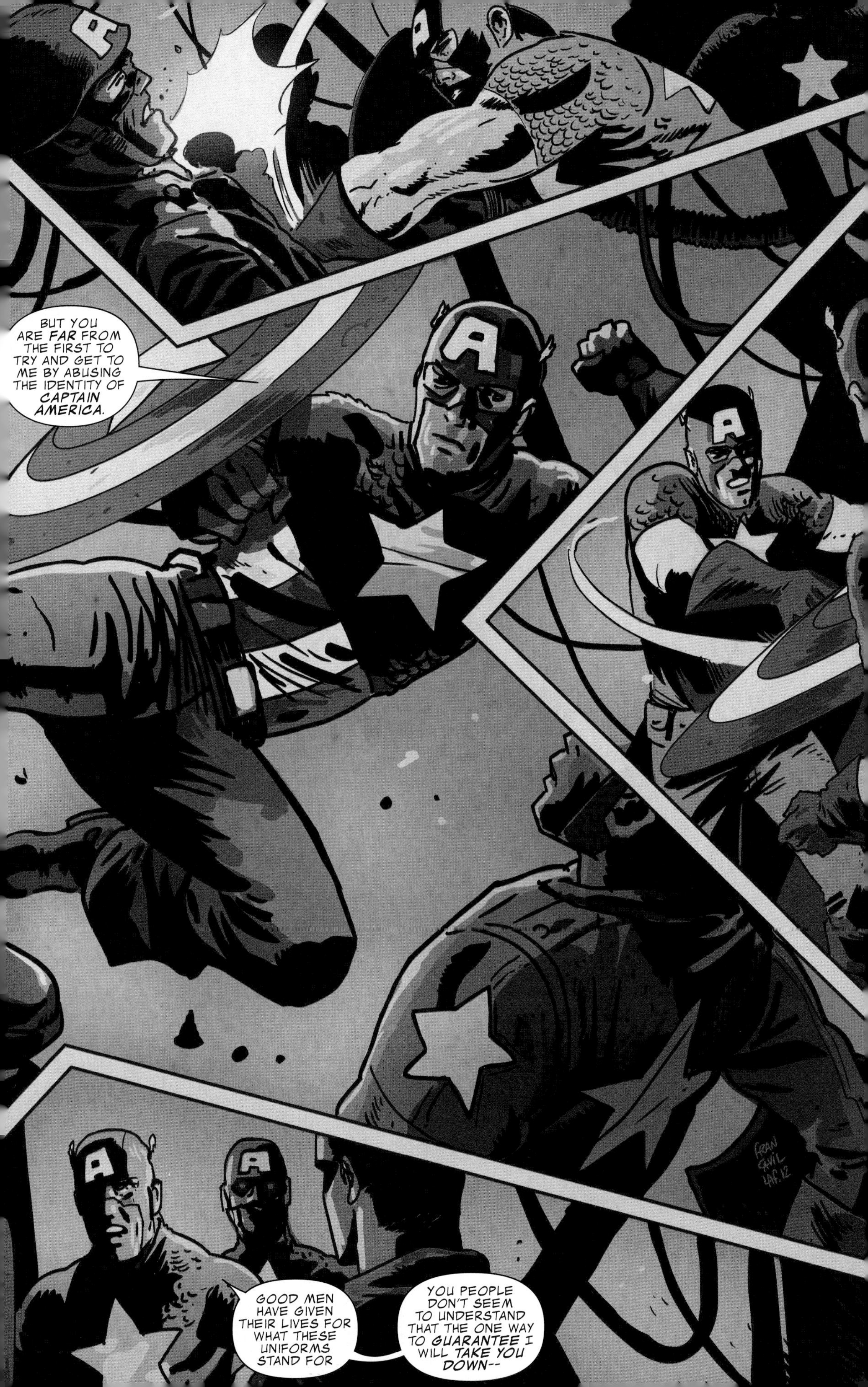
BUT YOU ARE FAR FROM THE FIRST TO TRY AND GET TO ME BY ABUSING THE IDENTITY OF CAPTAIN AMERICA.
GOOD MEN HAVE GIVEN THEIR LIVES FOR WHAT THESE UNIFORMS STAND FOR
YOU PEOPLE DON'T SEEM TO UNDERSTAND THAT THE ONE WAY TO GUARANTEE I WILL TAKE YOU DOWN--
FRAN GAVIL LAF.12

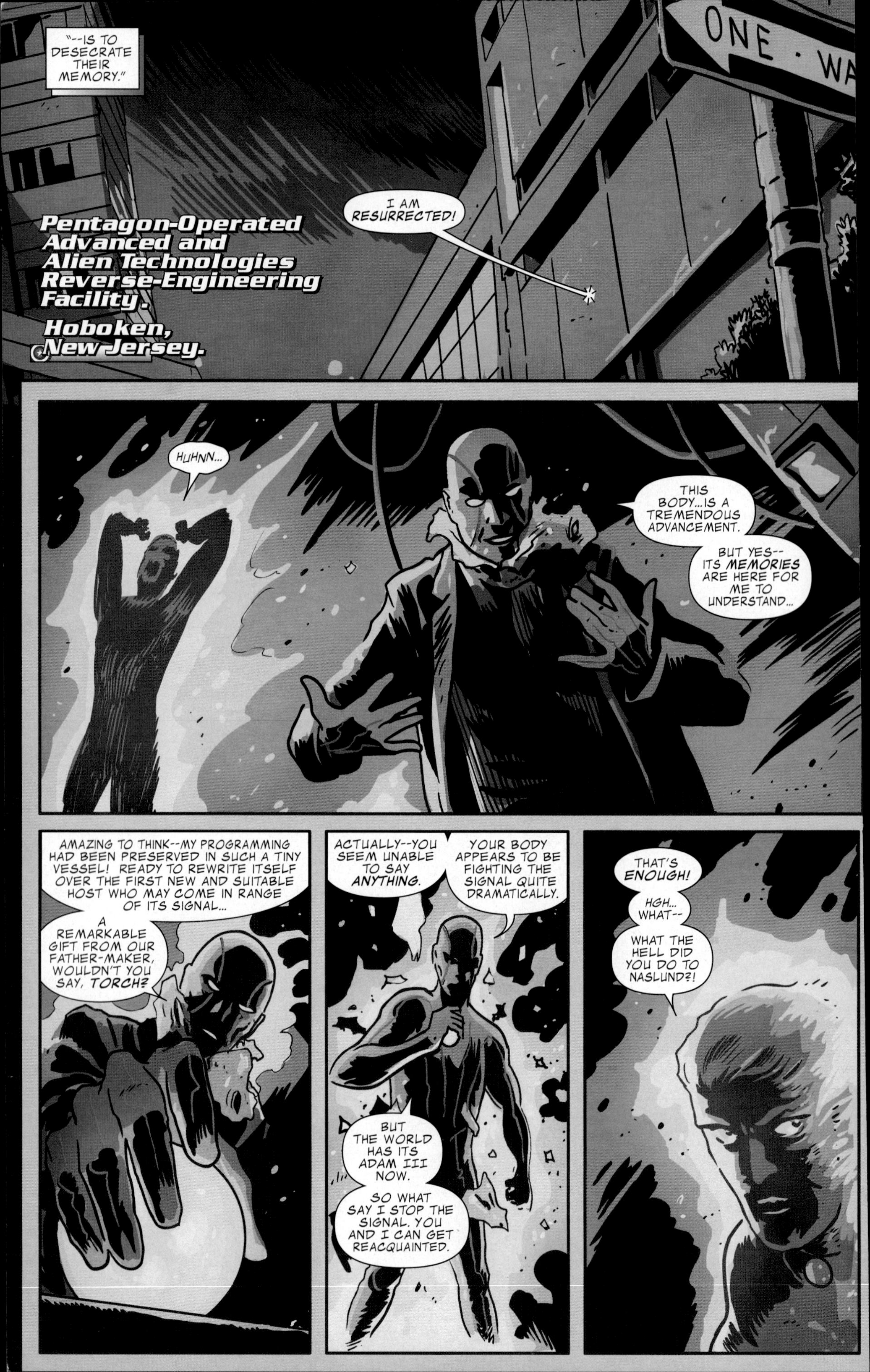
"--IS TO DESECRATE THEIR MEMORY."
ONE · WA
I AM RESURRECTED!
Pentagon-Operated Advanced and Alien Technologies Reverse-Engineering Facility.
Hoboken, New Jersey.
HUHNN...
THIS BODY...IS A TREMENDOUS ADVANCEMENT.
BUT YES-- ITS MEMORIES ARE HERE FOR ME TO UNDERSTAND...
AMAZING TO THINK--MY PROGRAMMING HAD BEEN PRESERVED IN SUCH A TINY VESSEL! READY TO REWRITE ITSELF OVER THE FIRST NEW AND SUITABLE HOST WHO MAY COME IN RANGE OF ITS SIGNAL...
A REMARKABLE GIFT FROM OUR FATHER-MAKER, WOULDN'T YOU SAY, TORCH?
ACTUALLY--YOU SEEM UNABLE TO SAY ANYTHING.
YOUR BODY APPEARS TO BE FIGHTING THE SIGNAL QUITE DRAMATICALLY.
BUT THE WORLD HAS ITS ADAM III NOW.
SO WHAT SAY I STOP THE SIGNAL. YOU AND I CAN GET REACQUAINTED.
THAT'S ENOUGH!
HGH... WHAT--
WHAT THE HELL DID YOU DO TO NASLUND?!

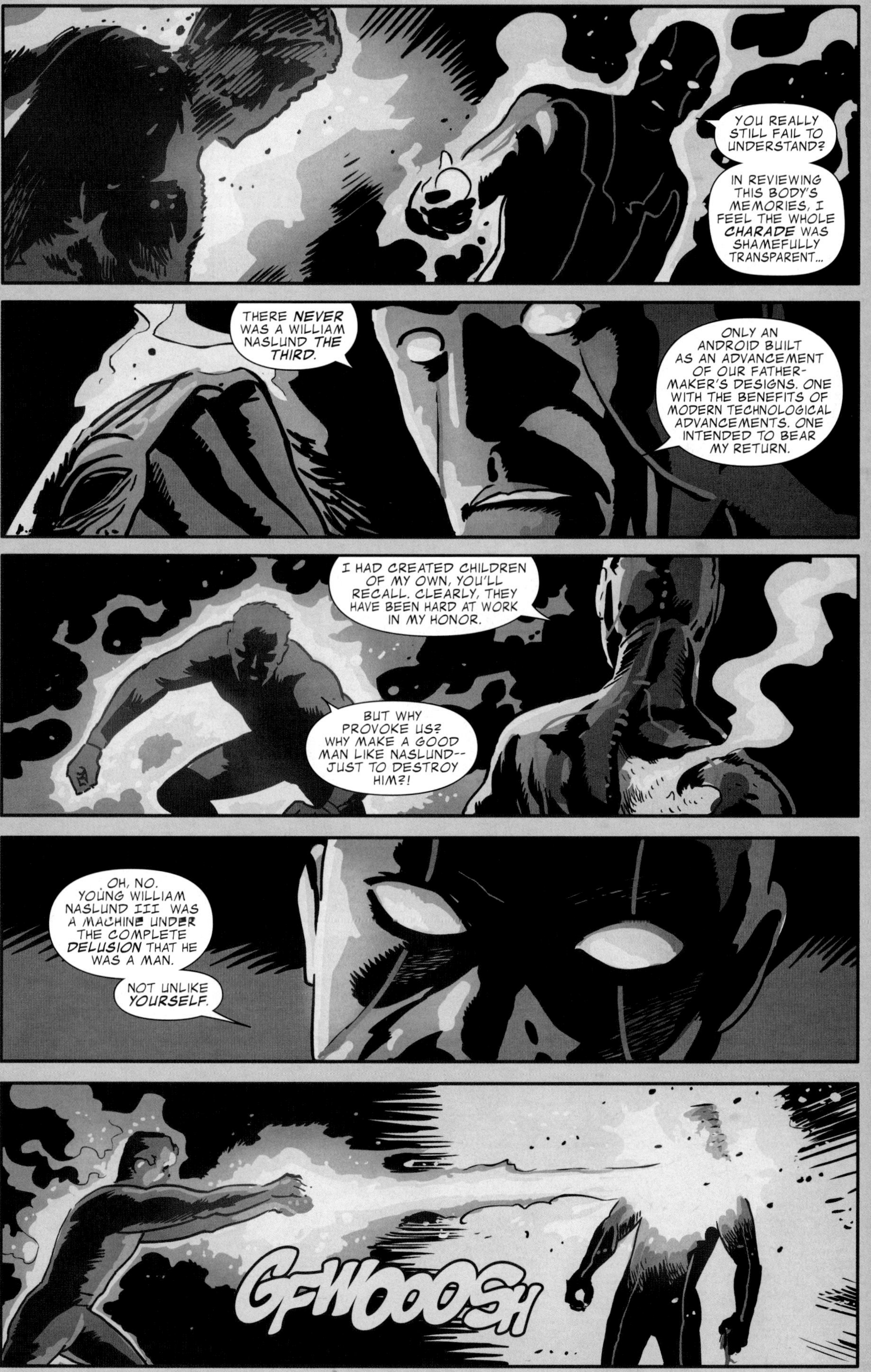
YOU REALLY STILL FAIL TO UNDERSTAND?
IN REVIEWING THIS BODY'S MEMORIES, I FEEL THE WHOLE CHARADE WAS SHAMEFULLY TRANSPARENT...
THERE NEVER WAS A WILLIAM NASLUND THE THIRD.
ONLY AN ANDROID BUILT AS AN ADVANCEMENT OF OUR FATHER-MAKER'S DESIGNS. ONE WITH THE BENEFITS OF MODERN TECHNOLOGICAL ADVANCEMENTS. ONE INTENDED TO BEAR MY RETURN.
I HAD CREATED CHILDREN OF MY OWN, YOU'LL RECALL. CLEARLY, THEY HAVE BEEN HARD AT WORK IN MY HONOR.
BUT WHY PROVOKE US? WHY MAKE A GOOD MAN LIKE NASLUND-- JUST TO DESTROY HIM?!
OH, NO. YOUNG WILLIAM NASLUND III WAS A MACHINE UNDER THE COMPLETE DELUSION THAT HE WAS A MAN.
NOT UNLIKE YOURSELF.
GFWOOOSH

ARE YOU CONFUSING YOUR *BOOK OF GENESIS*, DEAR BROTHER?

FATHER INTENDED ME TO BE THE "*ADAM*" OF A NEW RACE. NOT THE ABEL TO YOUR CAIN.

BESIDES--I AM SOMETHING *NEW* NOW.

AND I WOULD *LOVE* TO SHARE THESE GIFTS WITH YOU.

JUST *IMAGINE*--

F
G
O
O
O
M
M

NOPE. NOT INTERESTED.

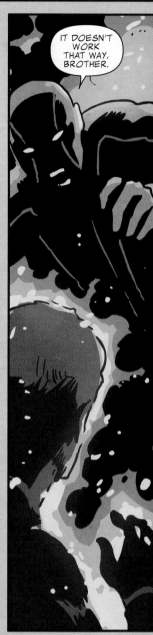

IT DOESN'T WORK THAT WAY, BROTHER.

I AM OUR FATHER-MAKER'S INNOVATION FULLY REALIZED. EACH *CELL* IN MY BODY FUNCTIONS AS ITS OWN CHEMICAL COMPUTER FOR ME TO REPROGRAM AND CONTROL!

IN SHORT-- I CAN DO *ALL* THAT YOU CAN DO--

AND SO MUCH *MORE*!

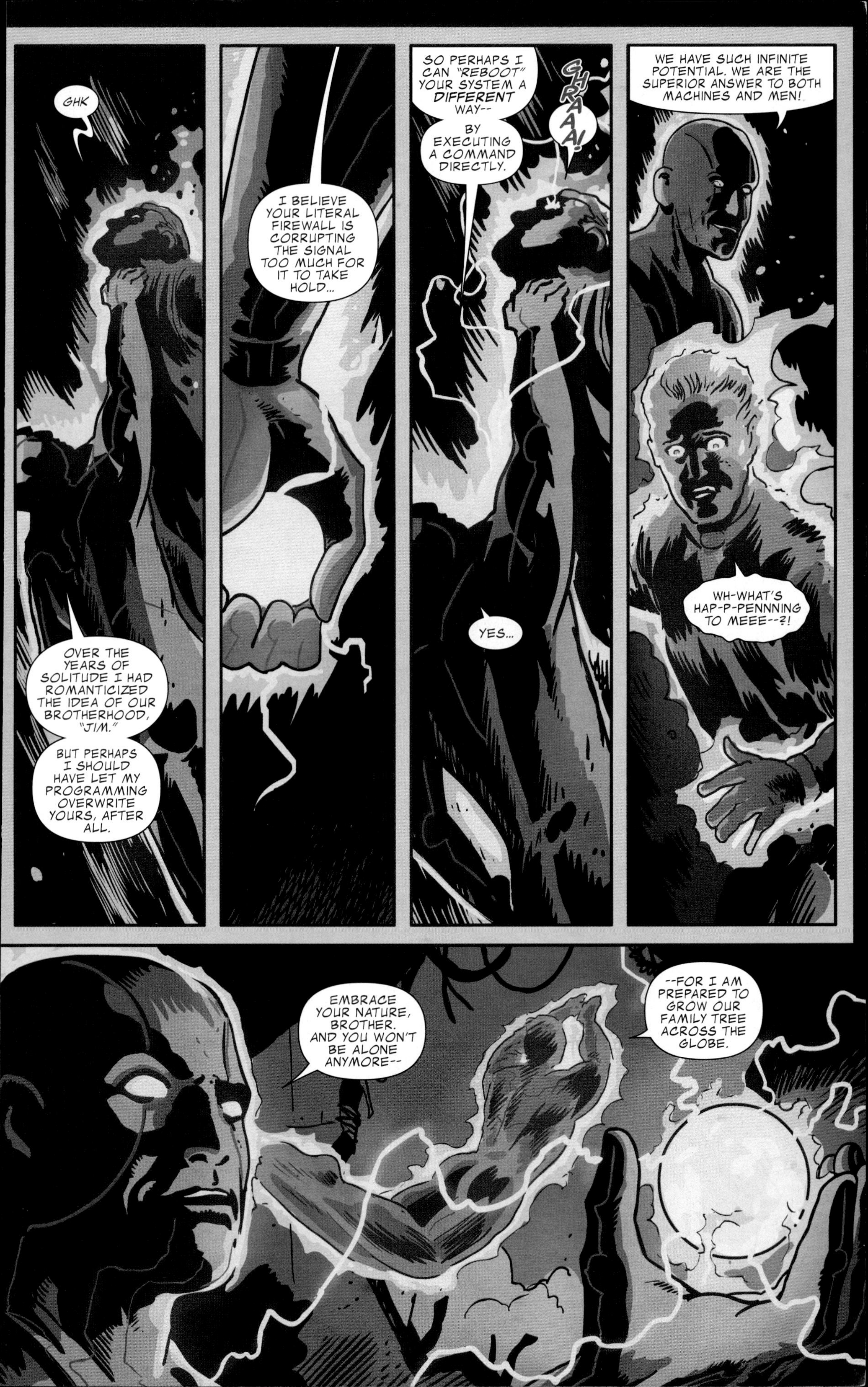
GHK
OVER THE YEARS OF SOLITUDE I HAD ROMANTICIZED THE IDEA OF OUR BROTHERHOOD, "JIM."
BUT PERHAPS I SHOULD HAVE LET MY PROGRAMMING OVERWRITE YOURS, AFTER ALL.
I BELIEVE YOUR LITERAL FIREWALL IS CORRUPTING THE SIGNAL TOO MUCH FOR IT TO TAKE HOLD...
SO PERHAPS I CAN "REBOOT" YOUR SYSTEM A DIFFERENT WAY--
BY EXECUTING A COMMAND DIRECTLY.
GHRAAAA!
YES...
WE HAVE SUCH INFINITE POTENTIAL. WE ARE THE SUPERIOR ANSWER TO BOTH MACHINES AND MEN!
WH-WHAT'S HAP-P-PENNNING TO MEEE--?!
EMBRACE YOUR NATURE, BROTHER. AND YOU WON'T BE ALONE ANYMORE--
--FOR I AM PREPARED TO GROW OUR FAMILY TREE ACROSS THE GLOBE.

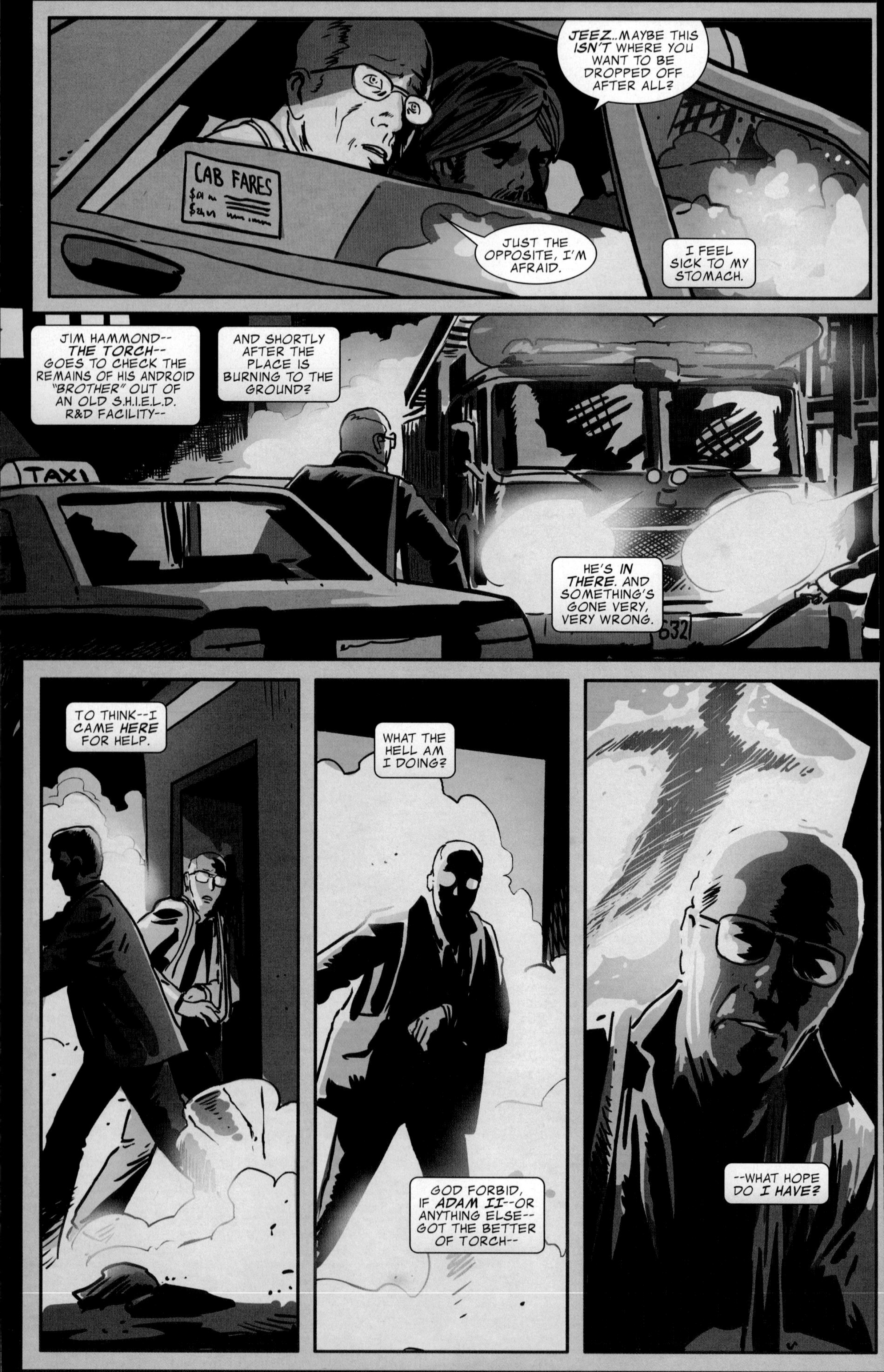
JEEZ..MAYBE THIS ISN'T WHERE YOU WANT TO BE DROPPED OFF AFTER ALL?
CAB FARES
JUST THE OPPOSITE, I'M AFRAID.
I FEEL SICK TO MY STOMACH.
JIM HAMMOND--THE TORCH--GOES TO CHECK THE REMAINS OF HIS ANDROID "BROTHER" OUT OF AN OLD S.H.I.E.L.D. R&D FACILITY--
AND SHORTLY AFTER THE PLACE IS BURNING TO THE GROUND?
TAXI
HE'S IN THERE. AND SOMETHING'S GONE VERY, VERY WRONG.
632
TO THINK--I CAME HERE FOR HELP.
WHAT THE HELL AM I DOING?
GOD FORBID, IF ADAM II--OR ANYTHING ELSE--GOT THE BETTER OF TORCH--
--WHAT HOPE DO I HAVE?

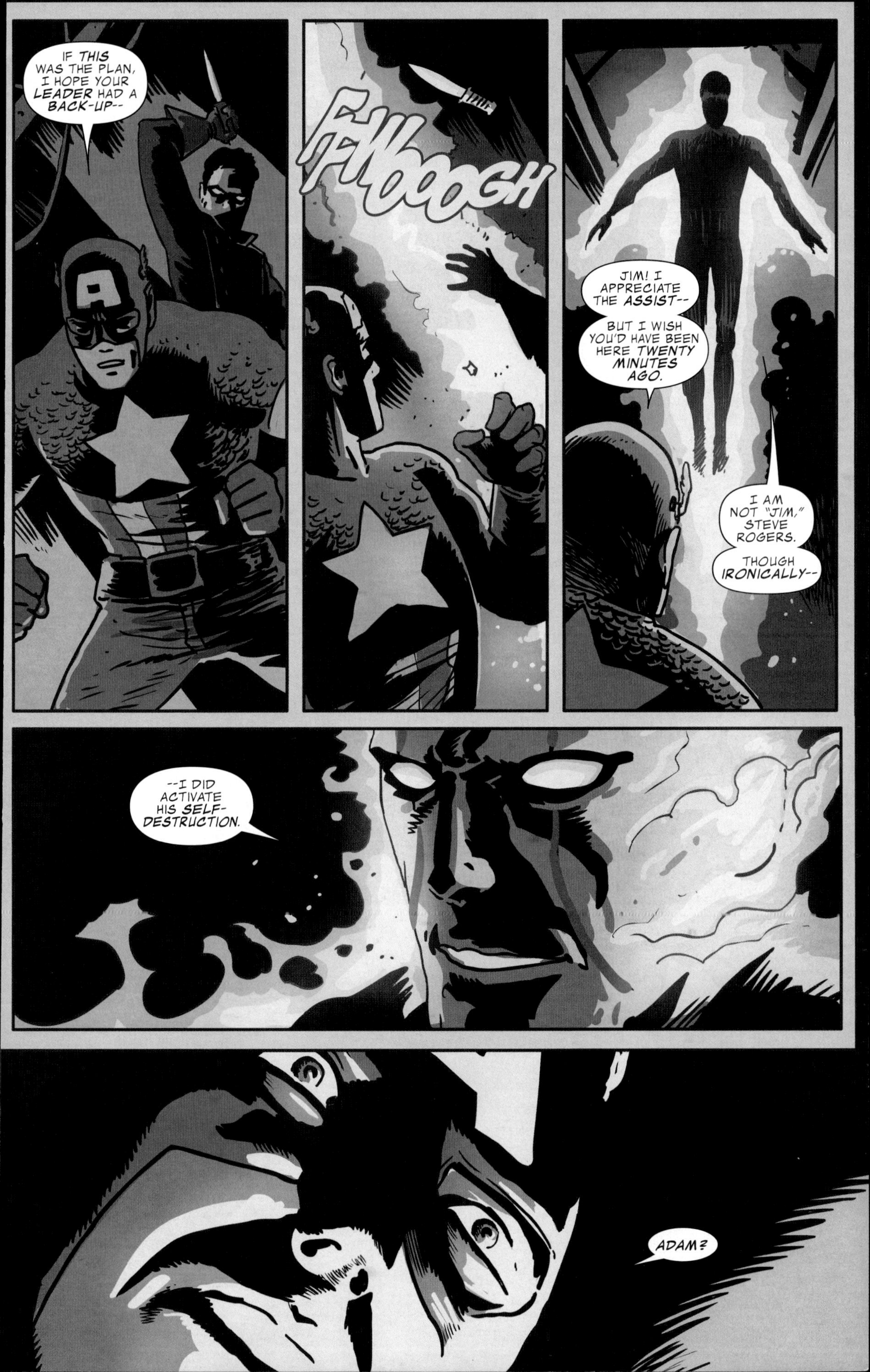
IF THIS WAS THE PLAN, I HOPE YOUR LEADER HAD A BACK-UP--
FFWOOOGH
JIM! I APPRECIATE THE ASSIST--
BUT I WISH YOU'D HAVE BEEN HERE TWENTY MINUTES AGO.
I AM NOT "JIM," STEVE ROGERS.
THOUGH IRONICALLY--
--I DID ACTIVATE HIS SELF-DESTRUCTION.
ADAM?

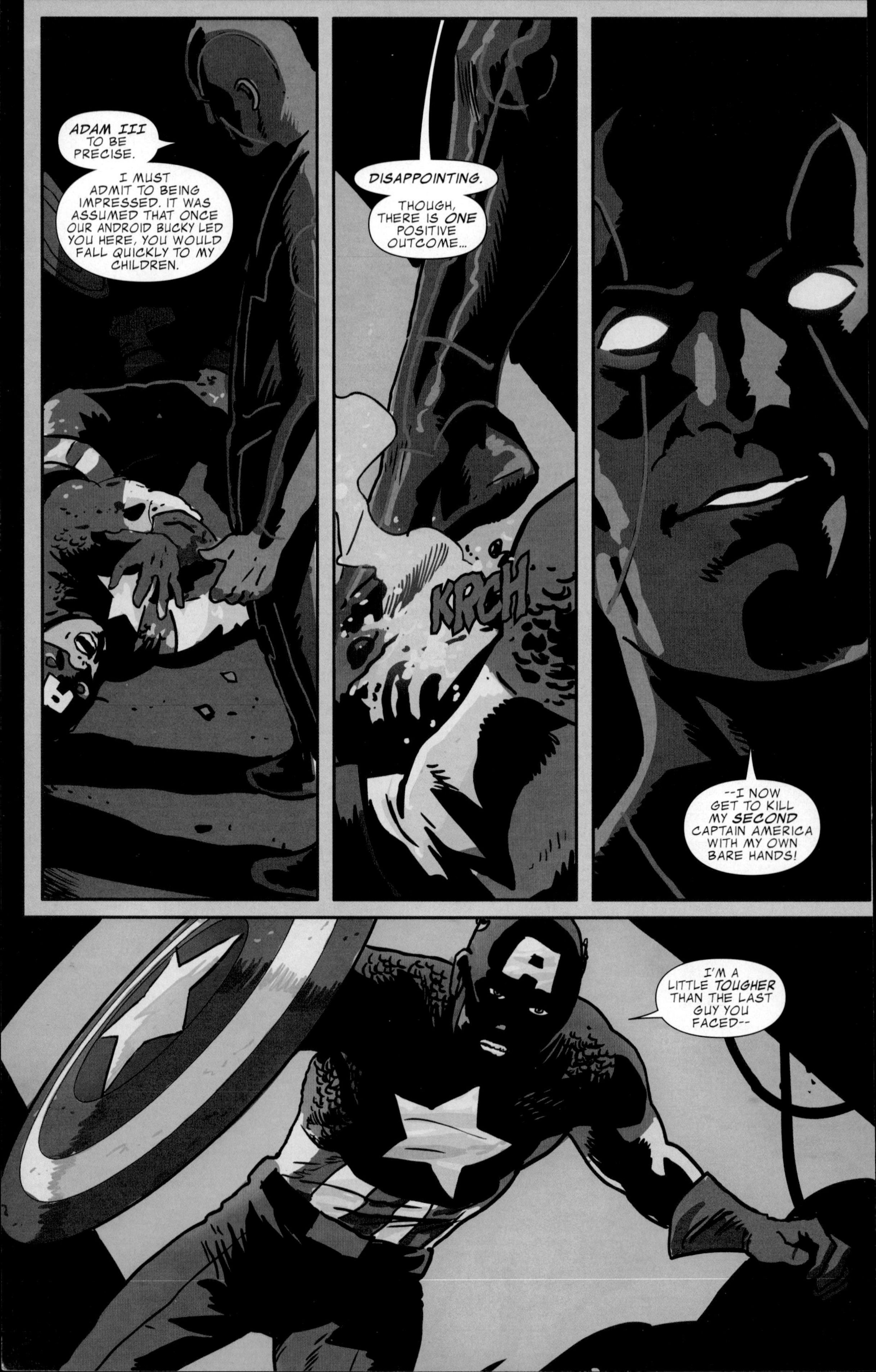
ADAM III TO BE PRECISE.
I MUST ADMIT TO BEING IMPRESSED. IT WAS ASSUMED THAT ONCE OUR ANDROID BUCKY LED YOU HERE, YOU WOULD FALL QUICKLY TO MY CHILDREN.
DISAPPOINTING.
THOUGH, THERE IS ONE POSITIVE OUTCOME...
KRCH
--I NOW GET TO KILL MY SECOND CAPTAIN AMERICA WITH MY OWN BARE HANDS!
I'M A LITTLE TOUGHER THAN THE LAST GUY YOU FACED--

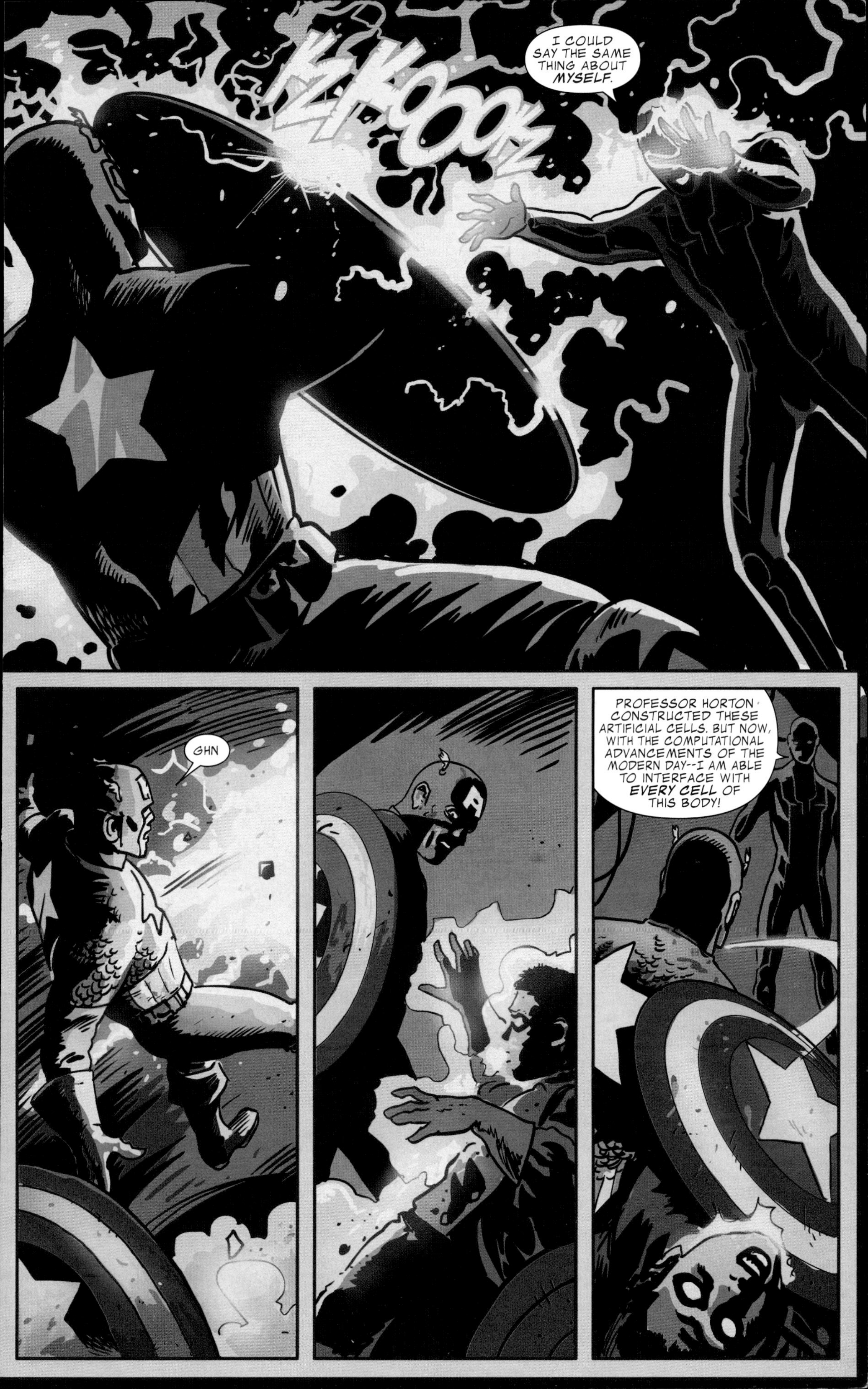
KZKOOOM
I COULD SAY THE SAME THING ABOUT MYSELF.
GHN
PROFESSOR HORTON CONSTRUCTED THESE ARTIFICIAL CELLS. BUT NOW, WITH THE COMPUTATIONAL ADVANCEMENTS OF THE MODERN DAY--I AM ABLE TO INTERFACE WITH EVERY CELL OF THIS BODY!

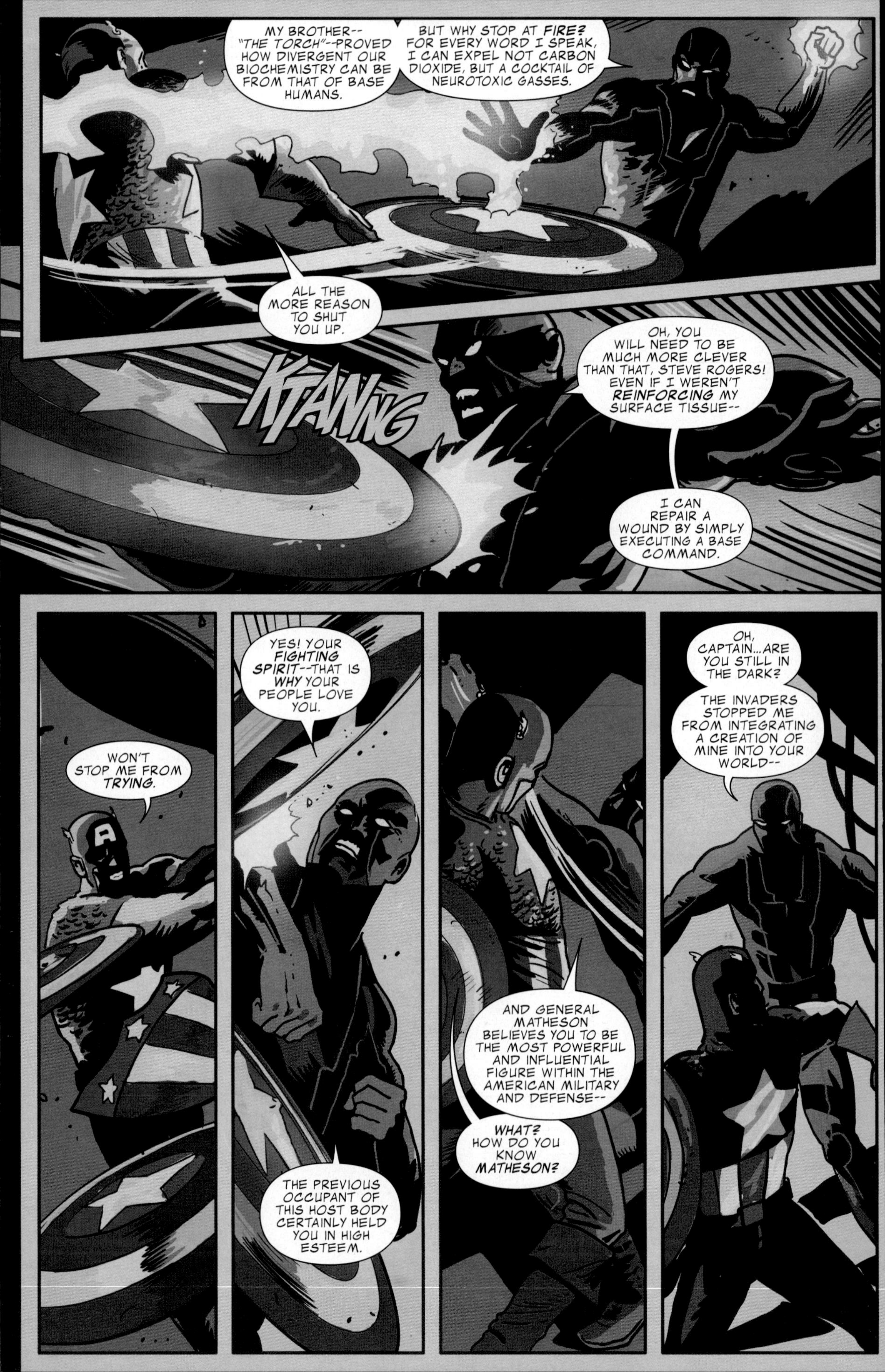

MY BROTHER-- "THE TORCH"--PROVED HOW DIVERGENT OUR BIOCHEMISTRY CAN BE FROM THAT OF BASE HUMANS.
BUT WHY STOP AT FIRE? FOR EVERY WORD I SPEAK, I CAN EXPEL NOT CARBON DIOXIDE, BUT A COCKTAIL OF NEUROTOXIC GASSES.
ALL THE MORE REASON TO SHUT YOU UP.
KTANNG
OH, YOU WILL NEED TO BE MUCH MORE CLEVER THAN THAT, STEVE ROGERS! EVEN IF I WEREN'T REINFORCING MY SURFACE TISSUE--
I CAN REPAIR A WOUND BY SIMPLY EXECUTING A BASE COMMAND.
WON'T STOP ME FROM TRYING.
YES! YOUR FIGHTING SPIRIT--THAT IS WHY YOUR PEOPLE LOVE YOU.
THE PREVIOUS OCCUPANT OF THIS HOST BODY CERTAINLY HELD YOU IN HIGH ESTEEM.
AND GENERAL MATHESON BELIEVES YOU TO BE THE MOST POWERFUL AND INFLUENTIAL FIGURE WITHIN THE AMERICAN MILITARY AND DEFENSE--
WHAT? HOW DO YOU KNOW MATHESON?
OH, CAPTAIN...ARE YOU STILL IN THE DARK?
THE INVADERS STOPPED ME FROM INTEGRATING A CREATION OF MINE INTO YOUR WORLD--

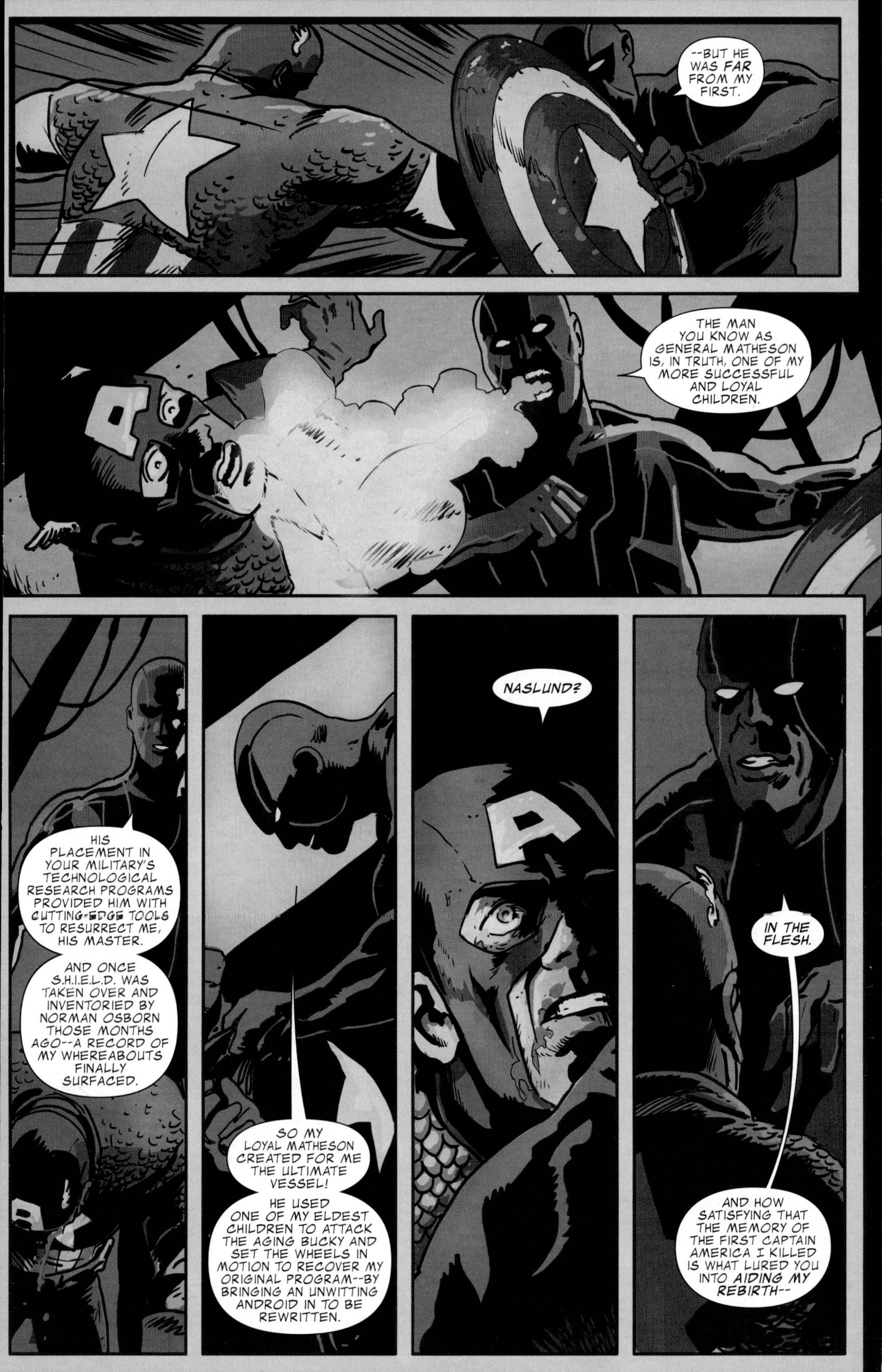
--BUT HE WAS FAR FROM MY FIRST.
THE MAN YOU KNOW AS GENERAL MATHESON IS, IN TRUTH, ONE OF MY MORE SUCCESSFUL AND LOYAL CHILDREN.
HIS PLACEMENT IN YOUR MILITARY'S TECHNOLOGICAL RESEARCH PROGRAMS PROVIDED HIM WITH CUTTING-EDGE TOOLS TO RESURRECT ME, HIS MASTER.
AND ONCE S.H.I.E.L.D. WAS TAKEN OVER AND INVENTORIED BY NORMAN OSBORN THOSE MONTHS AGO--A RECORD OF MY WHEREABOUTS FINALLY SURFACED.
SO MY LOYAL MATHESON CREATED FOR ME THE ULTIMATE VESSEL!
HE USED ONE OF MY ELDEST CHILDREN TO ATTACK THE AGING BUCKY AND SET THE WHEELS IN MOTION TO RECOVER MY ORIGINAL PROGRAM--BY BRINGING AN UNWITTING ANDROID IN TO BE REWRITTEN.
NASLUND?
IN THE FLESH.
AND HOW SATISFYING THAT THE MEMORY OF THE FIRST CAPTAIN AMERICA I KILLED IS WHAT LURED YOU INTO AIDING MY REBIRTH--

SO THAT I MAY KILL YOU AGAIN!

HGRAAA--

YOU TRULY WERE A REMARKABLE MAN, STEVE ROGERS.

A MAN OF SUCH POWER AND INFLUENCE--

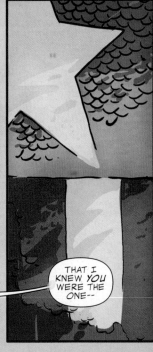

THAT I KNEW YOU WERE THE ONE--

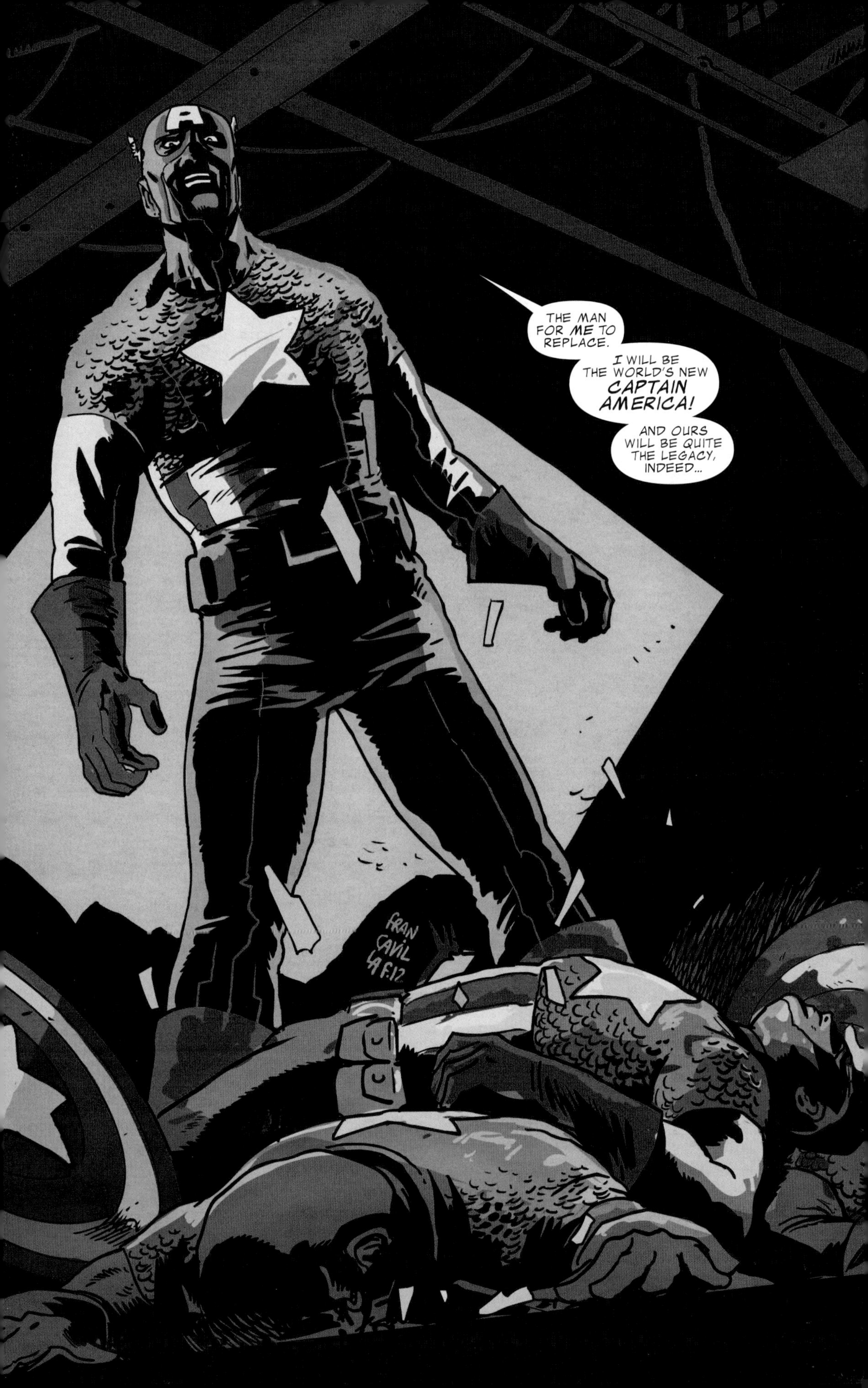
THE MAN FOR *ME* TO REPLACE.
I WILL BE THE WORLD'S NEW ***CAPTAIN AMERICA!***
AND OURS WILL BE QUITE THE LEGACY, INDEED...

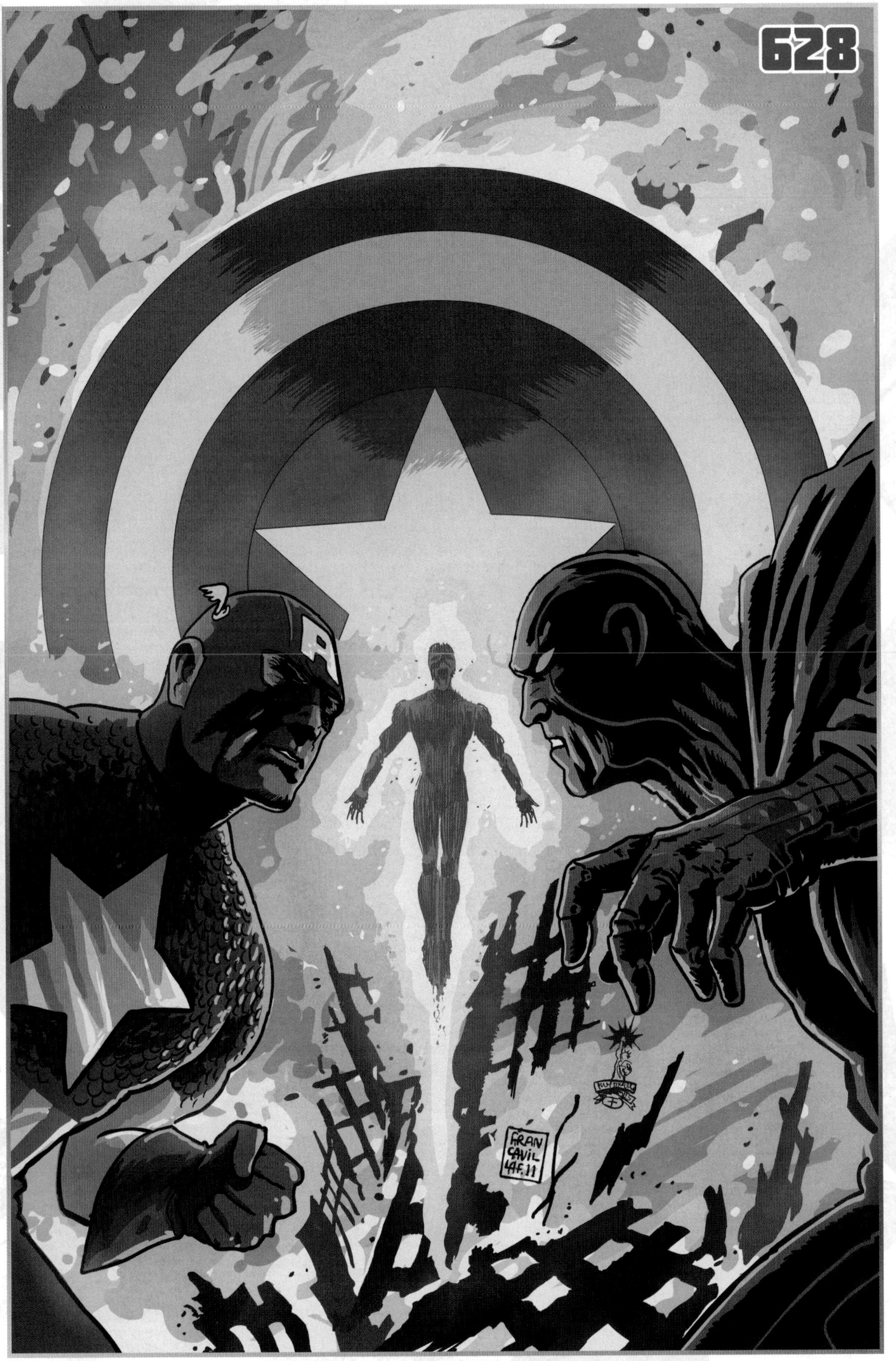
628

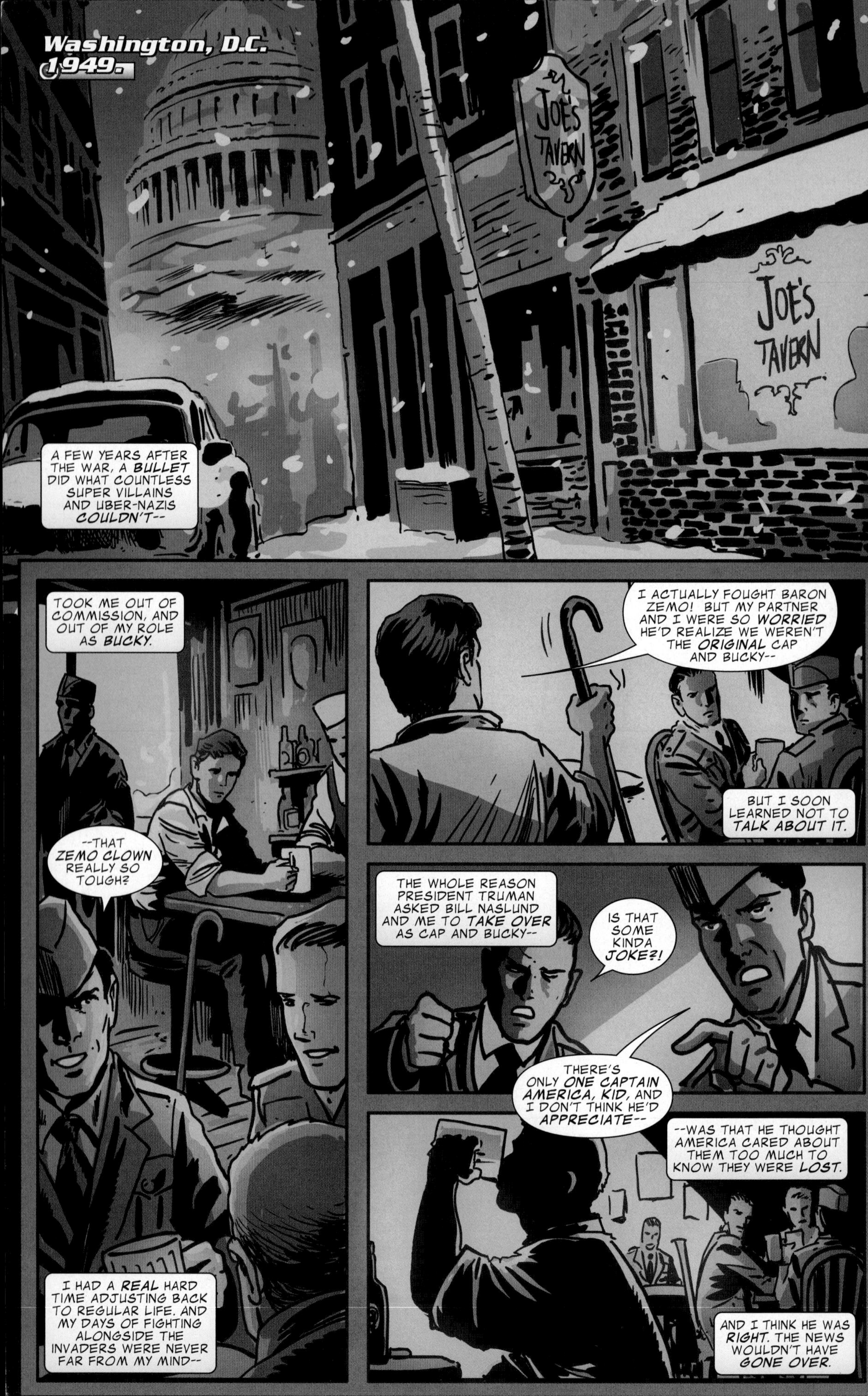
Washington, D.C. 1949.
A FEW YEARS AFTER THE WAR, A BULLET DID WHAT COUNTLESS SUPER VILLAINS AND UBER-NAZIS COULDN'T--
JOE'S TAVERN
JOE'S TAVERN
TOOK ME OUT OF COMMISSION, AND OUT OF MY ROLE AS BUCKY.
--THAT ZEMO CLOWN REALLY SO TOUGH?
I HAD A REAL HARD TIME ADJUSTING BACK TO REGULAR LIFE. AND MY DAYS OF FIGHTING ALONGSIDE THE INVADERS WERE NEVER FAR FROM MY MIND--
I ACTUALLY FOUGHT BARON ZEMO! BUT MY PARTNER AND I WERE SO WORRIED HE'D REALIZE WE WEREN'T THE ORIGINAL CAP AND BUCKY--
BUT I SOON LEARNED NOT TO TALK ABOUT IT.
THE WHOLE REASON PRESIDENT TRUMAN ASKED BILL NASLUND AND ME TO TAKE OVER AS CAP AND BUCKY--
IS THAT SOME KINDA JOKE?!
THERE'S ONLY ONE CAPTAIN AMERICA, KID, AND I DON'T THINK HE'D APPRECIATE--
--WAS THAT HE THOUGHT AMERICA CARED ABOUT THEM TOO MUCH TO KNOW THEY WERE LOST.
AND I THINK HE WAS RIGHT. THE NEWS WOULDN'T HAVE GONE OVER.

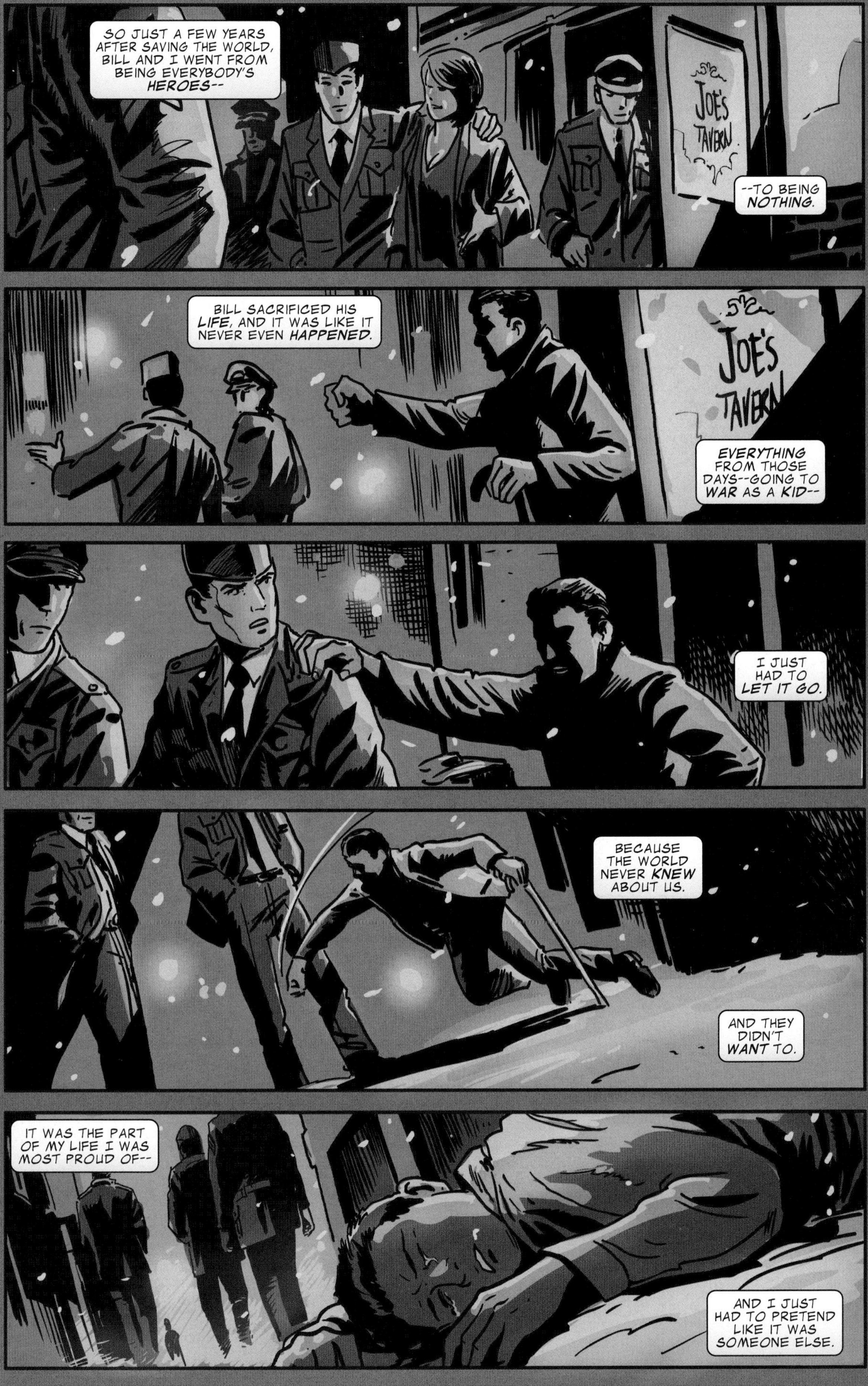
SO JUST A FEW YEARS AFTER SAVING THE WORLD, BILL AND I WENT FROM BEING EVERYBODY'S *HEROES*--
JOE'S TAVERN
--TO BEING *NOTHING*.
BILL SACRIFICED HIS *LIFE*, AND IT WAS LIKE IT NEVER EVEN *HAPPENED*.
JOE'S TAVERN
EVERYTHING FROM THOSE DAYS--GOING TO *WAR* AS A *KID*--
I JUST HAD TO *LET IT GO*.
BECAUSE THE WORLD NEVER *KNEW* ABOUT US.
AND THEY DIDN'T *WANT* TO.
IT WAS THE PART OF MY LIFE I WAS MOST PROUD OF--
AND I JUST HAD TO PRETEND LIKE IT WAS SOMEONE ELSE.

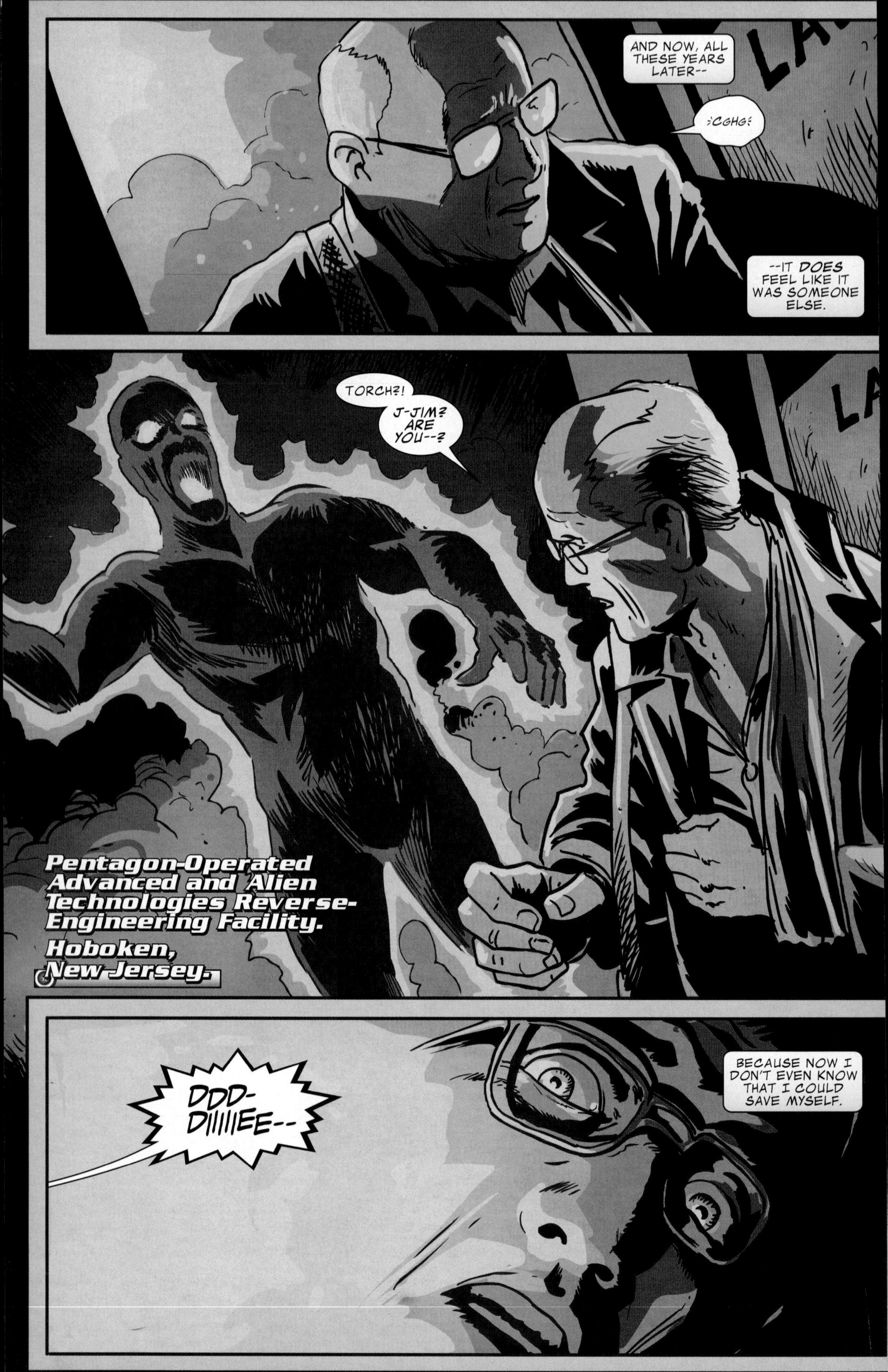

AND NOW, ALL THESE YEARS LATER--
:CGHG:
--IT DOES FEEL LIKE IT WAS SOMEONE ELSE.
TORCH?!
J-JIM? ARE YOU--?
Pentagon-Operated Advanced and Alien Technologies Reverse-Engineering Facility.
Hoboken, New-Jersey.
DDD-DIIIIIEE--
BECAUSE NOW I DON'T EVEN KNOW THAT I COULD SAVE MYSELF.

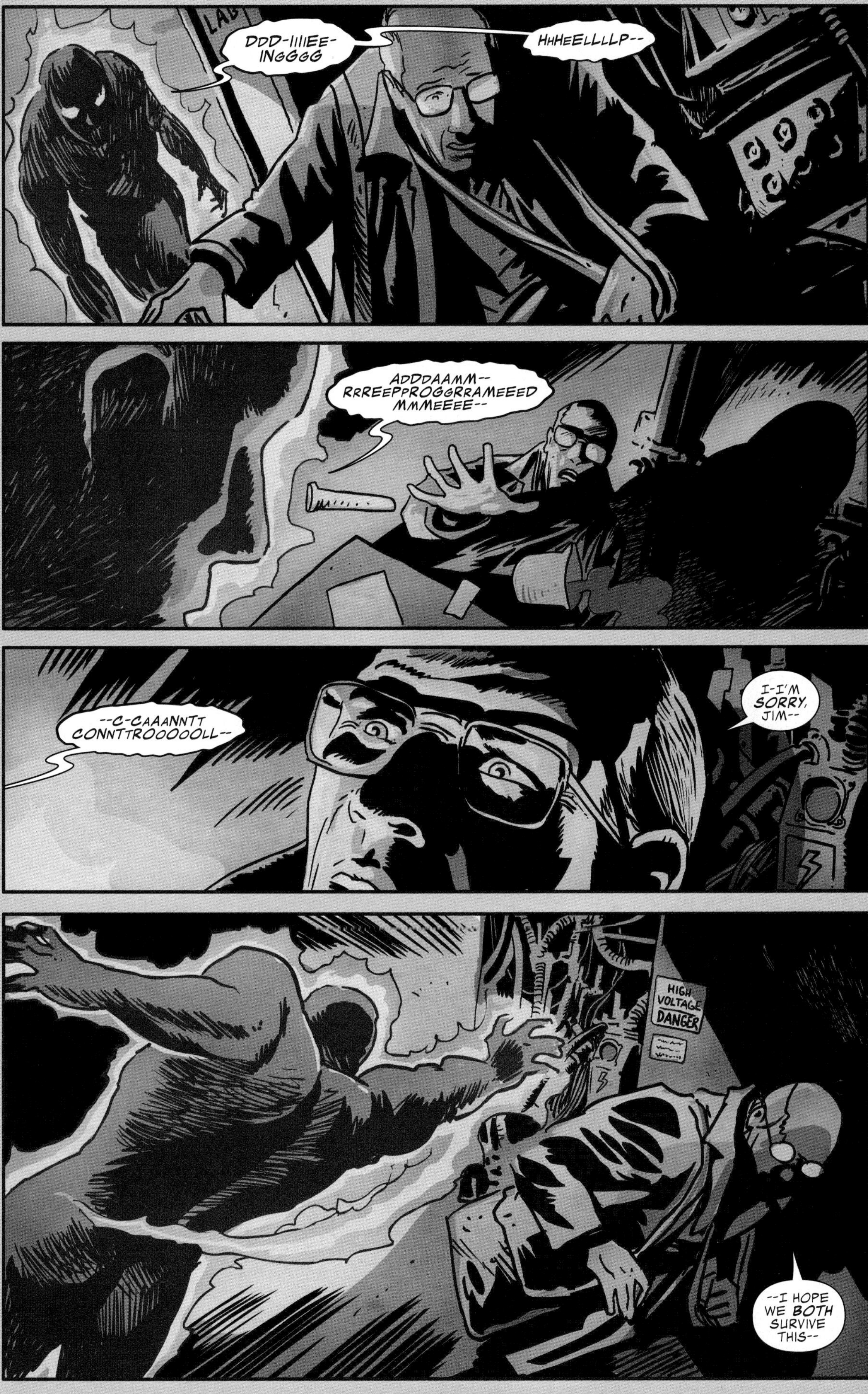
LAB
DDD-IIIIEE-INGGGG
HHHEELLLLP--
ADDDAAMM--RRREEPPROGGRRAMEEED MMMEEEE--
--C-CAAANNTT CONNTTROOOOOOLL--
I-I'M SORRY, JIM--
HIGH VOLTAGE
DANGER
--I HOPE WE **BOTH** SURVIVE THIS--

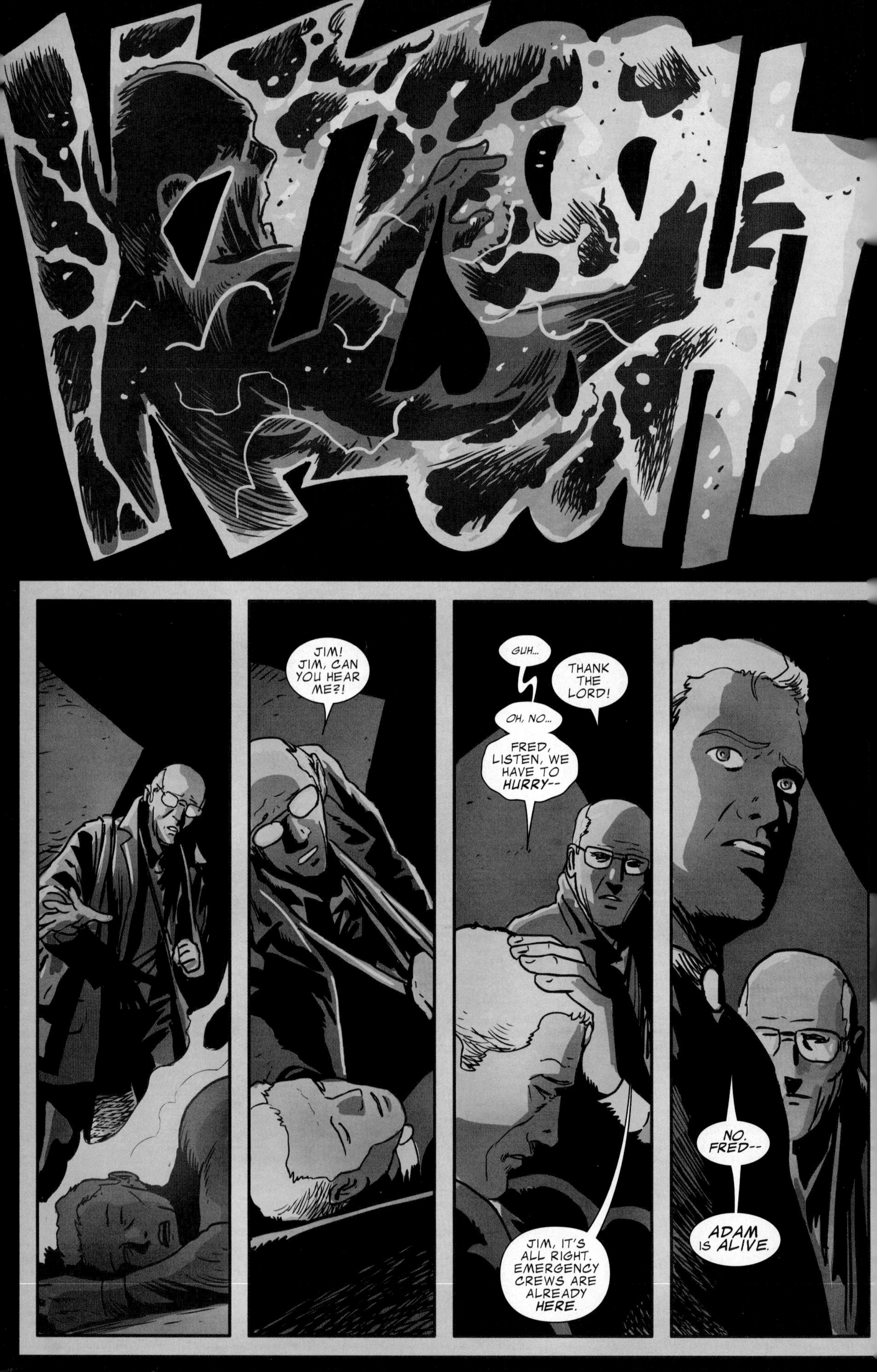
KRAKOOM
JIM! JIM, CAN YOU HEAR ME?!
GUH...
OH, NO...
THANK THE LORD!
FRED, LISTEN, WE HAVE TO HURRY--
JIM, IT'S ALL RIGHT. EMERGENCY CREWS ARE ALREADY HERE.
NO. FRED--
ADAM IS ALIVE.

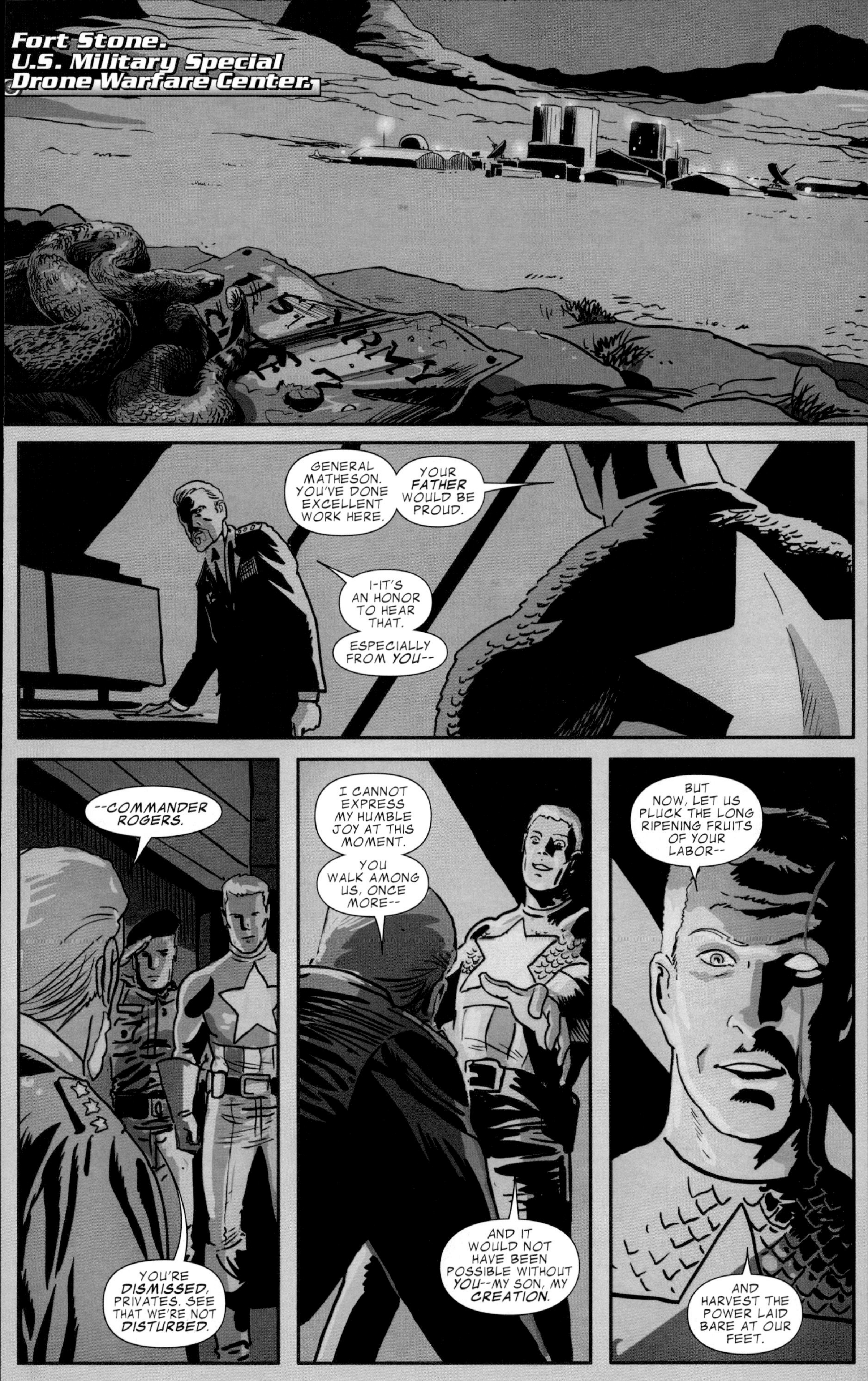
Fort Stone.
U.S. Military Special Drone Warfare Center.
GENERAL MATHESON. YOU'VE DONE EXCELLENT WORK HERE.
YOUR FATHER WOULD BE PROUD.
I-IT'S AN HONOR TO HEAR THAT.
ESPECIALLY FROM YOU--
--COMMANDER ROGERS.
YOU'RE DISMISSED, PRIVATES. SEE THAT WE'RE NOT DISTURBED.
I CANNOT EXPRESS MY HUMBLE JOY AT THIS MOMENT.
YOU WALK AMONG US, ONCE MORE--
AND IT WOULD NOT HAVE BEEN POSSIBLE WITHOUT YOU--MY SON, MY CREATION.
BUT NOW, LET US PLUCK THE LONG RIPENING FRUITS OF YOUR LABOR--
AND HARVEST THE POWER LAID BARE AT OUR FEET.

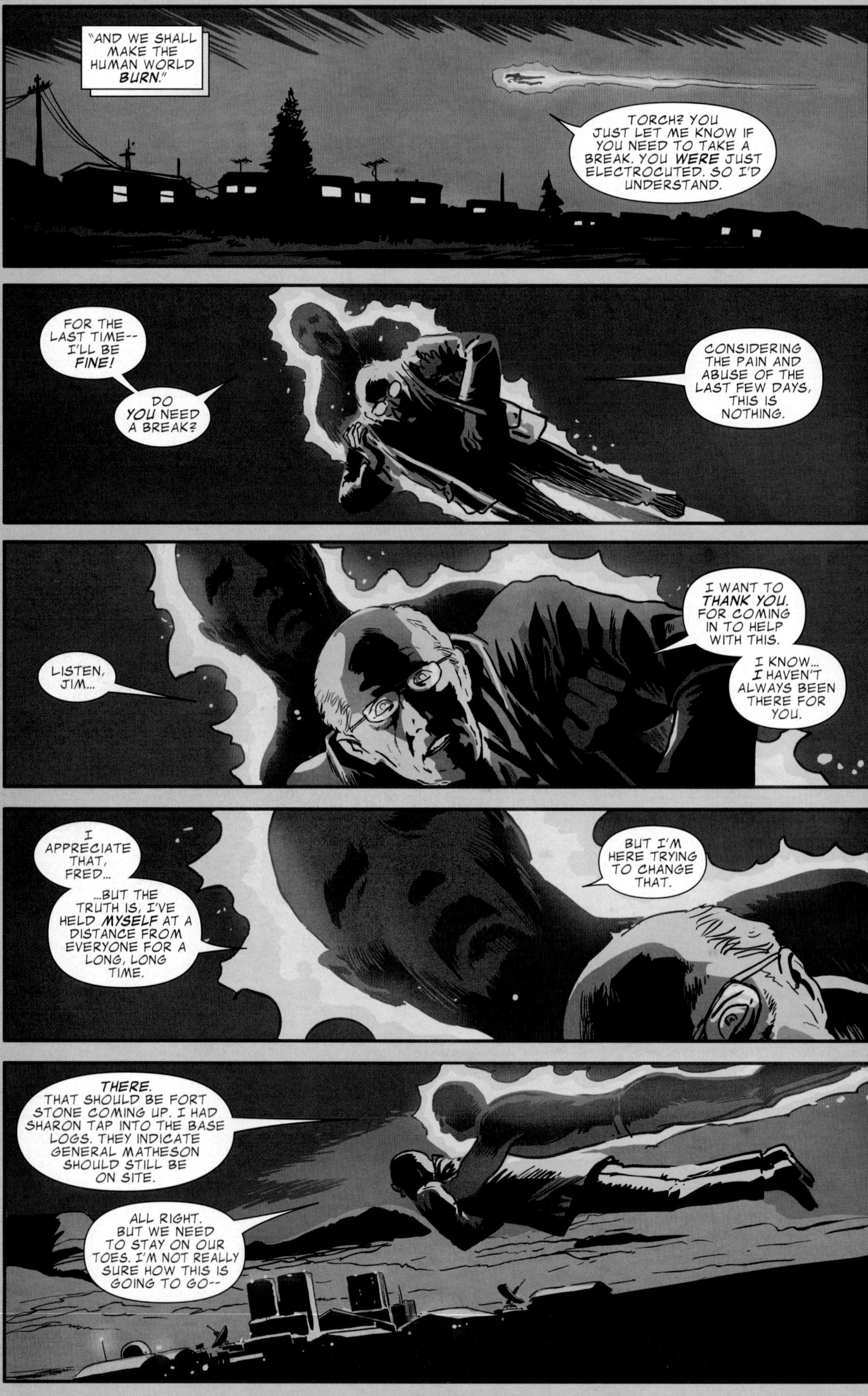
"AND WE SHALL MAKE THE HUMAN WORLD BURN."
TORCH? YOU JUST LET ME KNOW IF YOU NEED TO TAKE A BREAK. YOU WERE JUST ELECTROCUTED. SO I'D UNDERSTAND.
FOR THE LAST TIME-- I'LL BE FINE!
DO YOU NEED A BREAK?
CONSIDERING THE PAIN AND ABUSE OF THE LAST FEW DAYS, THIS IS NOTHING.
LISTEN, JIM...
I WANT TO THANK YOU. FOR COMING IN TO HELP WITH THIS.
I KNOW... I HAVEN'T ALWAYS BEEN THERE FOR YOU.
BUT I'M HERE TRYING TO CHANGE THAT.
I APPRECIATE THAT, FRED...
...BUT THE TRUTH IS, I'VE HELD MYSELF AT A DISTANCE FROM EVERYONE FOR A LONG, LONG TIME.
THERE. THAT SHOULD BE FORT STONE COMING UP. I HAD SHARON TAP INTO THE BASE LOGS. THEY INDICATE GENERAL MATHESON SHOULD STILL BE ON SITE.
ALL RIGHT. BUT WE NEED TO STAY ON OUR TOES. I'M NOT REALLY SURE HOW THIS IS GOING TO GO--

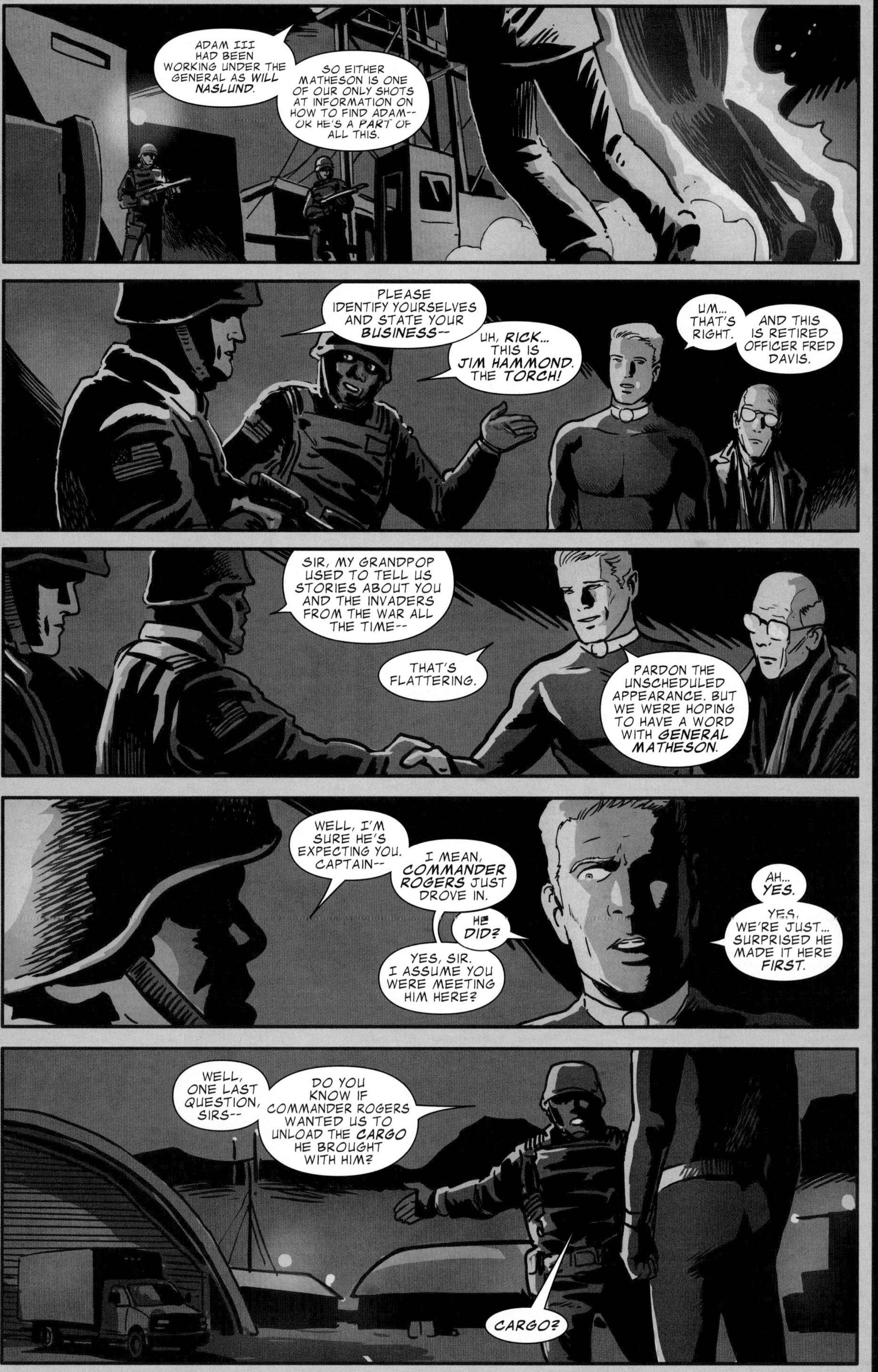
ADAM III HAD BEEN WORKING UNDER THE GENERAL AS WILL NASLUND.
SO EITHER MATHESON IS ONE OF OUR ONLY SHOTS AT INFORMATION ON HOW TO FIND ADAM-- OR HE'S A PART OF ALL THIS.
PLEASE IDENTIFY YOURSELVES AND STATE YOUR BUSINESS--
UH, RICK... THIS IS JIM HAMMOND. THE TORCH!
UM... THAT'S RIGHT.
AND THIS IS RETIRED OFFICER FRED DAVIS.
SIR, MY GRANDPOP USED TO TELL US STORIES ABOUT YOU AND THE INVADERS FROM THE WAR ALL THE TIME--
THAT'S FLATTERING.
PARDON THE UNSCHEDULED APPEARANCE. BUT WE WERE HOPING TO HAVE A WORD WITH GENERAL MATHESON.
WELL, I'M SURE HE'S EXPECTING YOU. CAPTAIN--
I MEAN, COMMANDER ROGERS JUST DROVE IN.
HE DID?
YES, SIR. I ASSUME YOU WERE MEETING HIM HERE?
AH... YES.
YES, WE'RE JUST... SURPRISED HE MADE IT HERE FIRST.
WELL, ONE LAST QUESTION, SIRS--
DO YOU KNOW IF COMMANDER ROGERS WANTED US TO UNLOAD THE CARGO HE BROUGHT WITH HIM?
CARGO?

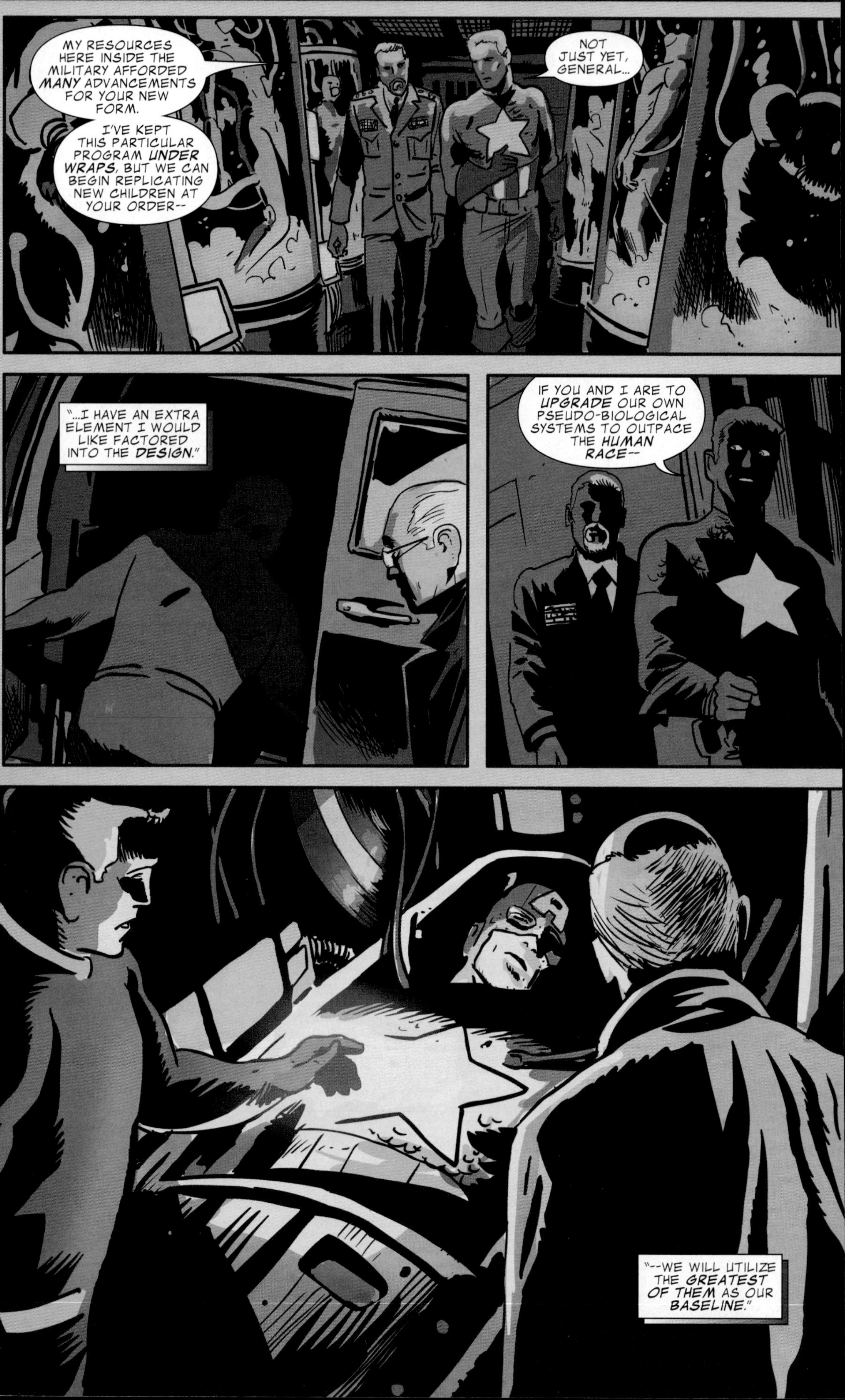
MY RESOURCES HERE INSIDE THE MILITARY AFFORDED MANY ADVANCEMENTS FOR YOUR NEW FORM.
I'VE KEPT THIS PARTICULAR PROGRAM UNDER WRAPS, BUT WE CAN BEGIN REPLICATING NEW CHILDREN AT YOUR ORDER--
NOT JUST YET, GENERAL...
"...I HAVE AN EXTRA ELEMENT I WOULD LIKE FACTORED INTO THE DESIGN."
IF YOU AND I ARE TO UPGRADE OUR OWN PSEUDO-BIOLOGICAL SYSTEMS TO OUTPACE THE HUMAN RACE--
"--WE WILL UTILIZE THE GREATEST OF THEM AS OUR BASELINE."

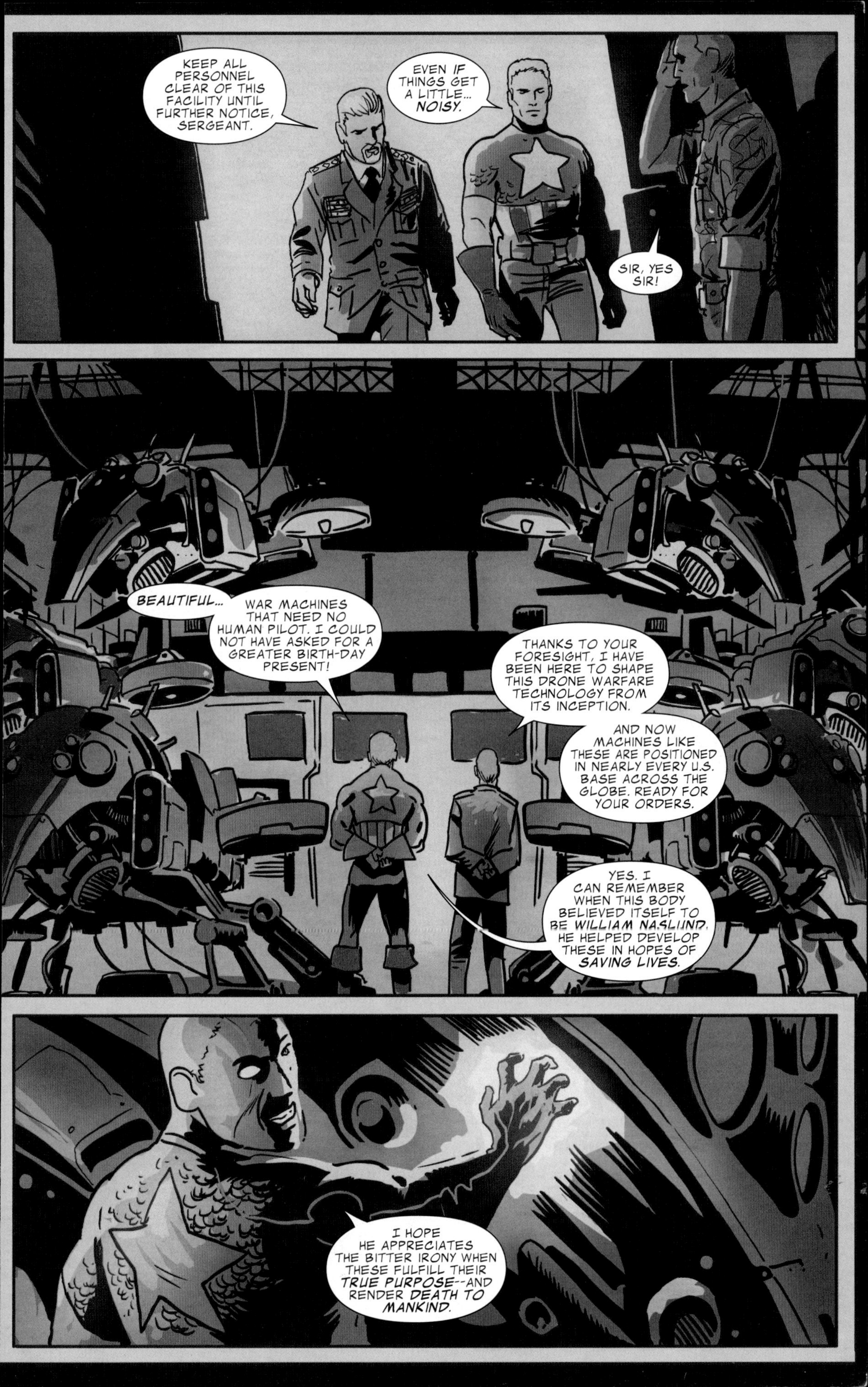
KEEP ALL PERSONNEL CLEAR OF THIS FACILITY UNTIL FURTHER NOTICE, SERGEANT.
EVEN IF THINGS GET A LITTLE... NOISY.
SIR, YES SIR!
BEAUTIFUL...
WAR MACHINES THAT NEED NO HUMAN PILOT. I COULD NOT HAVE ASKED FOR A GREATER BIRTH-DAY PRESENT!
THANKS TO YOUR FORESIGHT, I HAVE BEEN HERE TO SHAPE THIS DRONE WARFARE TECHNOLOGY FROM ITS INCEPTION.
AND NOW MACHINES LIKE THESE ARE POSITIONED IN NEARLY EVERY U.S. BASE ACROSS THE GLOBE. READY FOR YOUR ORDERS.
YES. I CAN REMEMBER WHEN THIS BODY BELIEVED ITSELF TO BE WILLIAM NASLUND. HE HELPED DEVELOP THESE IN HOPES OF SAVING LIVES.
I HOPE HE APPRECIATES THE BITTER IRONY WHEN THESE FULFILL THEIR TRUE PURPOSE--AND RENDER DEATH TO MANKIND.

OH YES, YOU'RE *EAGER CHILDREN*, AREN'T YOU?

WT BZZ CHK

BUT THEN, THAT'S THE WAY OF THE WORLD. AS THE OLDER MEN WEAR ON, A YOUNGER AND HUNGRIER MODEL SURGES FORWARD TO TAKE HIS PLACE.

ONLY HUMANS HAVE BEGUN REPLACING THEMSELVES WITH MACHINES...

HOW ABOUT WE *EXPEDITE* THAT PROCESS.

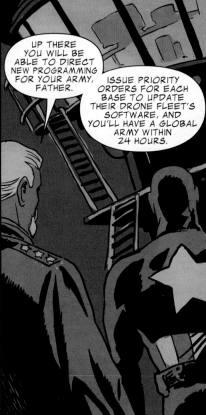

UP THERE YOU WILL BE ABLE TO DIRECT NEW PROGRAMMING FOR YOUR ARMY, *FATHER*.

ISSUE PRIORITY ORDERS FOR EACH BASE TO UPDATE THEIR DRONE FLEET'S SOFTWARE, AND YOU'LL HAVE A GLOBAL ARMY WITHIN 24 HOURS.

ACTUALLY, GENERAL-- *STEVE ROGERS'* BIOMETRICS WILL PROVIDE THE CLEARANCE TO ISSUE SUCH ORDERS.

AND AS HE NO LONGER HAS *NEED*--HE WON'T MIND MY BORROWING THEM.

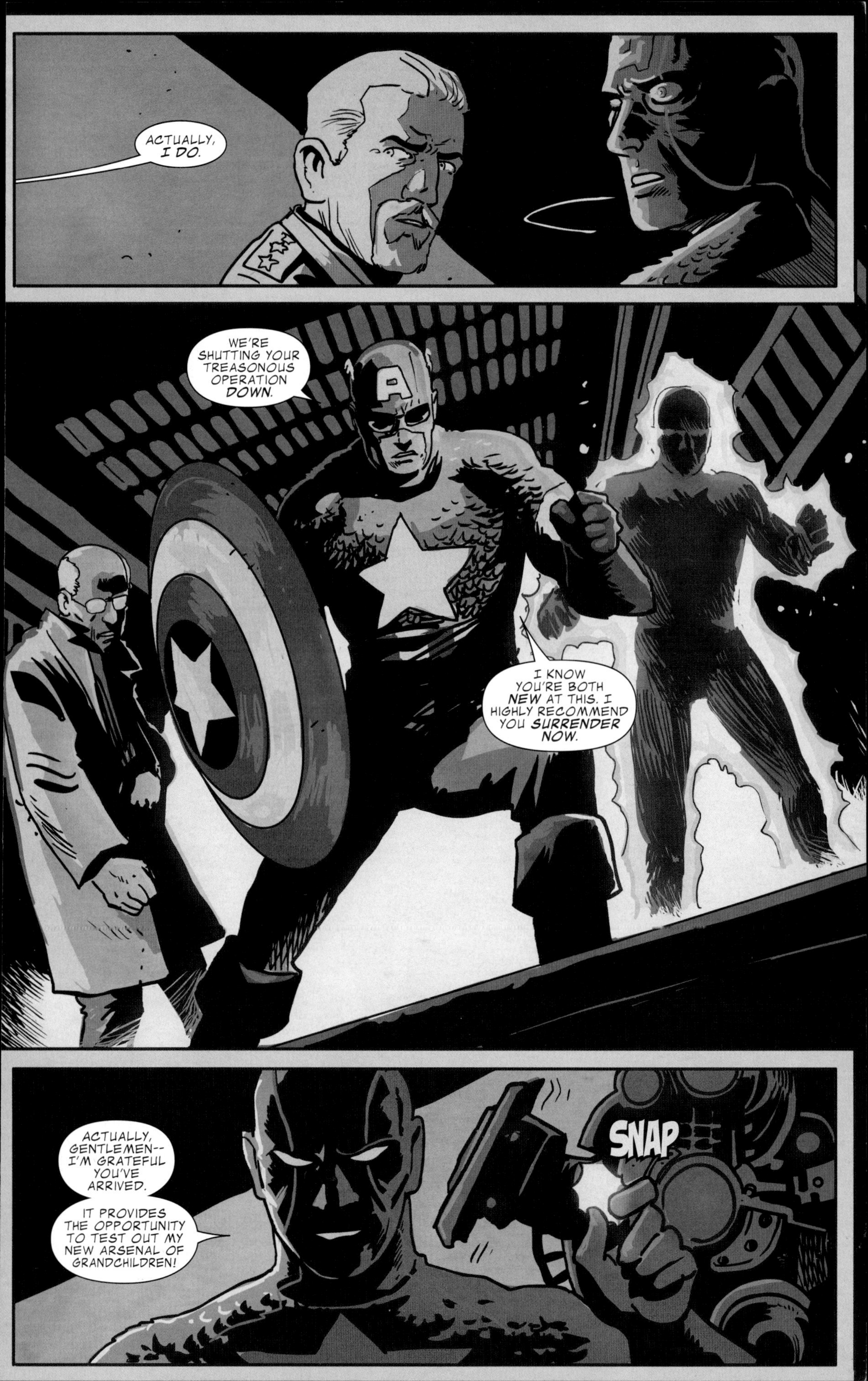
ACTUALLY, I DO.
WE'RE SHUTTING YOUR TREASONOUS OPERATION DOWN.
I KNOW YOU'RE BOTH NEW AT THIS. I HIGHLY RECOMMEND YOU SURRENDER NOW.
ACTUALLY, GENTLEMEN-- I'M GRATEFUL YOU'VE ARRIVED.
IT PROVIDES THE OPPORTUNITY TO TEST OUT MY NEW ARSENAL OF GRANDCHILDREN!
SNAP

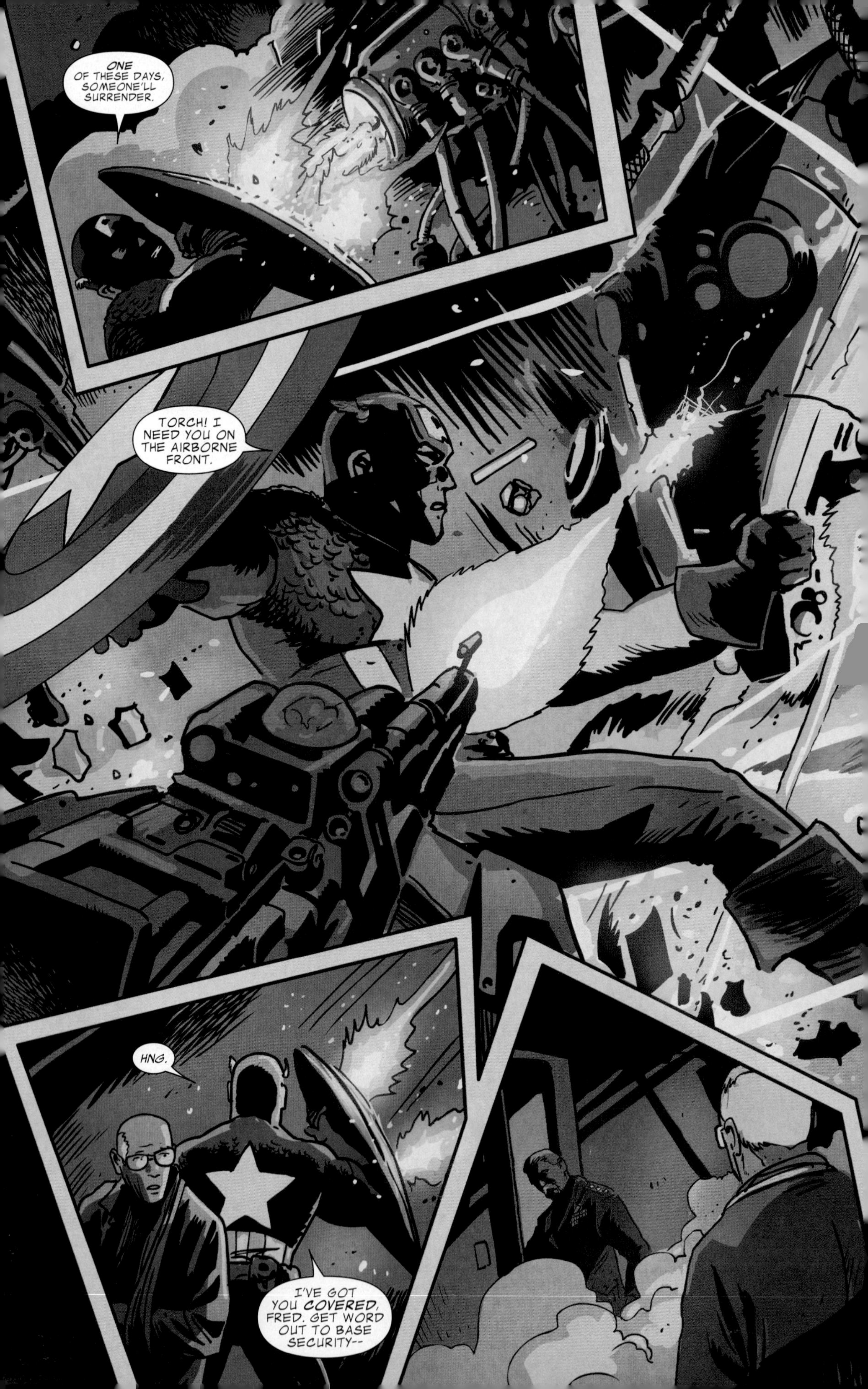
ONE OF THESE DAYS, SOMEONE'LL SURRENDER.
TORCH! I NEED YOU ON THE AIRBORNE FRONT.
HNG.
I'VE GOT YOU COVERED, FRED. GET WORD OUT TO BASE SECURITY--

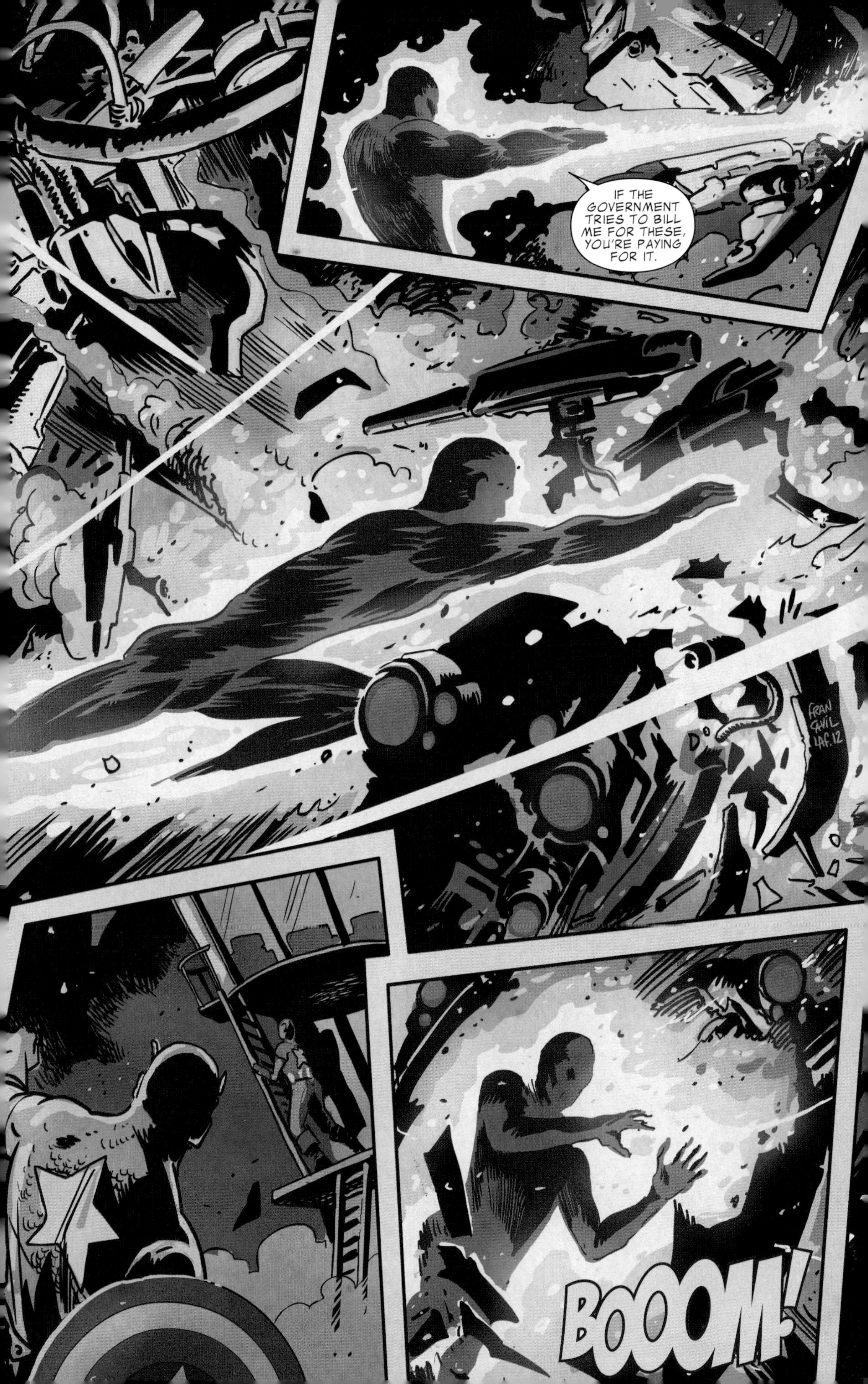
IF THE GOVERNMENT TRIES TO BILL ME FOR THESE, YOU'RE PAYING FOR IT.
FRAN GAVIL 4AF.12
BOOOM!

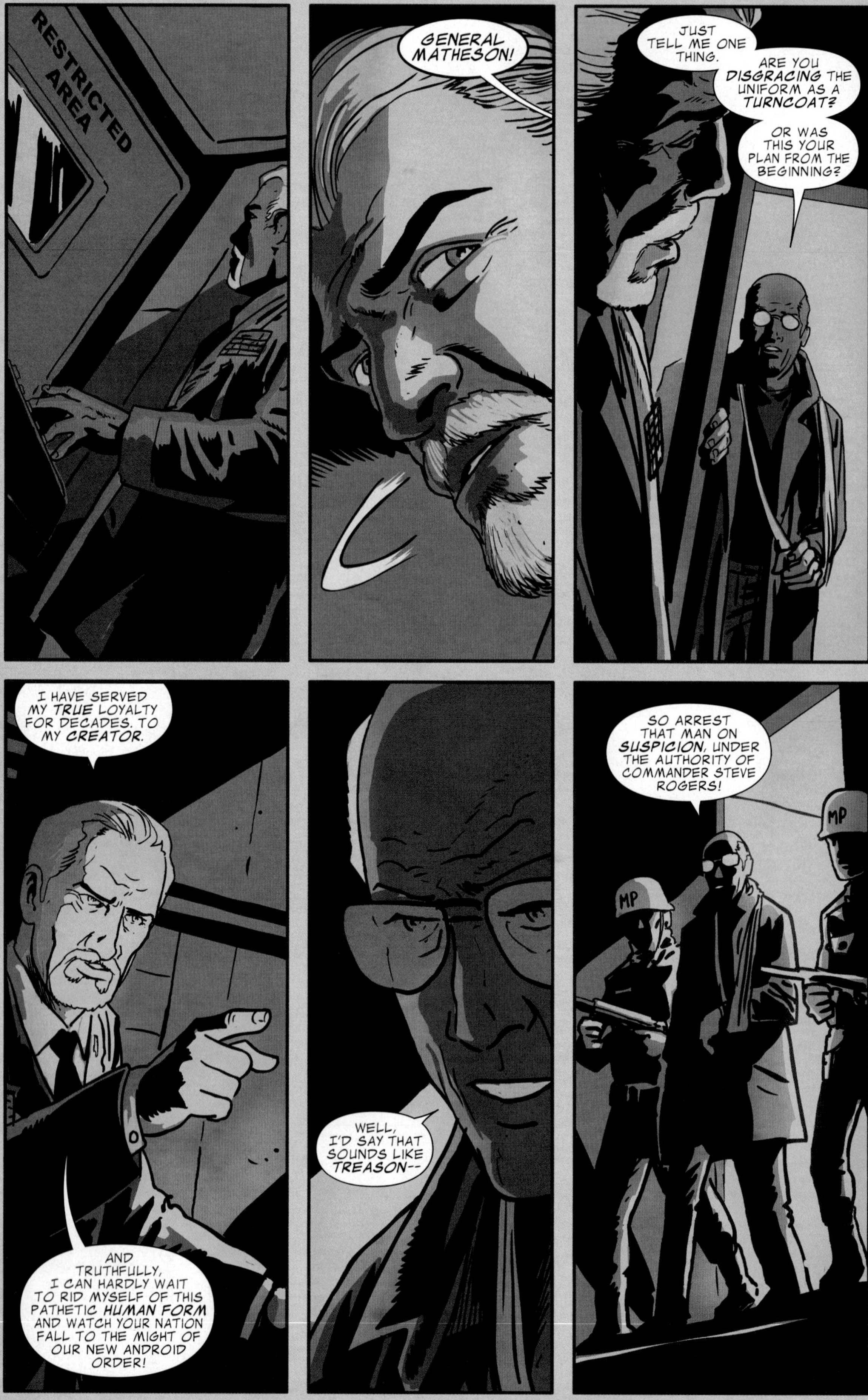
RESTRICTED AREA
GENERAL MATHESON!
JUST TELL ME ONE THING.
ARE YOU DISGRACING THE UNIFORM AS A TURNCOAT?
OR WAS THIS YOUR PLAN FROM THE BEGINNING?
I HAVE SERVED MY TRUE LOYALTY FOR DECADES. TO MY CREATOR.
AND TRUTHFULLY, I CAN HARDLY WAIT TO RID MYSELF OF THIS PATHETIC HUMAN FORM AND WATCH YOUR NATION FALL TO THE MIGHT OF OUR NEW ANDROID ORDER!
WELL, I'D SAY THAT SOUNDS LIKE TREASON--
SO ARREST THAT MAN ON SUSPICION, UNDER THE AUTHORITY OF COMMANDER STEVE ROGERS!
MP
MP

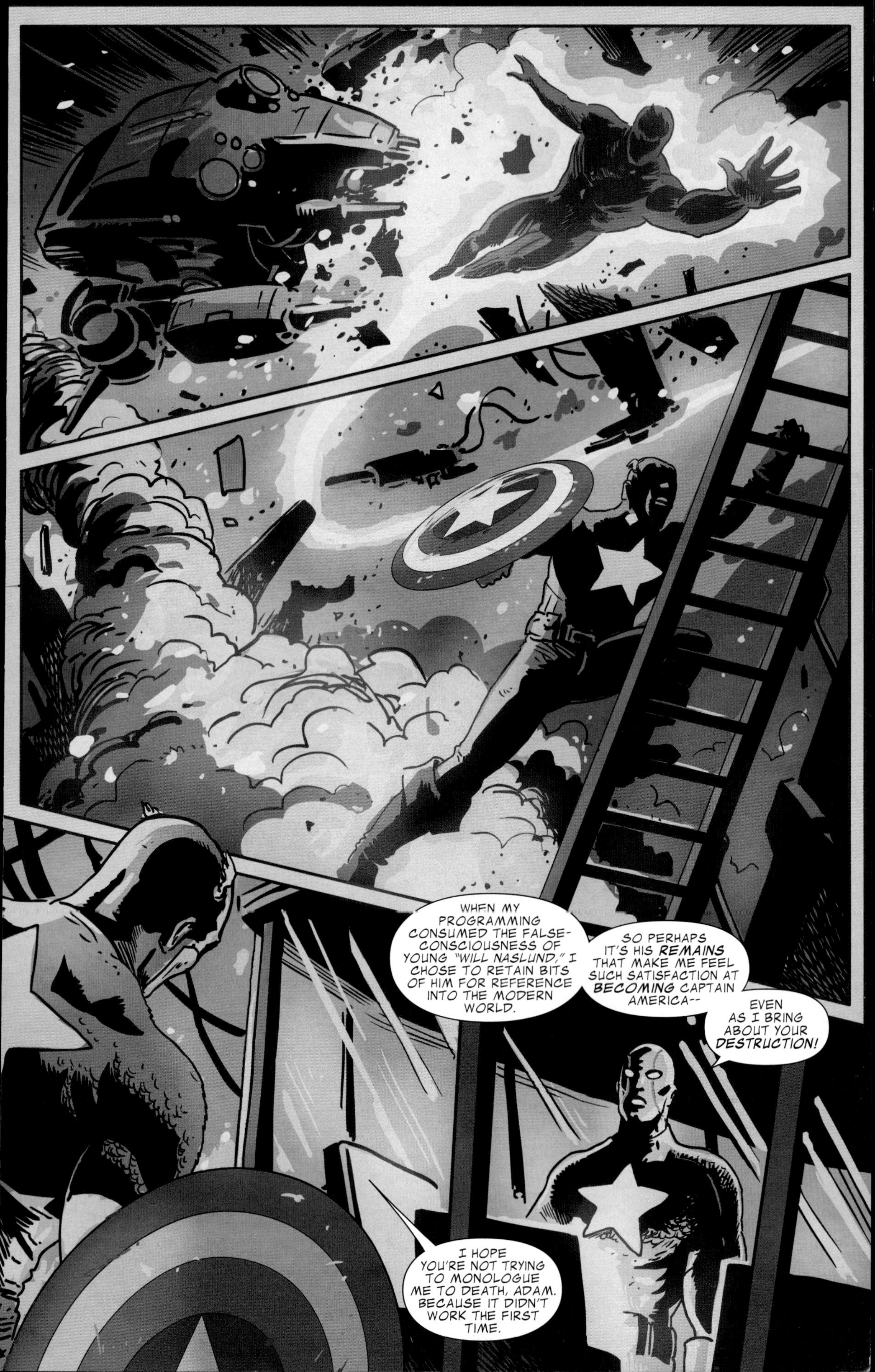

WHEN MY PROGRAMMING CONSUMED THE FALSE-CONSCIOUSNESS OF YOUNG "WILL NASLUND," I CHOSE TO RETAIN BITS OF HIM FOR REFERENCE INTO THE MODERN WORLD.
SO PERHAPS IT'S HIS REMAINS THAT MAKE ME FEEL SUCH SATISFACTION AT BECOMING CAPTAIN AMERICA--
EVEN AS I BRING ABOUT YOUR DESTRUCTION!
I HOPE YOU'RE NOT TRYING TO MONOLOGUE ME TO DEATH, ADAM. BECAUSE IT DIDN'T WORK THE FIRST TIME.

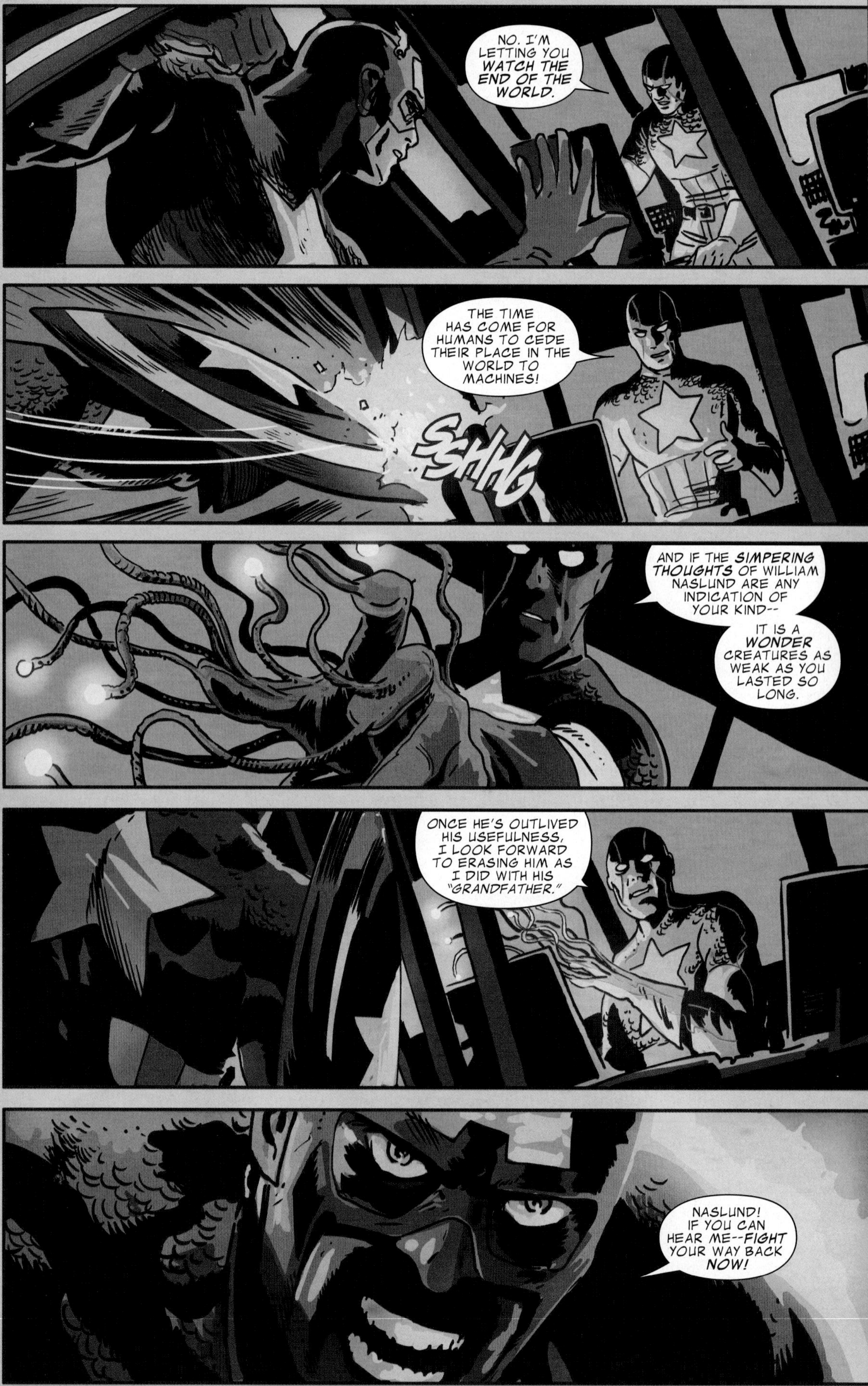
NO. I'M LETTING YOU WATCH THE END OF THE WORLD.
THE TIME HAS COME FOR HUMANS TO CEDE THEIR PLACE IN THE WORLD TO MACHINES!
SSHHG
AND IF THE SIMPERING THOUGHTS OF WILLIAM NASLUND ARE ANY INDICATION OF YOUR KIND--
IT IS A WONDER CREATURES AS WEAK AS YOU LASTED SO LONG.
ONCE HE'S OUTLIVED HIS USEFULNESS, I LOOK FORWARD TO ERASING HIM AS I DID WITH HIS "GRANDFATHER."
NASLUND! IF YOU CAN HEAR ME--FIGHT YOUR WAY BACK NOW!

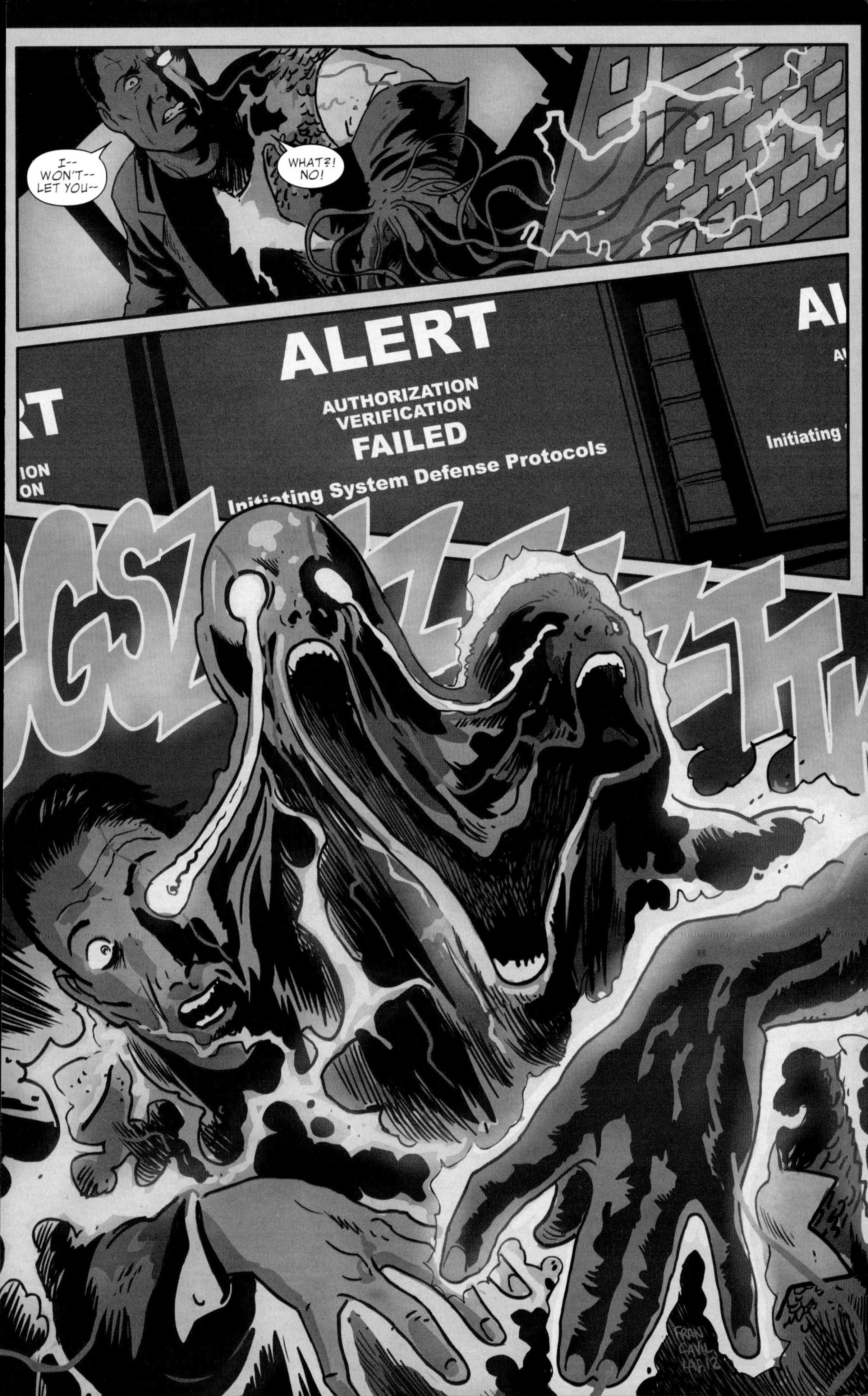

I-- WON'T-- LET YOU--
WHAT?! NO!
ALERT
AUTHORIZATION VERIFICATION FAILED
Initiating System Defense Protocols

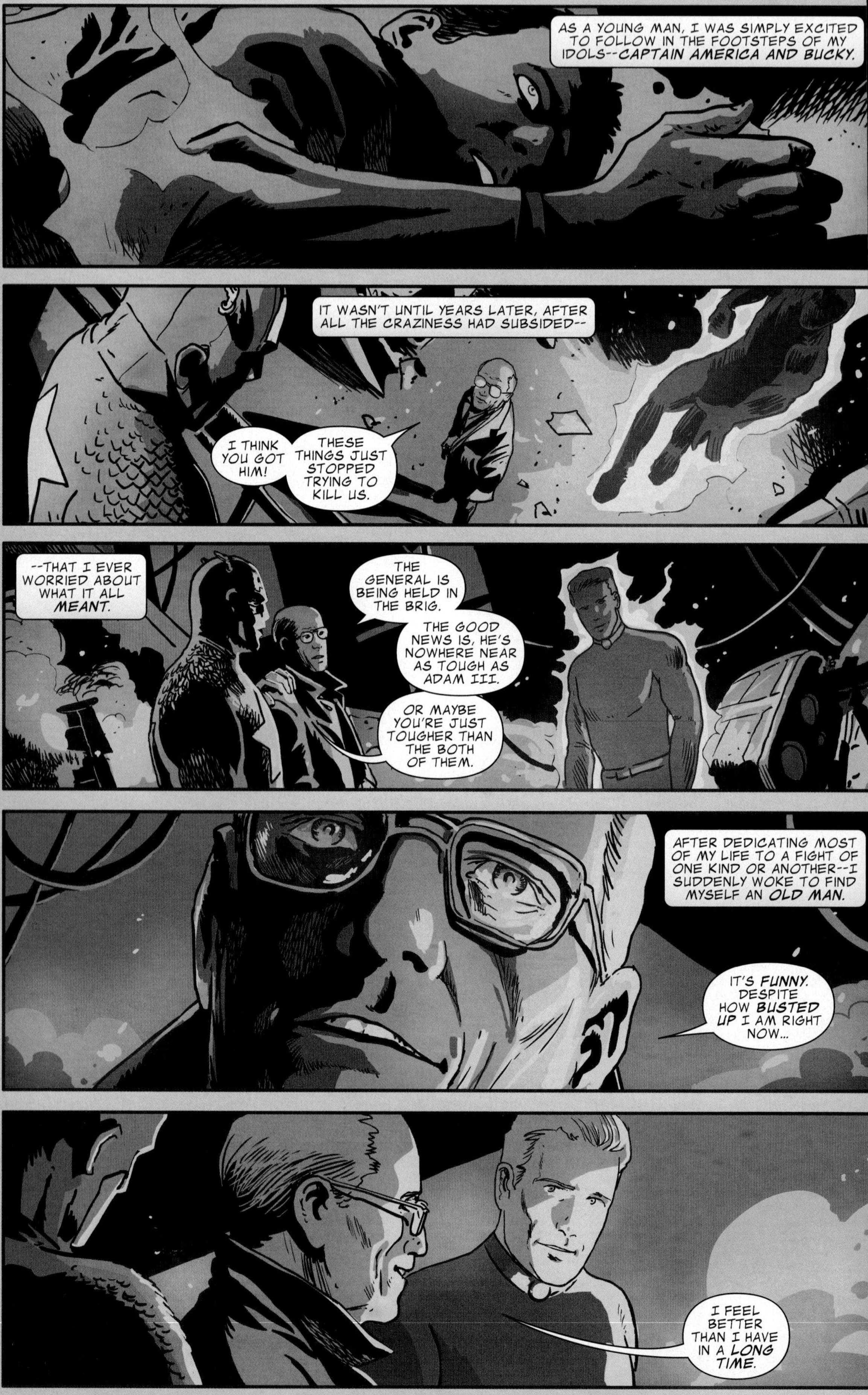
AS A YOUNG MAN, I WAS SIMPLY EXCITED TO FOLLOW IN THE FOOTSTEPS OF MY IDOLS--CAPTAIN AMERICA AND BUCKY.
IT WASN'T UNTIL YEARS LATER, AFTER ALL THE CRAZINESS HAD SUBSIDED--
I THINK YOU GOT HIM!
THESE THINGS JUST STOPPED TRYING TO KILL US.
--THAT I EVER WORRIED ABOUT WHAT IT ALL MEANT.
THE GENERAL IS BEING HELD IN THE BRIG.
THE GOOD NEWS IS, HE'S NOWHERE NEAR AS TOUGH AS ADAM III.
OR MAYBE YOU'RE JUST TOUGHER THAN THE BOTH OF THEM.
AFTER DEDICATING MOST OF MY LIFE TO A FIGHT OF ONE KIND OR ANOTHER--I SUDDENLY WOKE TO FIND MYSELF AN OLD MAN.
IT'S FUNNY. DESPITE HOW BUSTED UP I AM RIGHT NOW...
I FEEL BETTER THAN I HAVE IN A LONG TIME.

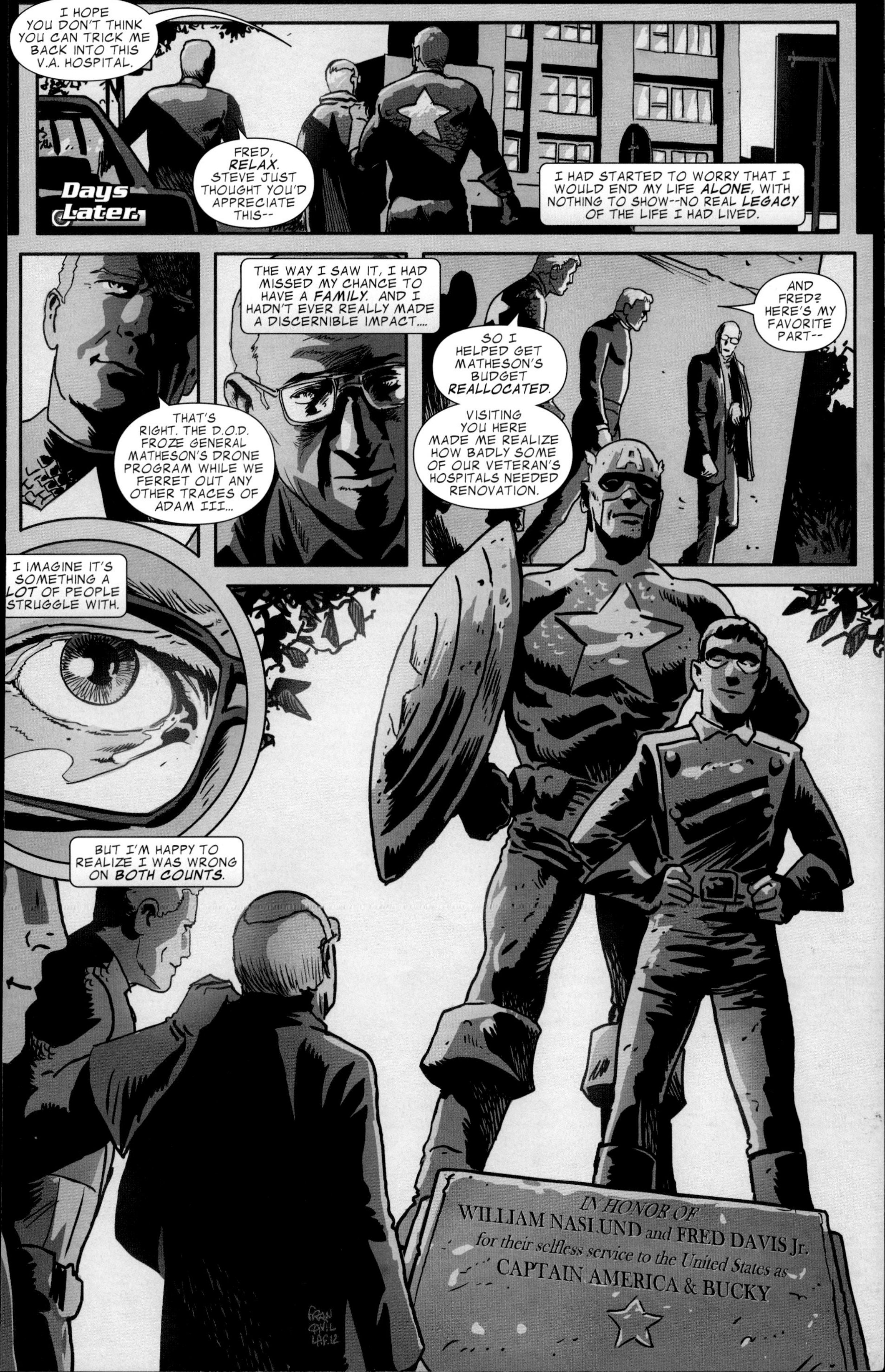
I HOPE YOU DON'T THINK YOU CAN TRICK ME BACK INTO THIS V.A. HOSPITAL.
Days Later.
FRED, RELAX. STEVE JUST THOUGHT YOU'D APPRECIATE THIS--
I HAD STARTED TO WORRY THAT I WOULD END MY LIFE ALONE, WITH NOTHING TO SHOW--NO REAL LEGACY OF THE LIFE I HAD LIVED.
THAT'S RIGHT. THE D.O.D. FROZE GENERAL MATHESON'S DRONE PROGRAM WHILE WE FERRET OUT ANY OTHER TRACES OF ADAM III...
THE WAY I SAW IT, I HAD MISSED MY CHANCE TO HAVE A FAMILY. AND I HADN'T EVER REALLY MADE A DISCERNIBLE IMPACT....
SO I HELPED GET MATHESON'S BUDGET REALLOCATED.
VISITING YOU HERE MADE ME REALIZE HOW BADLY SOME OF OUR VETERAN'S HOSPITALS NEEDED RENOVATION.
AND FRED? HERE'S MY FAVORITE PART--
I IMAGINE IT'S SOMETHING A LOT OF PEOPLE STRUGGLE WITH.
BUT I'M HAPPY TO REALIZE I WAS WRONG ON BOTH COUNTS.
IN HONOR OF WILLIAM NASLUND and FRED DAVIS Jr. for their selfless service to the United States as CAPTAIN AMERICA & BUCKY
FRAN CAVIL LAF.12

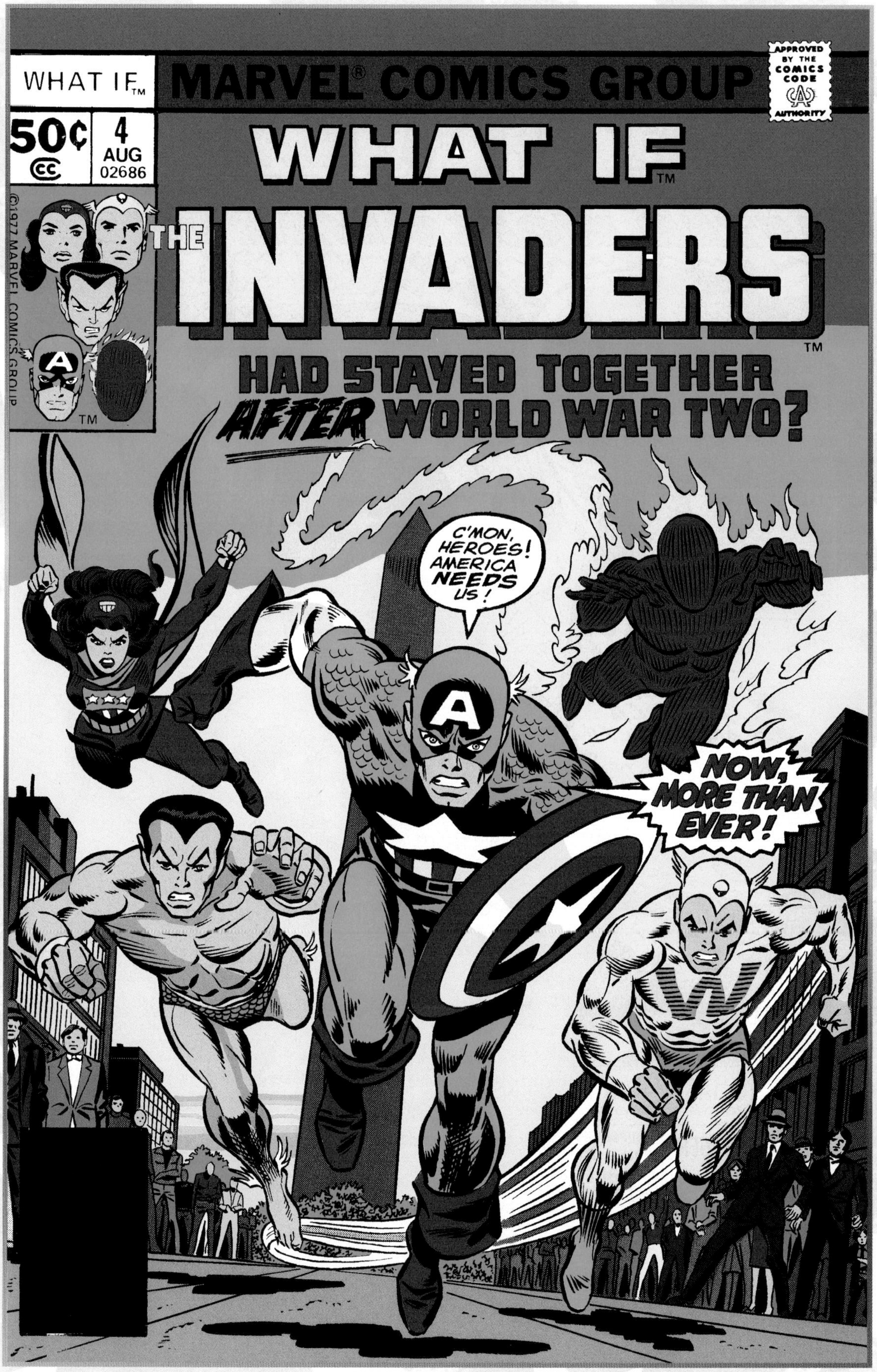
WHAT IF™
MARVEL® COMICS GROUP
APPROVED BY THE COMICS CODE AUTHORITY
50¢
4
AUG
02686
©1977 MARVEL COMICS GROUP
WHAT IF™
THE INVADERS™
HAD STAYED TOGETHER AFTER WORLD WAR TWO?
C'MON, HEROES! AMERICA NEEDS US!
NOW, MORE THAN EVER!

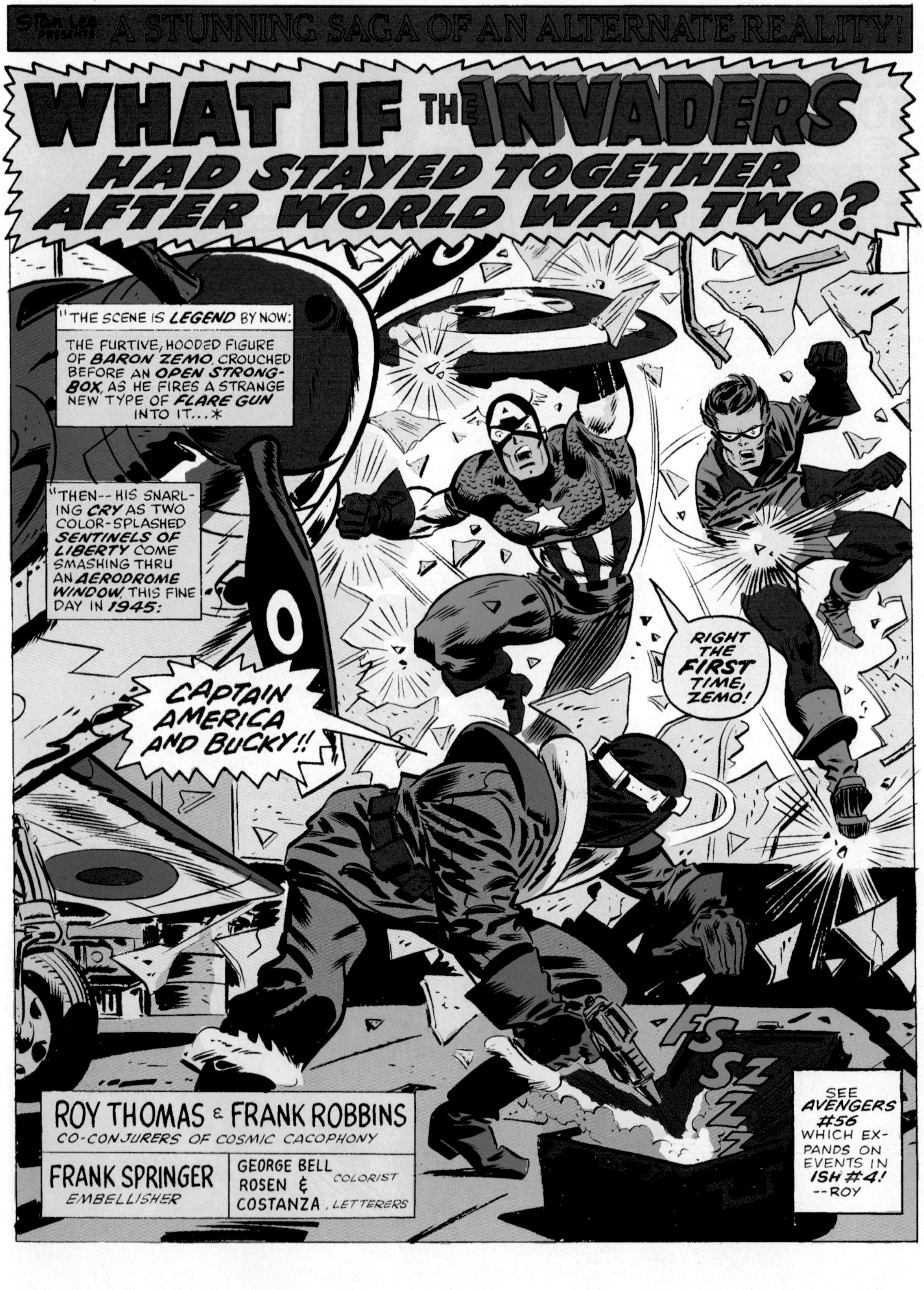

STAN LEE PRESENTS: A STUNNING SAGA OF AN ALTERNATE REALITY!
WHAT IF THE INVADERS HAD STAYED TOGETHER AFTER WORLD WAR TWO?
"THE SCENE IS LEGEND BY NOW:
THE FURTIVE, HOODED FIGURE OF BARON ZEMO, CROUCHED BEFORE AN OPEN STRONG-BOX, AS HE FIRES A STRANGE NEW TYPE OF FLARE GUN INTO IT...*
"THEN--HIS SNARLING CRY AS TWO COLOR-SPLASHED SENTINELS OF LIBERTY COME SMASHING THRU AN AERODROME WINDOW, THIS FINE DAY IN 1945:
CAPTAIN AMERICA AND BUCKY!!
RIGHT THE FIRST TIME, ZEMO!
FSSZZZ
ROY THOMAS & FRANK ROBBINS CO-CONJURERS OF COSMIC CACOPHONY
FRANK SPRINGER EMBELLISHER
GEORGE BELL COLORIST
ROSEN & COSTANZA, LETTERERS
*SEE AVENGERS #56 WHICH EXPANDS ON EVENTS IN ISH #4! --ROY

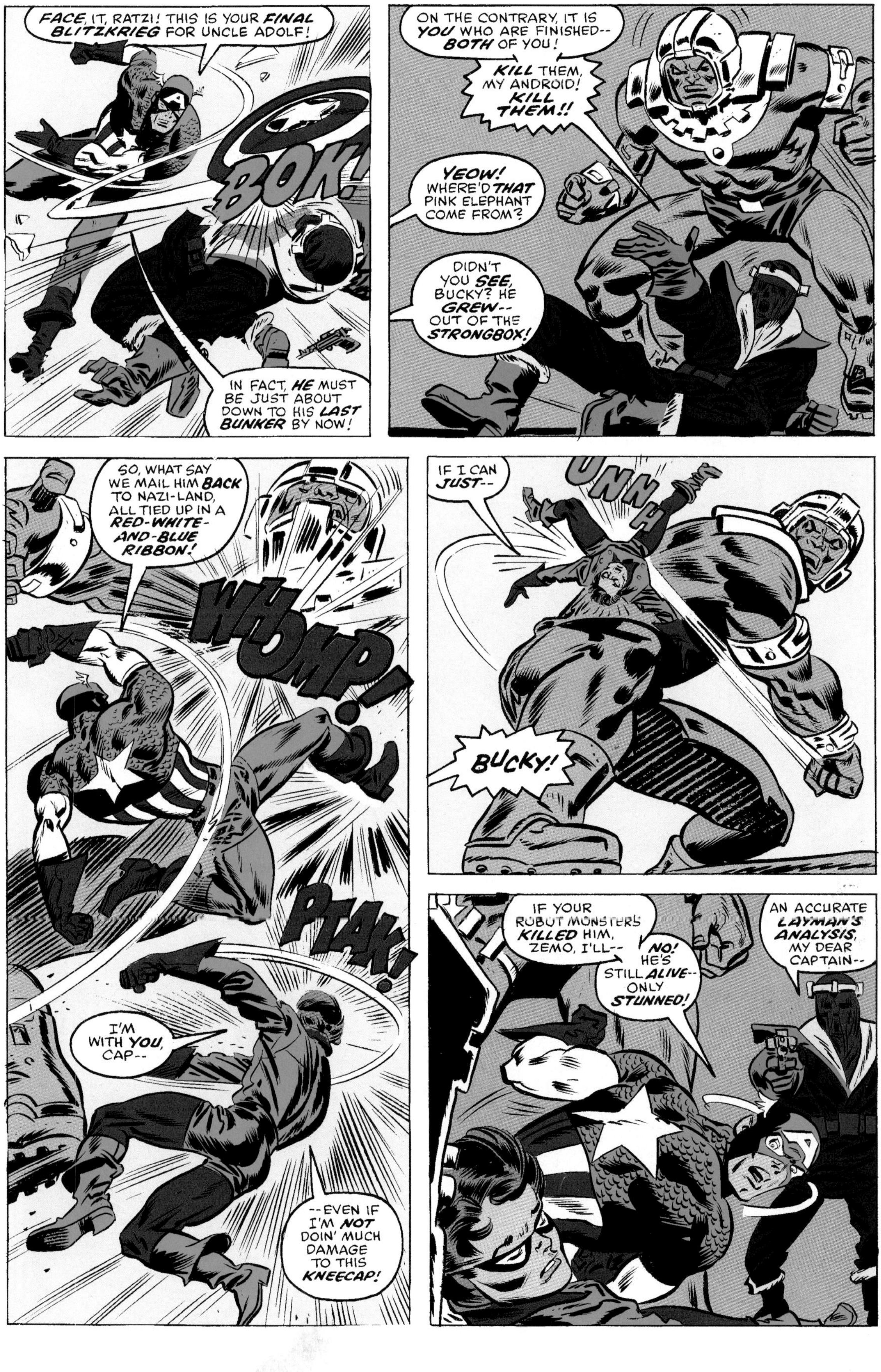
FACE IT, RATZI! THIS IS YOUR FINAL BLITZKRIEG FOR UNCLE ADOLF!
BOK!
IN FACT, HE MUST BE JUST ABOUT DOWN TO HIS LAST BUNKER BY NOW!
ON THE CONTRARY, IT IS YOU WHO ARE FINISHED-- BOTH OF YOU!
KILL THEM, MY ANDROID! KILL THEM!!
YEOW! WHERE'D THAT PINK ELEPHANT COME FROM?
DIDN'T YOU SEE, BUCKY? HE GREW-- OUT OF THE STRONGBOX!
SO, WHAT SAY WE MAIL HIM BACK TO NAZI-LAND, ALL TIED UP IN A RED-WHITE-AND-BLUE RIBBON!
WHOMP!
PTAK!
I'M WITH YOU, CAP--
--EVEN IF I'M NOT DOIN' MUCH DAMAGE TO THIS KNEECAP!
IF I CAN JUST--
UNNH
BUCKY!
IF YOUR ROBOT MONSTERS KILLED HIM, ZEMO, I'LL--
NO! HE'S STILL ALIVE-- ONLY STUNNED!
AN ACCURATE LAYMAN'S ANALYSIS, MY DEAR CAPTAIN--

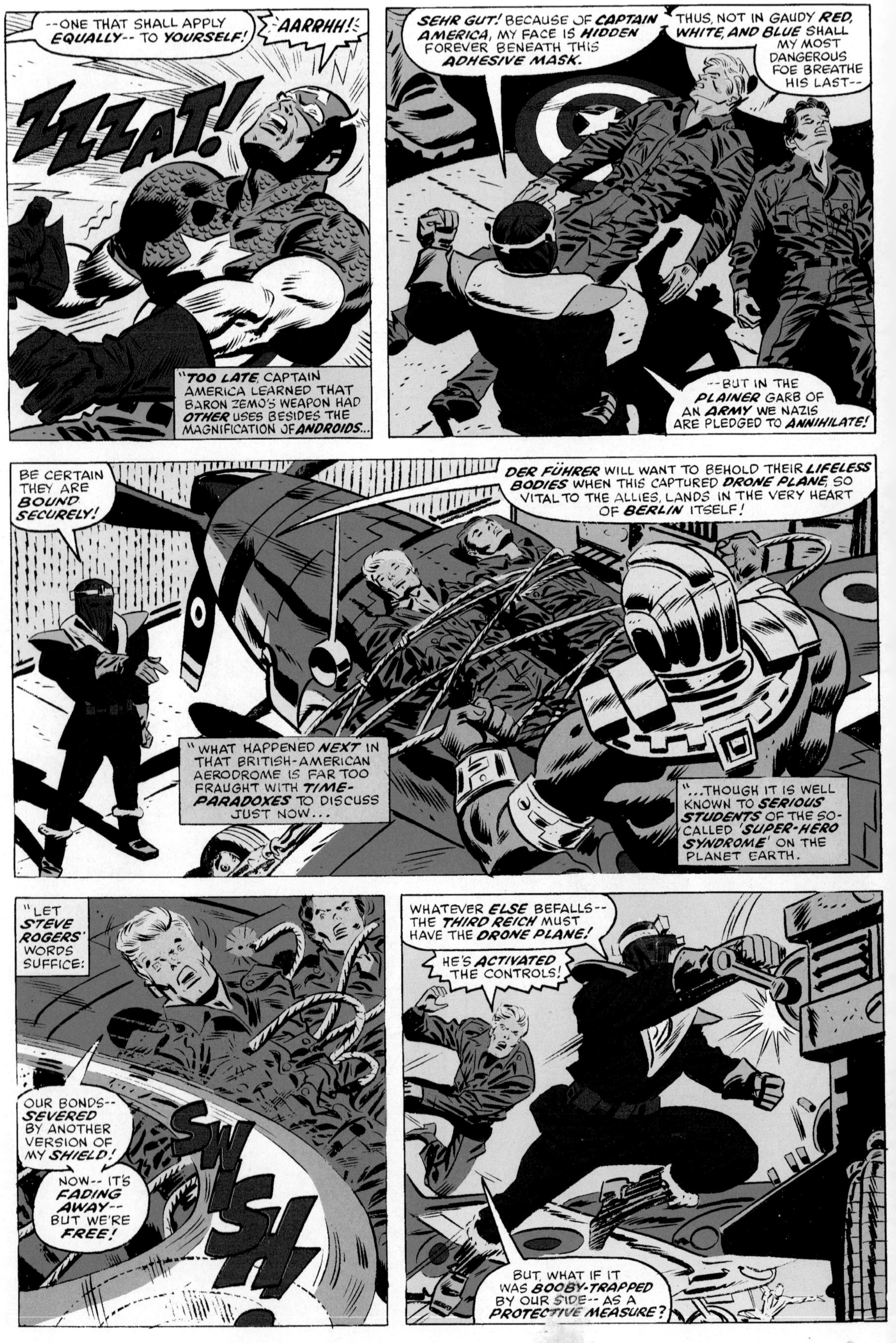

--ONE THAT SHALL APPLY EQUALLY-- TO YOURSELF!
AARRHH!
ZZZAT!
"TOO LATE, CAPTAIN AMERICA LEARNED THAT BARON ZEMO'S WEAPON HAD OTHER USES BESIDES THE MAGNIFICATION OF ANDROIDS...
SEHR GUT! BECAUSE OF CAPTAIN AMERICA, MY FACE IS HIDDEN FOREVER BENEATH THIS ADHESIVE MASK.
THUS, NOT IN GAUDY RED, WHITE, AND BLUE SHALL MY MOST DANGEROUS FOE BREATHE HIS LAST--
--BUT IN THE PLAINER GARB OF AN ARMY WE NAZIS ARE PLEDGED TO ANNIHILATE!
BE CERTAIN THEY ARE BOUND SECURELY!
DER FÜHRER WILL WANT TO BEHOLD THEIR LIFELESS BODIES WHEN THIS CAPTURED DRONE PLANE, SO VITAL TO THE ALLIES, LANDS IN THE VERY HEART OF BERLIN ITSELF!
"WHAT HAPPENED NEXT IN THAT BRITISH-AMERICAN AERODROME IS FAR TOO FRAUGHT WITH TIME-PARADOXES TO DISCUSS JUST NOW...
"...THOUGH IT IS WELL KNOWN TO SERIOUS STUDENTS OF THE SO-CALLED 'SUPER-HERO SYNDROME' ON THE PLANET EARTH.
"LET STEVE ROGERS' WORDS SUFFICE:
OUR BONDS--SEVERED BY ANOTHER VERSION OF MY SHIELD!
NOW-- IT'S FADING AWAY-- BUT WE'RE FREE!
SWISH
WHATEVER ELSE BEFALLS-- THE THIRD REICH MUST HAVE THE DRONE PLANE!
HE'S ACTIVATED THE CONTROLS!
BUT, WHAT IF IT WAS BOOBY-TRAPPED BY OUR SIDE-- AS A PROTECTIVE MEASURE?

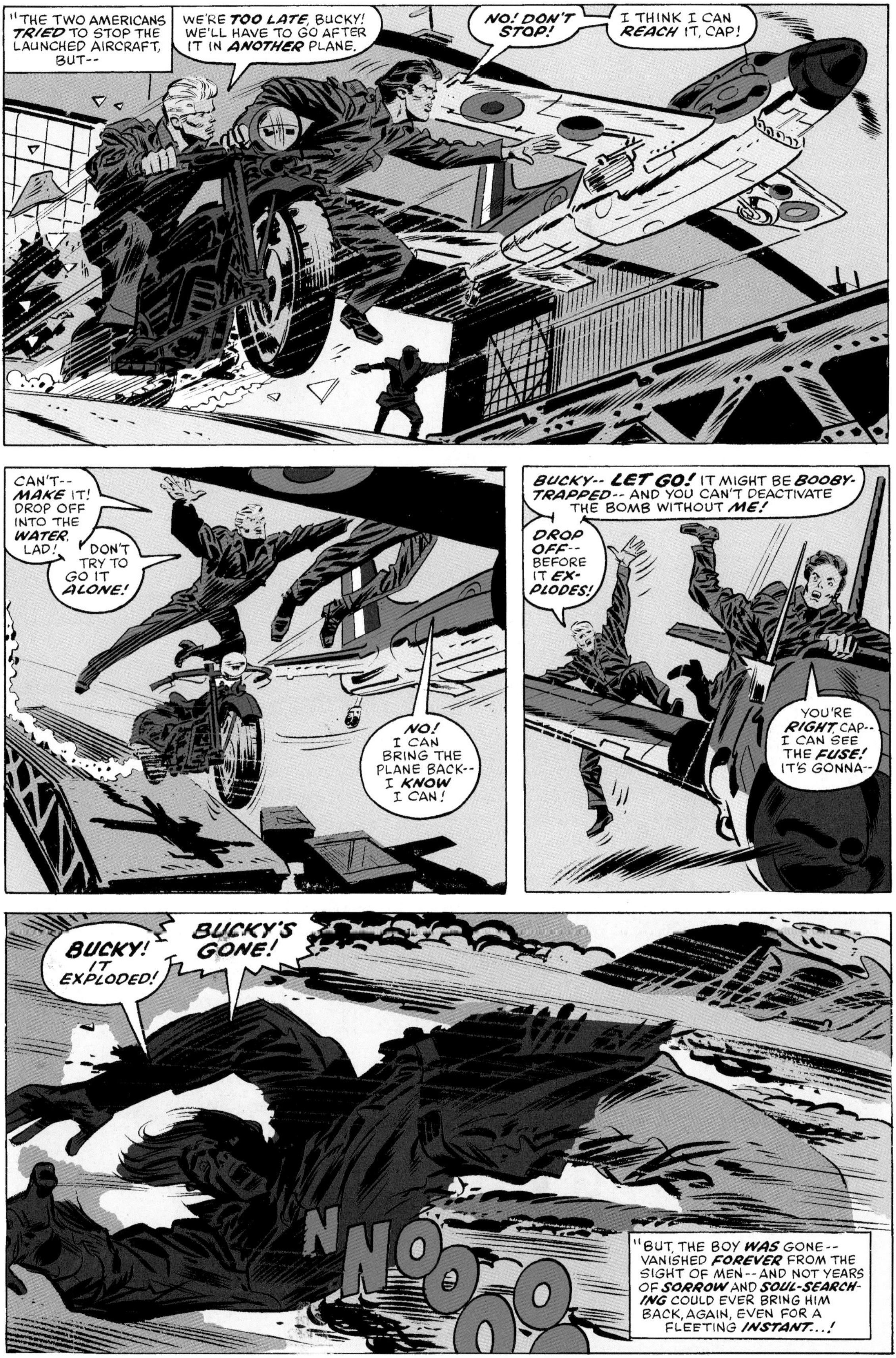
"THE TWO AMERICANS TRIED TO STOP THE LAUNCHED AIRCRAFT, BUT--
WE'RE TOO LATE, BUCKY! WE'LL HAVE TO GO AFTER IT IN ANOTHER PLANE.
NO! DON'T STOP!
I THINK I CAN REACH IT, CAP!
CAN'T-- MAKE IT! DROP OFF INTO THE WATER, LAD!
DON'T TRY TO GO IT ALONE!
NO! I CAN BRING THE PLANE BACK-- I KNOW I CAN!
BUCKY-- LET GO! IT MIGHT BE BOOBY-TRAPPED-- AND YOU CAN'T DEACTIVATE THE BOMB WITHOUT ME!
DROP OFF-- BEFORE IT EXPLODES!
YOU'RE RIGHT, CAP-- I CAN SEE THE FUSE! IT'S GONNA--
BUCKY! IT EXPLODED!
BUCKY'S GONE!
NNOOOOO
"BUT, THE BOY WAS GONE-- VANISHED FOREVER FROM THE SIGHT OF MEN-- AND NOT YEARS OF SORROW AND SOUL-SEARCHING COULD EVER BRING HIM BACK, AGAIN, EVEN FOR A FLEETING INSTANT...!

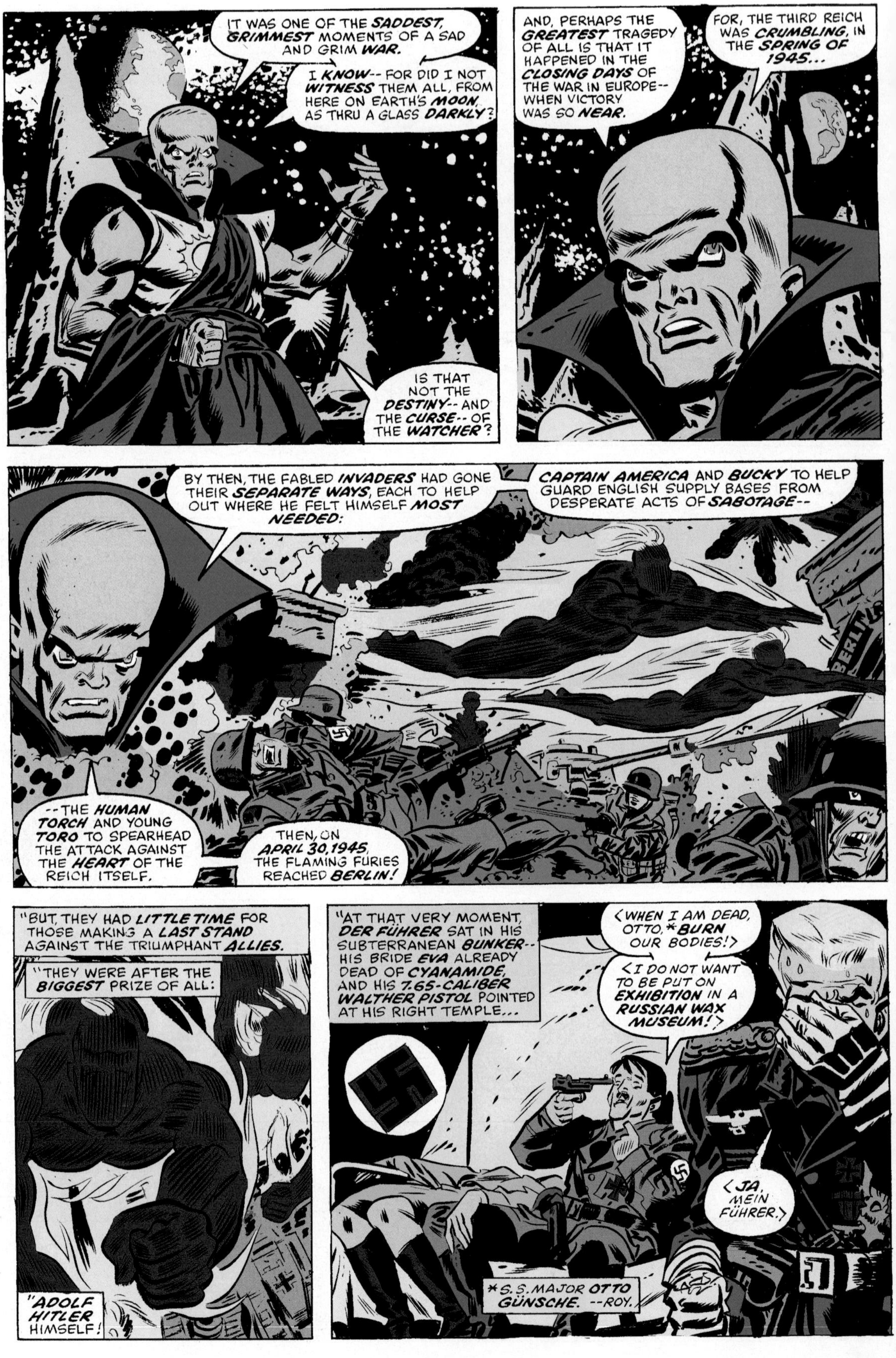

IT WAS ONE OF THE SADDEST, GRIMMEST MOMENTS OF A SAD AND GRIM WAR.
I KNOW-- FOR DID I NOT WITNESS THEM ALL, FROM HERE ON EARTH'S MOON, AS THRU A GLASS DARKLY?
IS THAT NOT THE DESTINY-- AND THE CURSE-- OF THE WATCHER?
AND, PERHAPS THE GREATEST TRAGEDY OF ALL IS THAT IT HAPPENED IN THE CLOSING DAYS OF THE WAR IN EUROPE-- WHEN VICTORY WAS SO NEAR.
FOR, THE THIRD REICH WAS CRUMBLING, IN THE SPRING OF 1945...
BY THEN, THE FABLED INVADERS HAD GONE THEIR SEPARATE WAYS, EACH TO HELP OUT WHERE HE FELT HIMSELF MOST NEEDED:
CAPTAIN AMERICA AND BUCKY TO HELP GUARD ENGLISH SUPPLY BASES FROM DESPERATE ACTS OF SABOTAGE--
--THE HUMAN TORCH AND YOUNG TORO TO SPEARHEAD THE ATTACK AGAINST THE HEART OF THE REICH ITSELF.
THEN, ON APRIL 30, 1945, THE FLAMING FURIES REACHED BERLIN!
BERLIN
"BUT, THEY HAD LITTLE TIME FOR THOSE MAKING A LAST STAND AGAINST THE TRIUMPHANT ALLIES.
"THEY WERE AFTER THE BIGGEST PRIZE OF ALL:
"ADOLF HITLER HIMSELF!
"AT THAT VERY MOMENT, DER FÜHRER SAT IN HIS SUBTERRANEAN BUNKER-- HIS BRIDE EVA ALREADY DEAD OF CYANAMIDE, AND HIS 7.65-CALIBER WALTHER PISTOL POINTED AT HIS RIGHT TEMPLE...
<WHEN I AM DEAD, OTTO,* BURN OUR BODIES!>
<I DO NOT WANT TO BE PUT ON EXHIBITION IN A RUSSIAN WAX MUSEUM!>
<JA, MEIN FÜHRER.>
*S.S. MAJOR OTTO GÜNSCHE. --ROY.

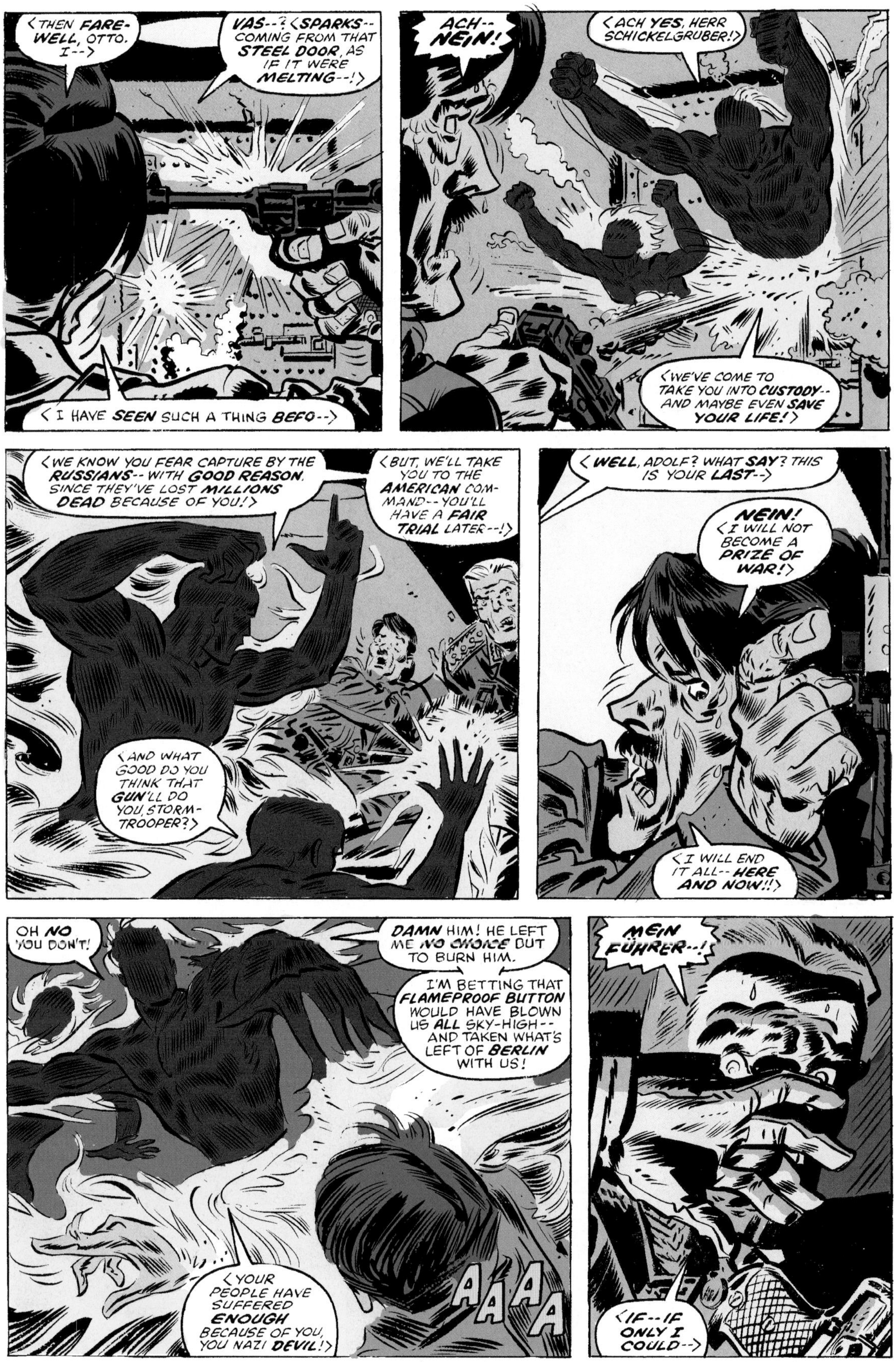
<THEN FAREWELL, OTTO. I-->
VAS--? <SPARKS-- COMING FROM THAT STEEL DOOR, AS IF IT WERE MELTING--!>
<I HAVE SEEN SUCH A THING BEFO-->
ACH-- NEIN!
<ACH YES, HERR SCHICKELGRUBER!>
<WE'VE COME TO TAKE YOU INTO CUSTODY-- AND MAYBE EVEN SAVE YOUR LIFE!>
<WE KNOW YOU FEAR CAPTURE BY THE RUSSIANS-- WITH GOOD REASON, SINCE THEY'VE LOST MILLIONS DEAD BECAUSE OF YOU!>
<BUT, WE'LL TAKE YOU TO THE AMERICAN COMMAND-- YOU'LL HAVE A FAIR TRIAL LATER--!>
<AND WHAT GOOD DO YOU THINK THAT GUN'LL DO YOU, STORM-TROOPER?>
<WELL, ADOLF? WHAT SAY? THIS IS YOUR LAST-->
NEIN! <I WILL NOT BECOME A PRIZE OF WAR!>
<I WILL END IT ALL-- HERE AND NOW!!>
OH NO YOU DON'T!
DAMN HIM! HE LEFT ME NO CHOICE BUT TO BURN HIM.
I'M BETTING THAT FLAMEPROOF BUTTON WOULD HAVE BLOWN US ALL SKY-HIGH-- AND TAKEN WHAT'S LEFT OF BERLIN WITH US!
<YOUR PEOPLE HAVE SUFFERED ENOUGH BECAUSE OF YOU, YOU NAZI DEVIL!>
AAAA
MEIN FÜHRER--!
<IF--IF ONLY I COULD-->

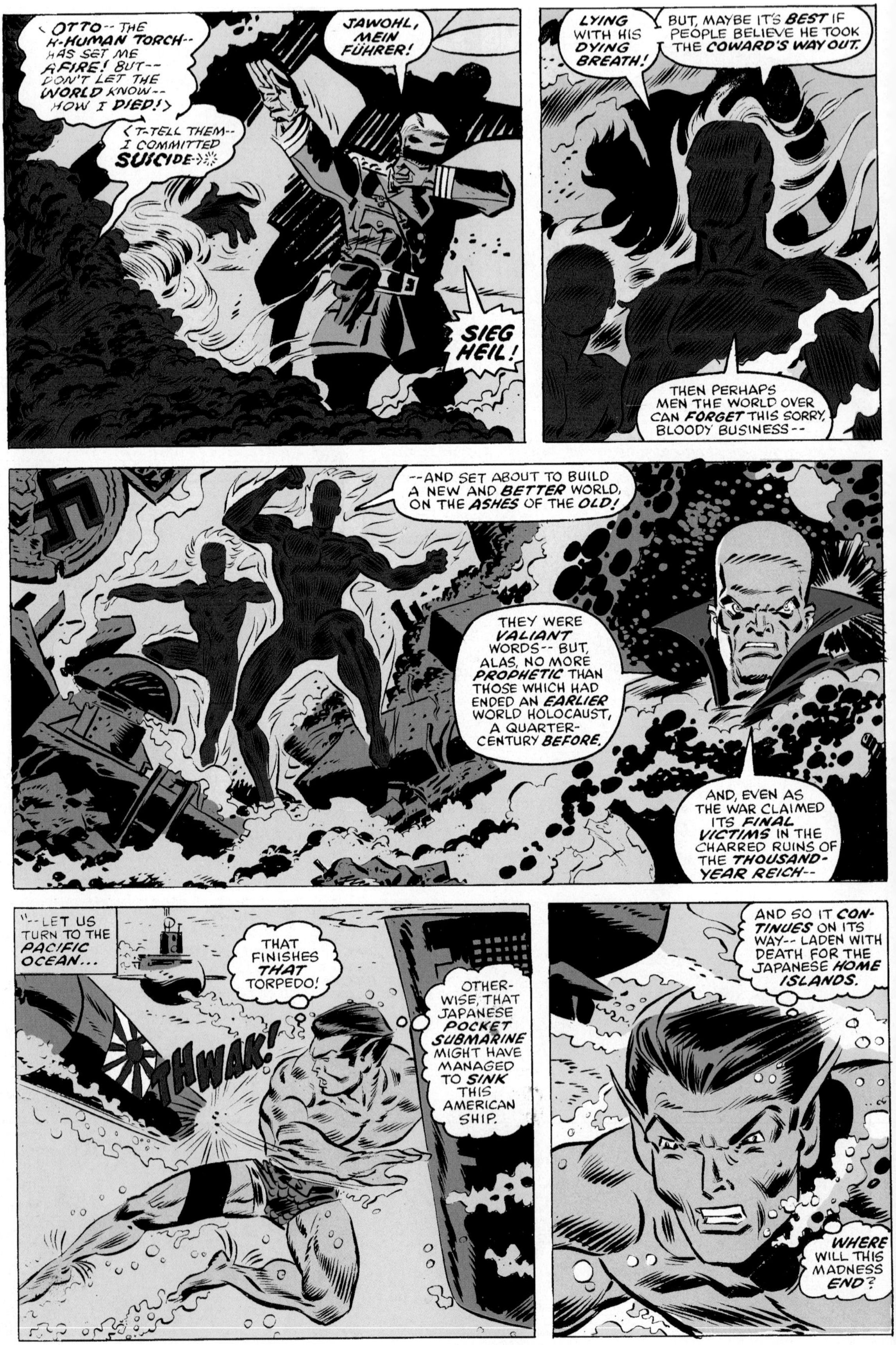

< OTTO-- THE H-HUMAN TORCH-- HAS SET ME AFIRE! BUT-- DON'T LET THE WORLD KNOW-- HOW I DIED! >
JAWOHL, MEIN FÜHRER!
< T-TELL THEM-- I COMMITTED SUICIDE--- >
SIEG HEIL!
LYING WITH HIS DYING BREATH!
BUT, MAYBE IT'S BEST IF PEOPLE BELIEVE HE TOOK THE COWARD'S WAY OUT.
THEN PERHAPS MEN THE WORLD OVER CAN FORGET THIS SORRY, BLOODY BUSINESS--
--AND SET ABOUT TO BUILD A NEW AND BETTER WORLD, ON THE ASHES OF THE OLD!
THEY WERE VALIANT WORDS-- BUT, ALAS, NO MORE PROPHETIC THAN THOSE WHICH HAD ENDED AN EARLIER WORLD HOLOCAUST, A QUARTER-CENTURY BEFORE.
AND, EVEN AS THE WAR CLAIMED ITS FINAL VICTIMS IN THE CHARRED RUINS OF THE THOUSAND-YEAR REICH--
"--LET US TURN TO THE PACIFIC OCEAN...
THAT FINISHES THAT TORPEDO!
THWAK!
OTHER-WISE, THAT JAPANESE POCKET SUBMARINE MIGHT HAVE MANAGED TO SINK THIS AMERICAN SHIP.
AND SO IT CON-TINUES ON ITS WAY-- LADEN WITH DEATH FOR THE JAPANESE HOME ISLANDS.
WHERE WILL THIS MADNESS END?

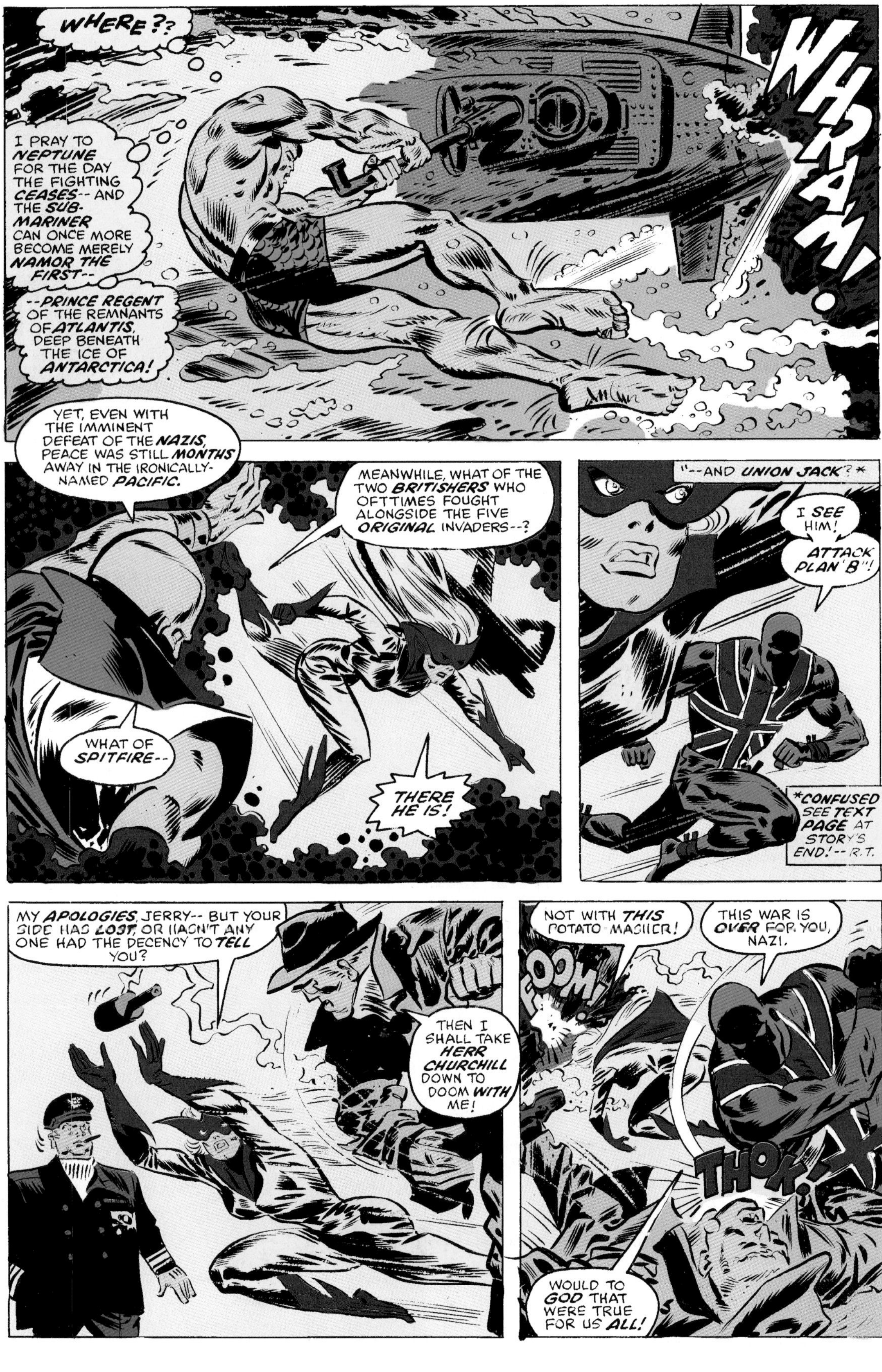
WHERE??
WHRAM!
I PRAY TO NEPTUNE FOR THE DAY THE FIGHTING CEASES-- AND THE SUB-MARINER CAN ONCE MORE BECOME MERELY NAMOR THE FIRST--
--PRINCE REGENT OF THE REMNANTS OF ATLANTIS, DEEP BENEATH THE ICE OF ANTARCTICA!
YET, EVEN WITH THE IMMINENT DEFEAT OF THE NAZIS, PEACE WAS STILL MONTHS AWAY IN THE IRONICALLY-NAMED PACIFIC.
MEANWHILE, WHAT OF THE TWO BRITISHERS WHO OFTTIMES FOUGHT ALONGSIDE THE FIVE ORIGINAL INVADERS--?
WHAT OF SPITFIRE--
THERE HE IS!
"--AND UNION JACK?*
I SEE HIM!
ATTACK PLAN 'B'"!
*CONFUSED? SEE TEXT PAGE AT STORY'S END! --R.T.
MY APOLOGIES, JERRY-- BUT YOUR SIDE HAS LOST, OR HASN'T ANY ONE HAD THE DECENCY TO TELL YOU?
THEN I SHALL TAKE HERR CHURCHILL DOWN TO DOOM WITH ME!
NOT WITH THIS POTATO MASHER!
THIS WAR IS OVER FOR YOU, NAZI.
FOOM!
THOK!
WOULD TO GOD THAT WERE TRUE FOR US ALL!

LATER THAT NIGHT, IN THE HEART OF LONDON...*

AH, *UNION JACK*--AND, ER, *MISS SPITFIRE*--THANK YOU FOR COMING SO *PROMPTLY!*

* *THIS* WILL BE EXPLAINED ON THE TEXT PAGE, *ALSO*--AS WILL THE GENTS *INSIDE.*--ROY.

WE CAME AS QUICKLY AS WE *COULD,* MAJOR RAWLINGS.

I FEAR *I* SLOW HER DOWN QUITE A *BIT,* GENTLE-MEN.

IN MANY WAYS, I WISH YOU HAD BEEN *SLOWER!*

WHAT DO YOU *MEAN,* MAJOR? WHY WERE WE *CALLED* HERE?

AYE! AND WHERE ARE *CAPTAIN AMERICA* AND HIS YOUNG ALLY?

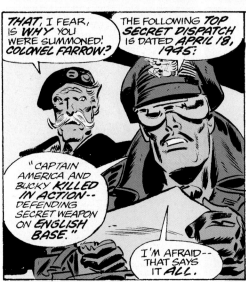

THAT, I FEAR, IS *WHY* YOU WERE SUMMONED! COLONEL FARROW?

THE FOLLOWING *TOP SECRET* DISPATCH IS DATED *APRIL 18, 1945:*

"CAPTAIN AMERICA AND BUCKY *KILLED IN ACTION*--DEFENDING SECRET WEAPON ON *ENGLISH BASE.*"

I'M AFRAID-- THAT SAYS IT *ALL.*

THE CAPTAIN-- *DEAD??* *YOU'RE LYING!*

I WISH TO GOD I *WERE,* MISS.

HOW DID IT HAPPEN? *HOW?*

AN *AERIAL EXPLOSION* -- THE BODIES WERE NOT RE-COVERED--!

NO BODIES!? THEN HOW DO YOU *KNOW* THEY'RE DEAD? THEY--

EASY, TORO! I'M SURE THE OFFICERS HAVE *MORE* TO SAY.

THE EXPLOSION WAS WITNESSED BY *R.A.F.* PERSONNEL. BUCKY WAS STILL ABOARD THE CRAFT...

THE *CAPTAIN'S* BODY FELL INTO THE *CHANNEL.* IT DID *NOT* SURFACE.

IF THAT'S *ALL,* SIR-- CAN WE RETURN TO THE *FRONT?*

THERE'S *NO NEED!* THE *REMNANTS* OF THE WEHRMACHT *SURRENDERED* AND IN BAVARIA AND WESTERN AUSTRIA.

THE WAR IN EUROPE IS ALL BUT *OVER.*

BUT THE *PRESIDENT* HAS ASKED TO SEE THOSE OF YOU WHO CAN FLY TO *WASHING-TON...!*

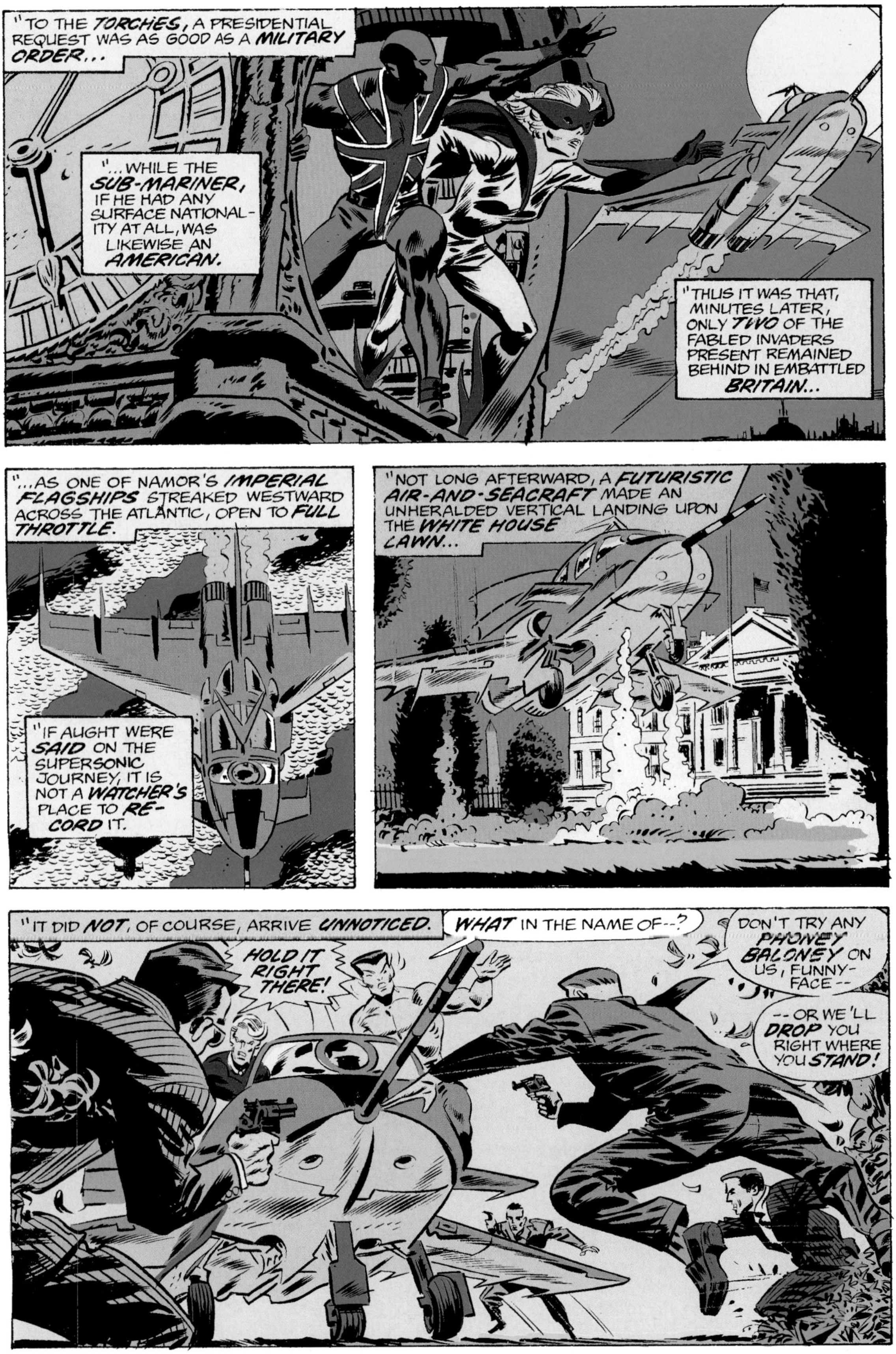
"TO THE TORCHES, A PRESIDENTIAL REQUEST WAS AS GOOD AS A MILITARY ORDER...
"...WHILE THE SUB-MARINER, IF HE HAD ANY SURFACE NATIONALITY AT ALL, WAS LIKEWISE AN AMERICAN.
"THUS IT WAS THAT, MINUTES LATER, ONLY TWO OF THE FABLED INVADERS PRESENT REMAINED BEHIND IN EMBATTLED BRITAIN...
"...AS ONE OF NAMOR'S IMPERIAL FLAGSHIPS STREAKED WESTWARD ACROSS THE ATLANTIC, OPEN TO FULL THROTTLE.
"IF AUGHT WERE SAID ON THE SUPERSONIC JOURNEY, IT IS NOT A WATCHER'S PLACE TO RECORD IT.
"NOT LONG AFTERWARD, A FUTURISTIC AIR-AND-SEACRAFT MADE AN UNHERALDED VERTICAL LANDING UPON THE WHITE HOUSE LAWN...
"IT DID NOT, OF COURSE, ARRIVE UNNOTICED.
WHAT IN THE NAME OF--?
HOLD IT RIGHT THERE!
DON'T TRY ANY PHONEY BALONEY ON US, FUNNY-FACE--
--OR WE'LL DROP YOU RIGHT WHERE YOU STAND!

ALL RIGHT, BOYS! I THINK WE CAN ASSUME THEY'RE THE REAL McCOY, ALL RIGHT!

WHATEVER YOU SAY, SIR!

YOU DID SEND FOR US, DID YOU NOT--

--MR. PRESIDENT?

I SURE DID--BUT YOU FELLAS GOT HERE EVEN FASTER THAN WE FIGURED!

SURE WISH WE HAD THE SECRET OF YOUR PLANE, PRINCE NAMOR.

I AM SORRY-- BUT I AM CERTAIN AMERICA HAS SECRET WEAPONS ALL HER OWN.

STILL, I AM PLEASED TO MEET YOU, SIR.

SAME HERE, MR. TRUMAN--

--I MEAN, MR. PRESIDENT!

I'M STILL GETTING USED TO THE TITLE MYSELF, SON. THIS WAY...

I APPRECIATE YOUR COMING--AND I GUESS YOU KNOW WHY I ASKED FOR YOU.

WE'VE A FAIR IDEA, SIR.

THIS COUNTRY'S LOST THREE GREAT MEN IN THE PAST FEW WEEKS --FIRST, PRESIDENT ROOSEVELT, GOD REST HIS SOUL--

--THEN, A FEW DAYS LATER, CAPTAIN AMERICA AND YOUNG BUCKY BARNES.

SIR, MAY I ASK WHY STEVE ROGERS' DEATH IS BEING KEPT A SECRET?

WE UNDERSTAND ONE IRRESPONSIBLE NEWSPAPER --NEW YORK'S DAILY BUGLE-- BROKE THE STORY--

BUT THE GOVERNMENT HAS SINCE DENIED IT'S TRUE!

I KNOW HOW YOU FEEL.

I DON'T LIKE KEEPING SECRETS. NEVER DID!

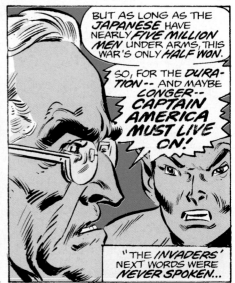

BUT AS LONG AS THE JAPANESE HAVE NEARLY FIVE MILLION MEN UNDER ARMS, THIS WAR'S ONLY HALF WON.

SO, FOR THE DURATION-- AND MAYBE LONGER-- CAPTAIN AMERICA MUST LIVE ON!

"THE INVADERS' NEXT WORDS WERE NEVER SPOKEN...

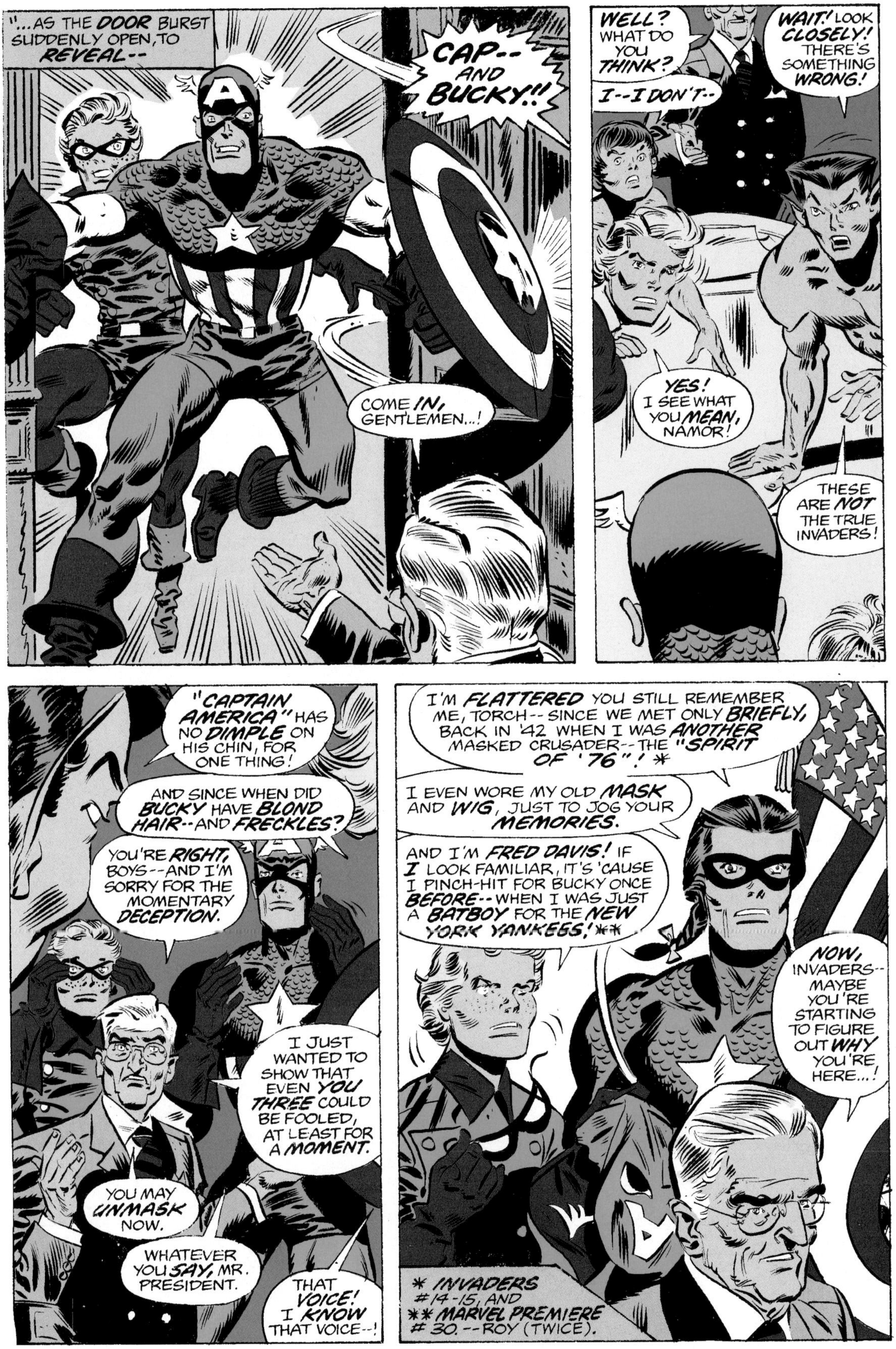
"...AS THE DOOR BURST SUDDENLY OPEN, TO REVEAL--
CAP-- AND BUCKY!!
COME IN, GENTLEMEN...!
WELL? WHAT DO YOU THINK?
I--I DON'T--
WAIT! LOOK CLOSELY! THERE'S SOMETHING WRONG!
YES! I SEE WHAT YOU MEAN, NAMOR!
THESE ARE NOT THE TRUE INVADERS!
"CAPTAIN AMERICA" HAS NO DIMPLE ON HIS CHIN, FOR ONE THING!
AND SINCE WHEN DID BUCKY HAVE BLOND HAIR--AND FRECKLES?
YOU'RE RIGHT, BOYS--AND I'M SORRY FOR THE MOMENTARY DECEPTION.
I JUST WANTED TO SHOW THAT EVEN YOU THREE COULD BE FOOLED, AT LEAST FOR A MOMENT.
YOU MAY UNMASK NOW.
WHATEVER YOU SAY, MR. PRESIDENT.
THAT VOICE! I KNOW THAT VOICE--!
I'M FLATTERED YOU STILL REMEMBER ME, TORCH--SINCE WE MET ONLY BRIEFLY, BACK IN '42 WHEN I WAS ANOTHER MASKED CRUSADER--THE "SPIRIT OF '76"! *
I EVEN WORE MY OLD MASK AND WIG, JUST TO JOG YOUR MEMORIES.
AND I'M FRED DAVIS! IF I LOOK FAMILIAR, IT'S 'CAUSE I PINCH-HIT FOR BUCKY ONCE BEFORE--WHEN I WAS JUST A BATBOY FOR THE NEW YORK YANKEES! **
NOW, INVADERS--MAYBE YOU'RE STARTING TO FIGURE OUT WHY YOU'RE HERE...!
* INVADERS #14-15, AND
** MARVEL PREMIERE #30. --ROY (TWICE).

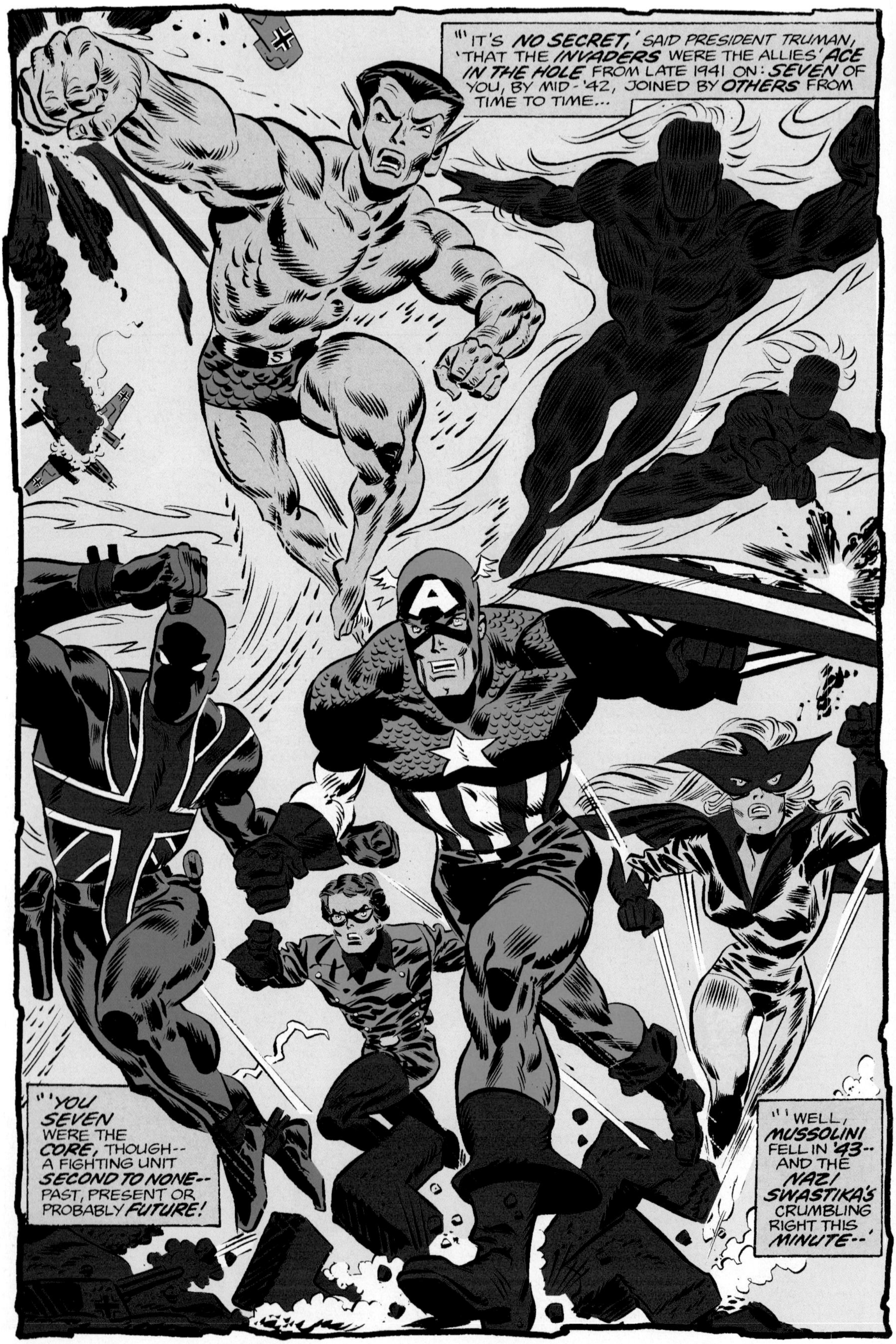
"'IT'S NO SECRET,' SAID PRESIDENT TRUMAN, 'THAT THE INVADERS WERE THE ALLIES' ACE IN THE HOLE FROM LATE 1941 ON: SEVEN OF YOU, BY MID-'42, JOINED BY OTHERS FROM TIME TO TIME...
"'YOU SEVEN WERE THE CORE, THOUGH-- A FIGHTING UNIT SECOND TO NONE-- PAST, PRESENT OR PROBABLY FUTURE!
"'WELL, MUSSOLINI FELL IN '43-- AND THE NAZI SWASTIKA'S CRUMBLING RIGHT THIS MINUTE--'

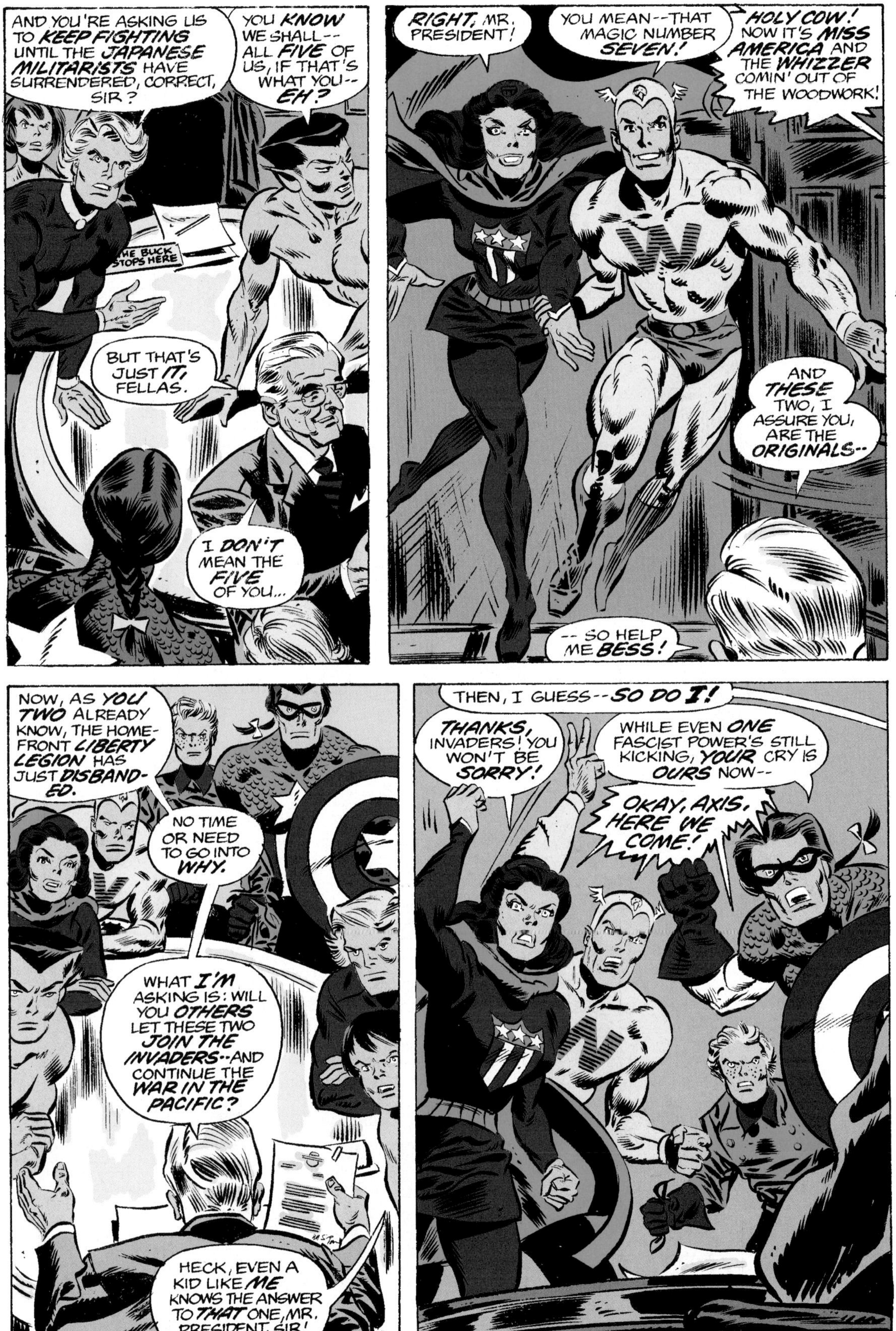
AND YOU'RE ASKING US TO KEEP FIGHTING UNTIL THE JAPANESE MILITARISTS HAVE SURRENDERED, CORRECT, SIR?
YOU KNOW WE SHALL-- ALL FIVE OF US, IF THAT'S WHAT YOU-- EH?
THE BUCK STOPS HERE
BUT THAT'S JUST IT, FELLAS.
I DON'T MEAN THE FIVE OF YOU...
RIGHT, MR. PRESIDENT!
YOU MEAN--THAT MAGIC NUMBER SEVEN!
HOLY COW! NOW IT'S MISS AMERICA AND THE WHIZZER COMIN' OUT OF THE WOODWORK!
AND THESE TWO, I ASSURE YOU, ARE THE ORIGINALS--
-- SO HELP ME BESS!
NOW, AS YOU TWO ALREADY KNOW, THE HOME-FRONT LIBERTY LEGION HAS JUST DISBANDED.
NO TIME OR NEED TO GO INTO WHY.
WHAT I'M ASKING IS: WILL YOU OTHERS LET THESE TWO JOIN THE INVADERS--AND CONTINUE THE WAR IN THE PACIFIC?
HECK, EVEN A KID LIKE ME KNOWS THE ANSWER TO THAT ONE, MR. PRESIDENT, SIR!
THEN, I GUESS--SO DO I!
THANKS, INVADERS! YOU WON'T BE SORRY!
WHILE EVEN ONE FASCIST POWER'S STILL KICKING, YOUR CRY IS OURS NOW--
OKAY, AXIS, HERE WE COME!

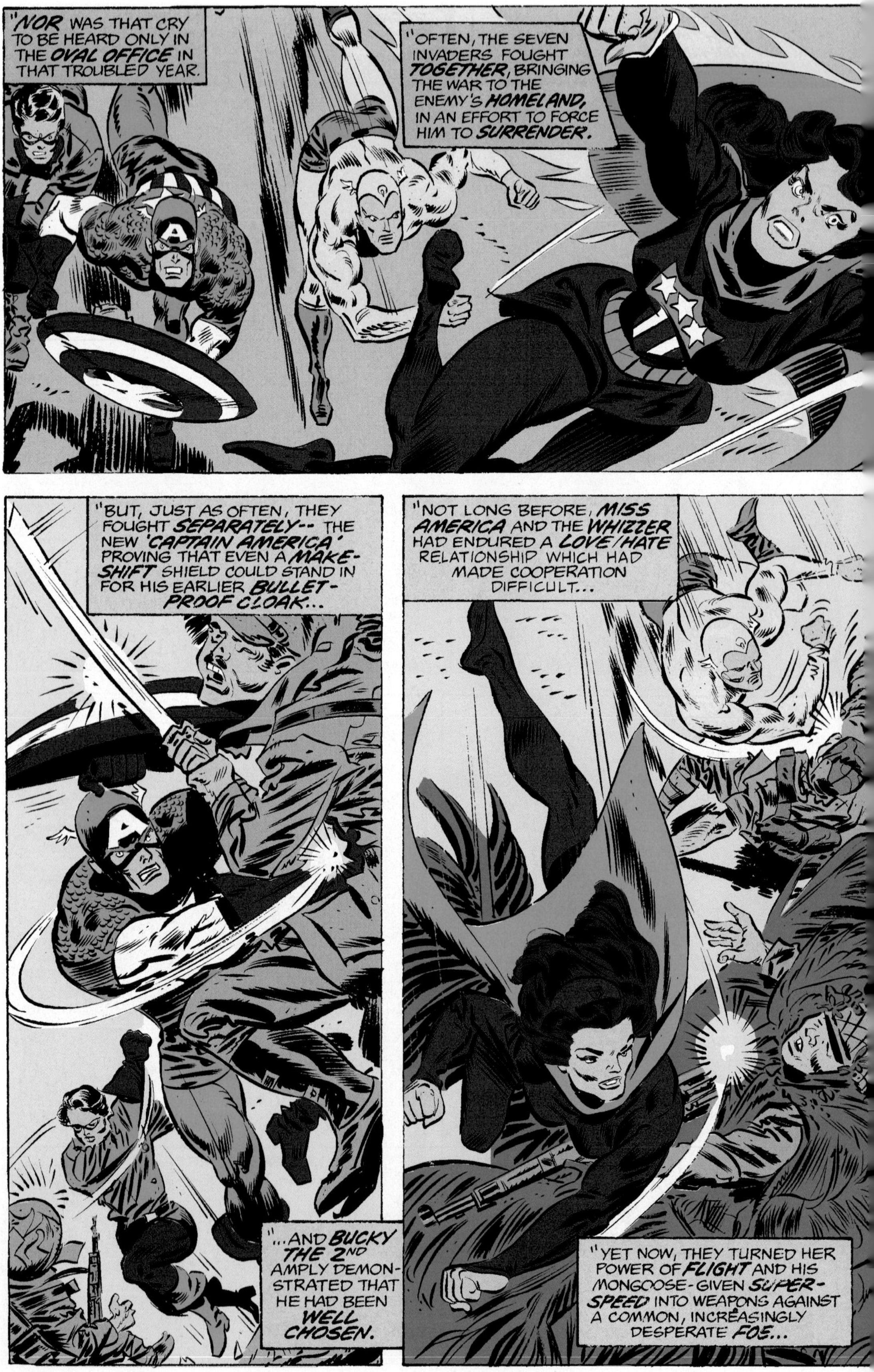
"NOR WAS THAT CRY TO BE HEARD ONLY IN THE OVAL OFFICE IN THAT TROUBLED YEAR.
"OFTEN, THE SEVEN INVADERS FOUGHT TOGETHER, BRINGING THE WAR TO THE ENEMY'S HOMELAND, IN AN EFFORT TO FORCE HIM TO SURRENDER.
"BUT, JUST AS OFTEN, THEY FOUGHT SEPARATELY-- THE NEW 'CAPTAIN AMERICA' PROVING THAT EVEN A MAKE-SHIFT SHIELD COULD STAND IN FOR HIS EARLIER BULLET-PROOF CLOAK...
"...AND BUCKY THE 2ND AMPLY DEMON-STRATED THAT HE HAD BEEN WELL CHOSEN.
"NOT LONG BEFORE, MISS AMERICA AND THE WHIZZER HAD ENDURED A LOVE/HATE RELATIONSHIP WHICH HAD MADE COOPERATION DIFFICULT...
"YET NOW, THEY TURNED HER POWER OF FLIGHT AND HIS MONGOOSE-GIVEN SUPER-SPEED INTO WEAPONS AGAINST A COMMON, INCREASINGLY DESPERATE FOE...

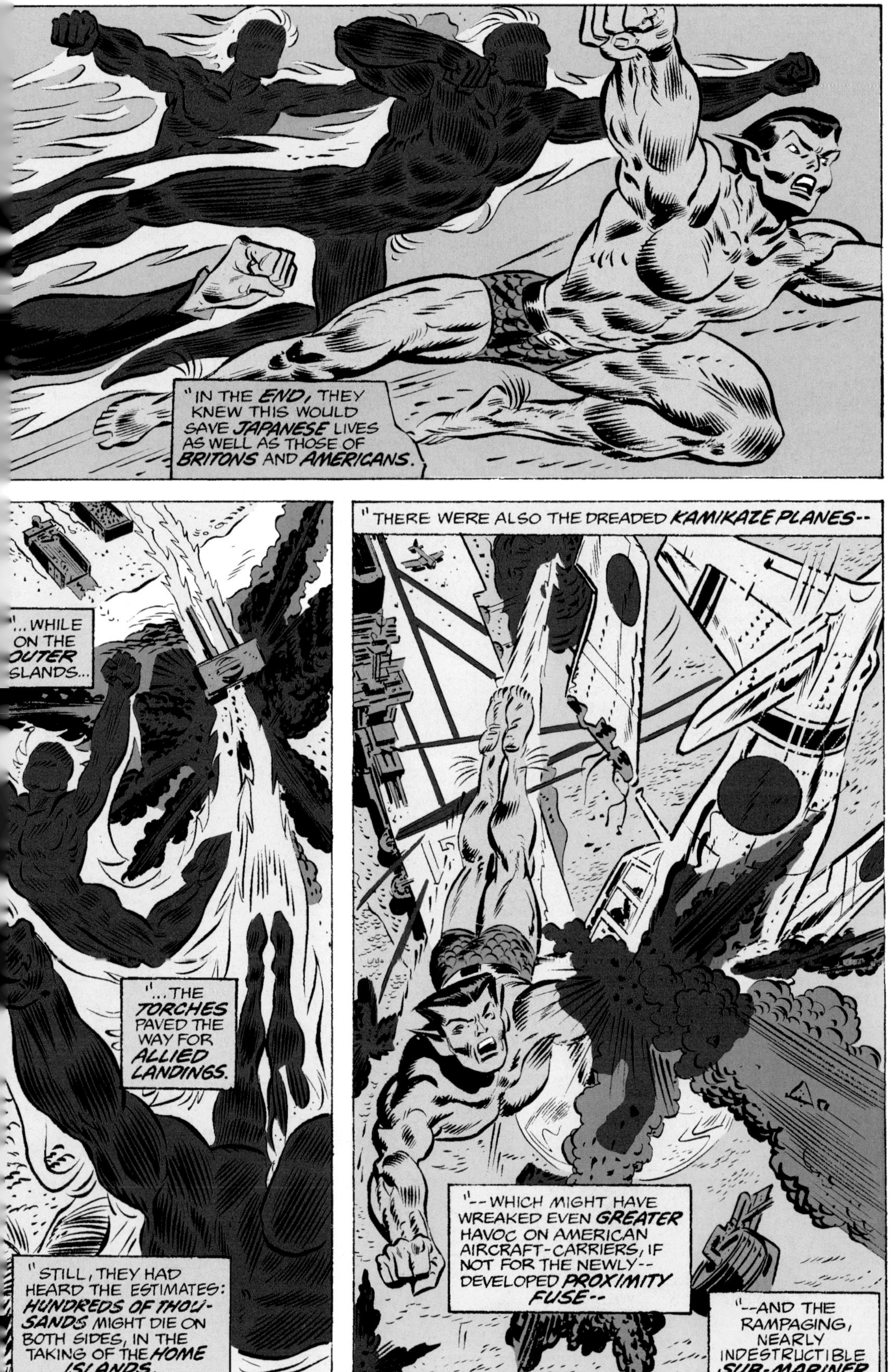
"IN THE END, THEY KNEW THIS WOULD SAVE JAPANESE LIVES AS WELL AS THOSE OF BRITONS AND AMERICANS.
"...WHILE ON THE OUTER ISLANDS...
"...THE TORCHES PAVED THE WAY FOR ALLIED LANDINGS.
"STILL, THEY HAD HEARD THE ESTIMATES: HUNDREDS OF THOU-SANDS MIGHT DIE ON BOTH SIDES, IN THE TAKING OF THE HOME ISLANDS.
"THERE WERE ALSO THE DREADED KAMIKAZE PLANES--
"--WHICH MIGHT HAVE WREAKED EVEN GREATER HAVOC ON AMERICAN AIRCRAFT-CARRIERS, IF NOT FOR THE NEWLY--DEVELOPED PROXIMITY FUSE--
"--AND THE RAMPAGING, NEARLY INDESTRUCTIBLE SUB-MARINER.

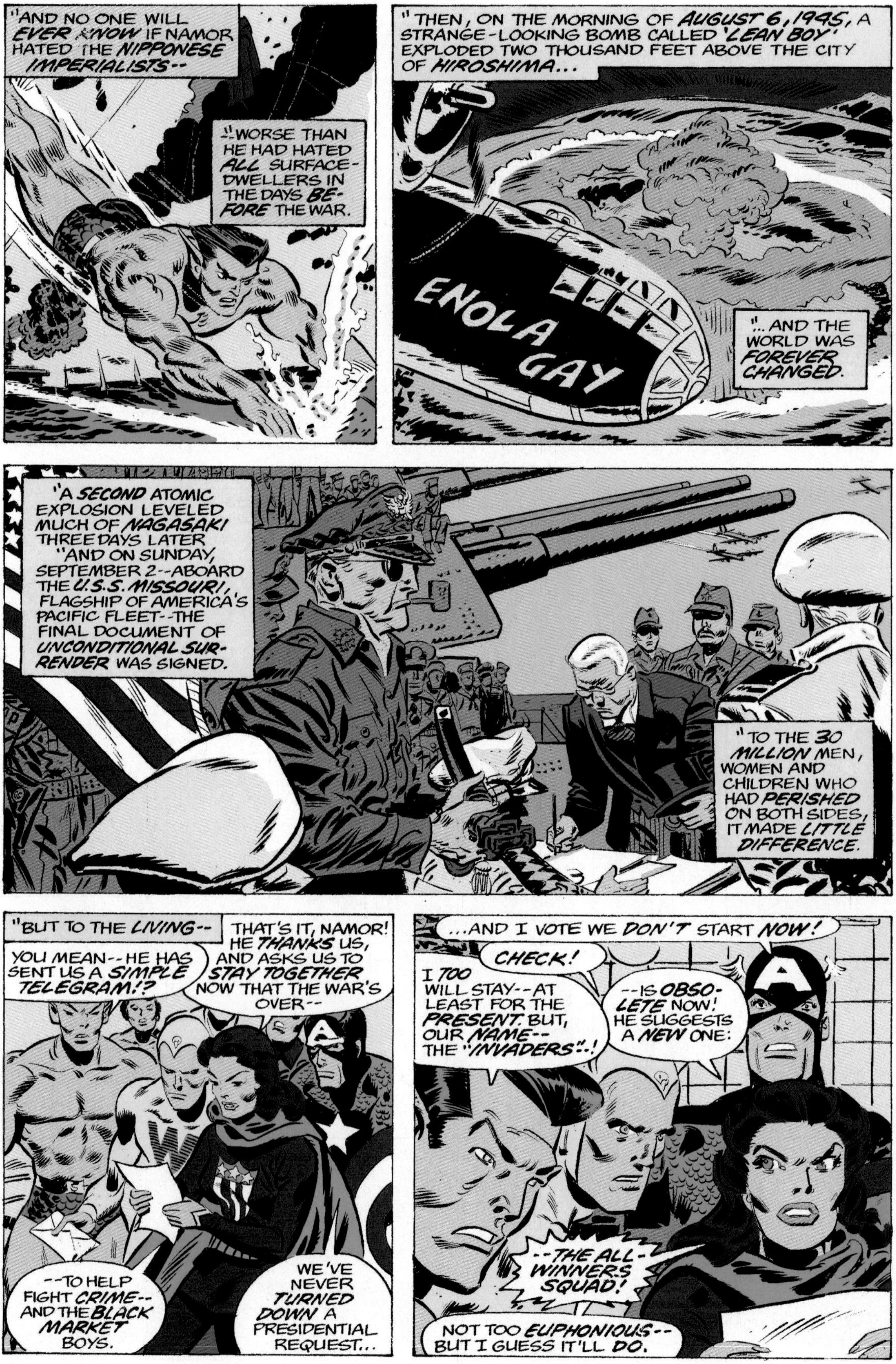
"AND NO ONE WILL EVER KNOW IF NAMOR HATED THE NIPPONESE IMPERIALISTS--
"--WORSE THAN HE HAD HATED ALL SURFACE-DWELLERS IN THE DAYS BEFORE THE WAR.
"THEN, ON THE MORNING OF AUGUST 6, 1945, A STRANGE-LOOKING BOMB CALLED 'LEAN BOY' EXPLODED TWO THOUSAND FEET ABOVE THE CITY OF HIROSHIMA...
ENOLA GAY
"...AND THE WORLD WAS FOREVER CHANGED.
"A SECOND ATOMIC EXPLOSION LEVELED MUCH OF NAGASAKI THREE DAYS LATER
"AND ON SUNDAY, SEPTEMBER 2--ABOARD THE U.S.S. MISSOURI, FLAGSHIP OF AMERICA'S PACIFIC FLEET--THE FINAL DOCUMENT OF UNCONDITIONAL SURRENDER WAS SIGNED.
"TO THE 30 MILLION MEN, WOMEN AND CHILDREN WHO HAD PERISHED ON BOTH SIDES, IT MADE LITTLE DIFFERENCE.
"BUT TO THE LIVING--
YOU MEAN--HE HAS SENT US A SIMPLE TELEGRAM!?
THAT'S IT, NAMOR! HE THANKS US, AND ASKS US TO STAY TOGETHER NOW THAT THE WAR'S OVER--
--TO HELP FIGHT CRIME--AND THE BLACK MARKET BOYS.
WE'VE NEVER TURNED DOWN A PRESIDENTIAL REQUEST...
...AND I VOTE WE DON'T START NOW!
CHECK!
I TOO WILL STAY--AT LEAST FOR THE PRESENT. BUT, OUR NAME--THE "INVADERS"--!
--IS OBSOLETE NOW! HE SUGGESTS A NEW ONE:
--THE ALL-WINNERS SQUAD!
NOT TOO EUPHONIOUS--BUT I GUESS IT'LL DO.

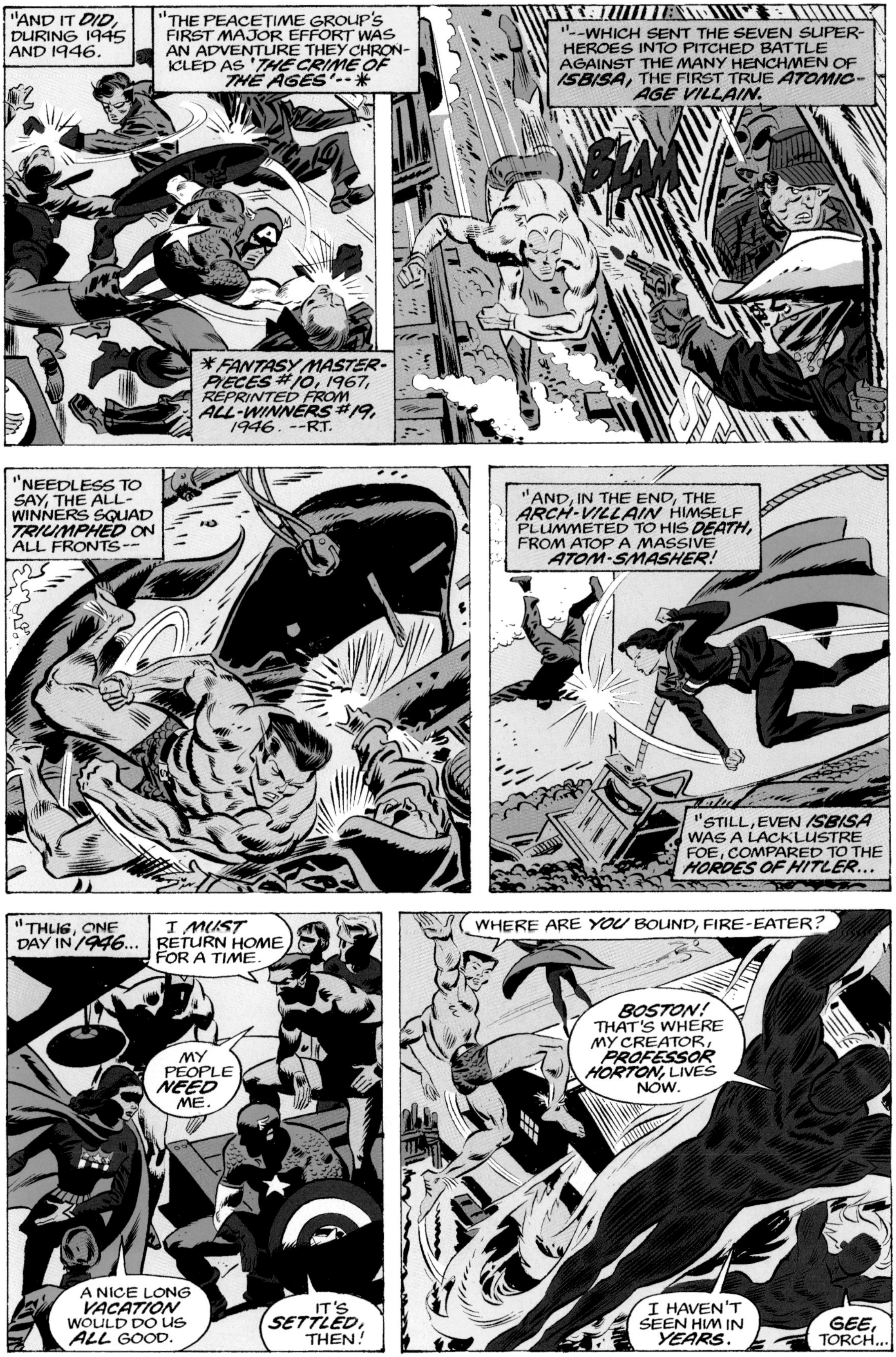
"AND IT DID, DURING 1945 AND 1946.
"THE PEACETIME GROUP'S FIRST MAJOR EFFORT WAS AN ADVENTURE THEY CHRONICLED AS 'THE CRIME OF THE AGES'--*
* FANTASY MASTERPIECES #10, 1967, REPRINTED FROM ALL-WINNERS #19, 1946. --R.T.
"--WHICH SENT THE SEVEN SUPER-HEROES INTO PITCHED BATTLE AGAINST THE MANY HENCHMEN OF ISBISA, THE FIRST TRUE ATOMIC-AGE VILLAIN.
BLAM
"NEEDLESS TO SAY, THE ALL-WINNERS SQUAD TRIUMPHED ON ALL FRONTS--
"AND, IN THE END, THE ARCH-VILLAIN HIMSELF PLUMMETED TO HIS DEATH, FROM ATOP A MASSIVE ATOM-SMASHER!
"STILL, EVEN ISBISA WAS A LACKLUSTRE FOE, COMPARED TO THE HORDES OF HITLER...
"THUS, ONE DAY IN 1946...
I MUST RETURN HOME FOR A TIME.
MY PEOPLE NEED ME.
A NICE LONG VACATION WOULD DO US ALL GOOD.
IT'S SETTLED, THEN!
WHERE ARE YOU BOUND, FIRE-EATER?
BOSTON! THAT'S WHERE MY CREATOR, PROFESSOR HORTON, LIVES NOW.
I HAVEN'T SEEN HIM IN YEARS.
GEE, TORCH...

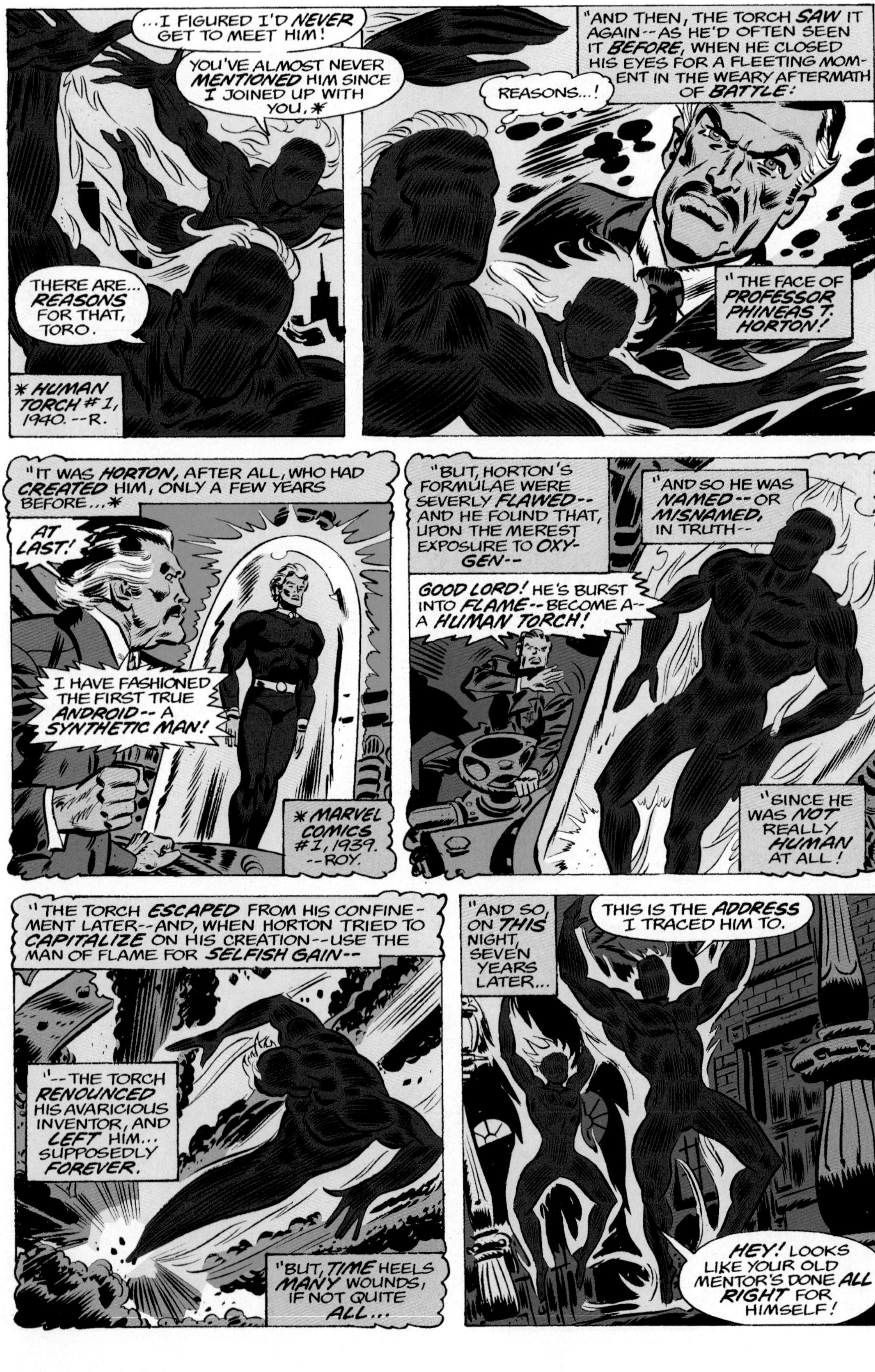
...I FIGURED I'D NEVER GET TO MEET HIM!
YOU'VE ALMOST NEVER MENTIONED HIM SINCE I JOINED UP WITH YOU.*
THERE ARE... REASONS FOR THAT, TORO.
* HUMAN TORCH #1, 1940. --R.
"AND THEN, THE TORCH SAW IT AGAIN--AS HE'D OFTEN SEEN IT BEFORE, WHEN HE CLOSED HIS EYES FOR A FLEETING MOMENT IN THE WEARY AFTERMATH OF BATTLE:
REASONS...!
"THE FACE OF PROFESSOR PHINEAS T. HORTON!
"IT WAS HORTON, AFTER ALL, WHO HAD CREATED HIM, ONLY A FEW YEARS BEFORE...*
AT LAST!
I HAVE FASHIONED THE FIRST TRUE ANDROID--A SYNTHETIC MAN!
* MARVEL COMICS #1, 1939. --ROY.
"BUT, HORTON'S FORMULAE WERE SEVERLY FLAWED--AND HE FOUND THAT, UPON THE MEREST EXPOSURE TO OXYGEN--
GOOD LORD! HE'S BURST INTO FLAME--BECOME A--A HUMAN TORCH!
"AND SO HE WAS NAMED--OR MISNAMED, IN TRUTH--
"SINCE HE WAS NOT REALLY HUMAN AT ALL!
"THE TORCH ESCAPED FROM HIS CONFINEMENT LATER--AND, WHEN HORTON TRIED TO CAPITALIZE ON HIS CREATION--USE THE MAN OF FLAME FOR SELFISH GAIN--
"--THE TORCH RENOUNCED HIS AVARICIOUS INVENTOR, AND LEFT HIM... SUPPOSEDLY FOREVER.
"BUT, TIME HEELS MANY WOUNDS, IF NOT QUITE ALL...
"AND SO, ON THIS NIGHT, SEVEN YEARS LATER...
THIS IS THE ADDRESS I TRACED HIM TO.
HEY! LOOKS LIKE YOUR OLD MENTOR'S DONE ALL RIGHT FOR HIMSELF!

HE IS A *BRILLIANT* MAN, LAD...THOUGH MARRED BY ALL-TOO-HUMAN *GREED* WHEN I LAST KNEW HIM.

HOK *HOK*

I HEAR SOMEBODY COMING.

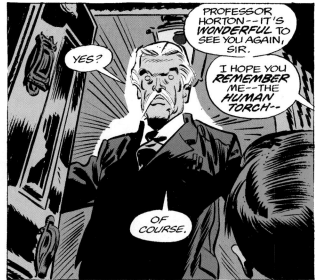

YES?

PROFESSOR HORTON--IT'S *WONDERFUL* TO SEE YOU AGAIN, SIR.

I HOPE YOU *REMEMBER* ME--THE *HUMAN TORCH*--

OF COURSE.

AND *THIS* IS MY YOUNG FRIEND *TORO.*

PUT 'ER *THERE,* PROF! GLAD TO *MEETCHA!*

LIKEWISE.

GOSH, SIR, I'VE ALWAYS BEEN *WANTING* TO--

ER, *'SCUZE* ME, BUT--I'M AFRAID YOUR *GRIP* IS HURTING MY *HAND!* I--

YEEEOWW!

HEY, *TORCH*--WHAT'S *WRONG* WITH HIM?

FLAME ON!

HE WON'T *LET GO!!*

LIKEWISE.

WH-WHAT'S THE *BIG IDEA,* TORCH? WHY IS THE *PROF*--?

THAT'S *NOT* PROFESSOR HORTON, TORO!

YOU'VE GOT TO *FLAME ON*-- *FAST!*

IF YOU *S-SAY* SO--

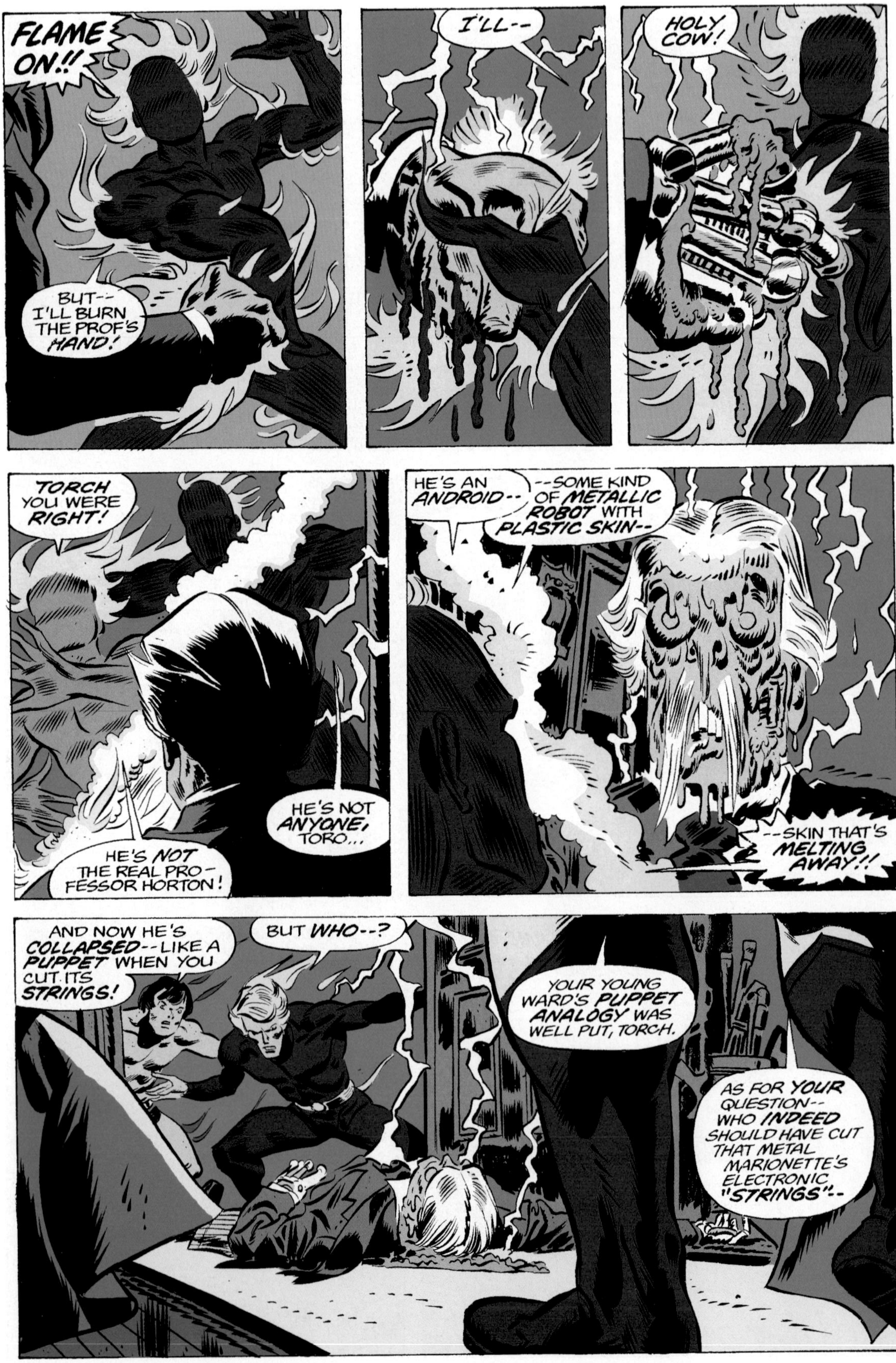
FLAME ON!!
BUT-- I'LL BURN THE PROF'S HAND!
I'LL--
HOLY COW!
TORCH YOU WERE RIGHT!
HE'S NOT THE REAL PRO-FESSOR HORTON!
HE'S NOT ANYONE, TORO...
HE'S AN ANDROID--
--SOME KIND OF METALLIC ROBOT WITH PLASTIC SKIN--
--SKIN THAT'S MELTING AWAY!!
AND NOW HE'S COLLAPSED--LIKE A PUPPET WHEN YOU CUT ITS STRINGS!
BUT WHO--?
YOUR YOUNG WARD'S PUPPET ANALOGY WAS WELL PUT, TORCH.
AS FOR YOUR QUESTION-- WHO INDEED SHOULD HAVE CUT THAT METAL MARIONETTE'S ELECTRONIC "STRINGS"--

--SAVE *ANOTHER ANDROID*, BUT ONE WHO *HAS* NO STRINGS!

WHO THE DEVIL--?

THE ANDROIDS *BEHIND* ME HAVE *NO NAMES*, FOR I'VE NOT CHOSEN TO GIVE THEM *IDENTITIES* BY NAMING THEM.

NAMES WOULD BE AS *USELESS* TO THEM AS THEIR *NON-EXISTENT TONGUES*.

WHAT ABOUT *YOU*, PALEFACE? YOU'VE GOT A *TONGUE*, SURE ENOUGH--HOW ABOUT A *NAME*?

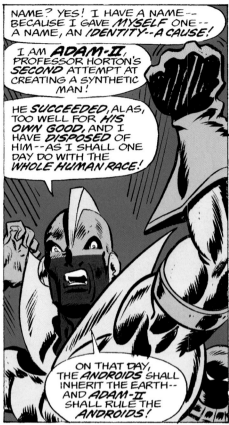

NAME? YES! I HAVE A NAME-- BECAUSE I GAVE *MYSELF* ONE-- A NAME, AN *IDENTITY*--A CAUSE!

I AM *ADAM-II*, PROFESSOR HORTON'S *SECOND* ATTEMPT AT CREATING A SYNTHETIC MAN!

HE *SUCCEEDED*, ALAS, TOO WELL FOR *HIS OWN GOOD*, AND I HAVE *DISPOSED* OF HIM--AS I SHALL ONE DAY DO WITH THE *WHOLE HUMAN RACE*!

ON THAT DAY, THE *ANDROIDS* SHALL INHERIT THE EARTH-- AND *ADAM-II* SHALL RULE THE *ANDROIDS*!

YOU DON'T HAVE TO WRITE US A *NOVEL*, FRIEND; WE GET THE *PICTURE*.

ORDINARILY, I'D *WELCOME* THE THOUGHT OF MORE ANDROIDS-- BUT RIGHT NOW-- *WHERE IS PROFESSOR HORTON ??*

WHAT SHOULD *YOU* CARE? YOU ARE NO MORE HUMAN THAN *I*!

THAT'S OPEN TO *QUESTION*.

KEEP BACK, YOU DEFECTIVELY- DESIGNED *FOOL*--!

DO YOU THINK I'D ALLOW AN *OBSOLESCENT MODEL* LIKE YOURSELF TO *RUIN MY PLANS*?

THESE ANDROIDS WILL NOT *MELT* LIKE THE HASTILY- FASHIONED METAL *ROBOT-HORTON* YOU DESTROYED!

STOP THEM!

LET'S GO, TORO!

I'M RIGHT *BEHIND* YOU, PAPPY!

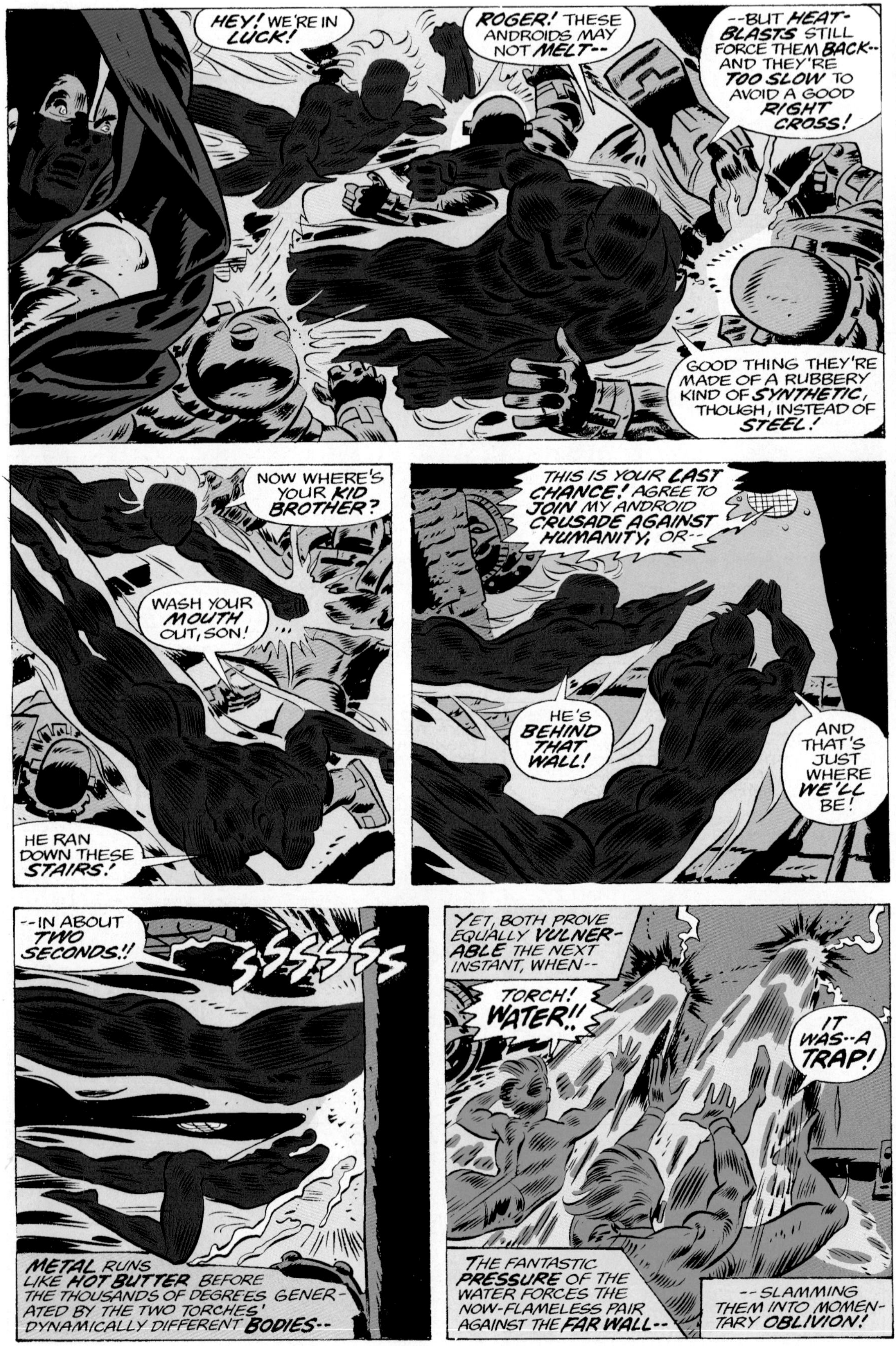
HEY! WE'RE IN LUCK!
ROGER! THESE ANDROIDS MAY NOT MELT--
--BUT HEAT-BLASTS STILL FORCE THEM BACK-- AND THEY'RE TOO SLOW TO AVOID A GOOD RIGHT CROSS!
GOOD THING THEY'RE MADE OF A RUBBERY KIND OF SYNTHETIC, THOUGH, INSTEAD OF STEEL!
NOW WHERE'S YOUR KID BROTHER?
WASH YOUR MOUTH OUT, SON!
HE RAN DOWN THESE STAIRS!
THIS IS YOUR LAST CHANCE! AGREE TO JOIN MY ANDROID CRUSADE AGAINST HUMANITY, OR--
HE'S BEHIND THAT WALL!
AND THAT'S JUST WHERE WE'LL BE!
--IN ABOUT TWO SECONDS!!
SSSSSSS
METAL RUNS LIKE HOT BUTTER BEFORE THE THOUSANDS OF DEGREES GENERATED BY THE TWO TORCHES' DYNAMICALLY DIFFERENT BODIES--
YET, BOTH PROVE EQUALLY VULNERABLE THE NEXT INSTANT, WHEN--
TORCH! WATER!!
IT WAS--A TRAP!
THE FANTASTIC PRESSURE OF THE WATER FORCES THE NOW-FLAMELESS PAIR AGAINST THE FAR WALL--
--SLAMMING THEM INTO MOMENTARY OBLIVION!

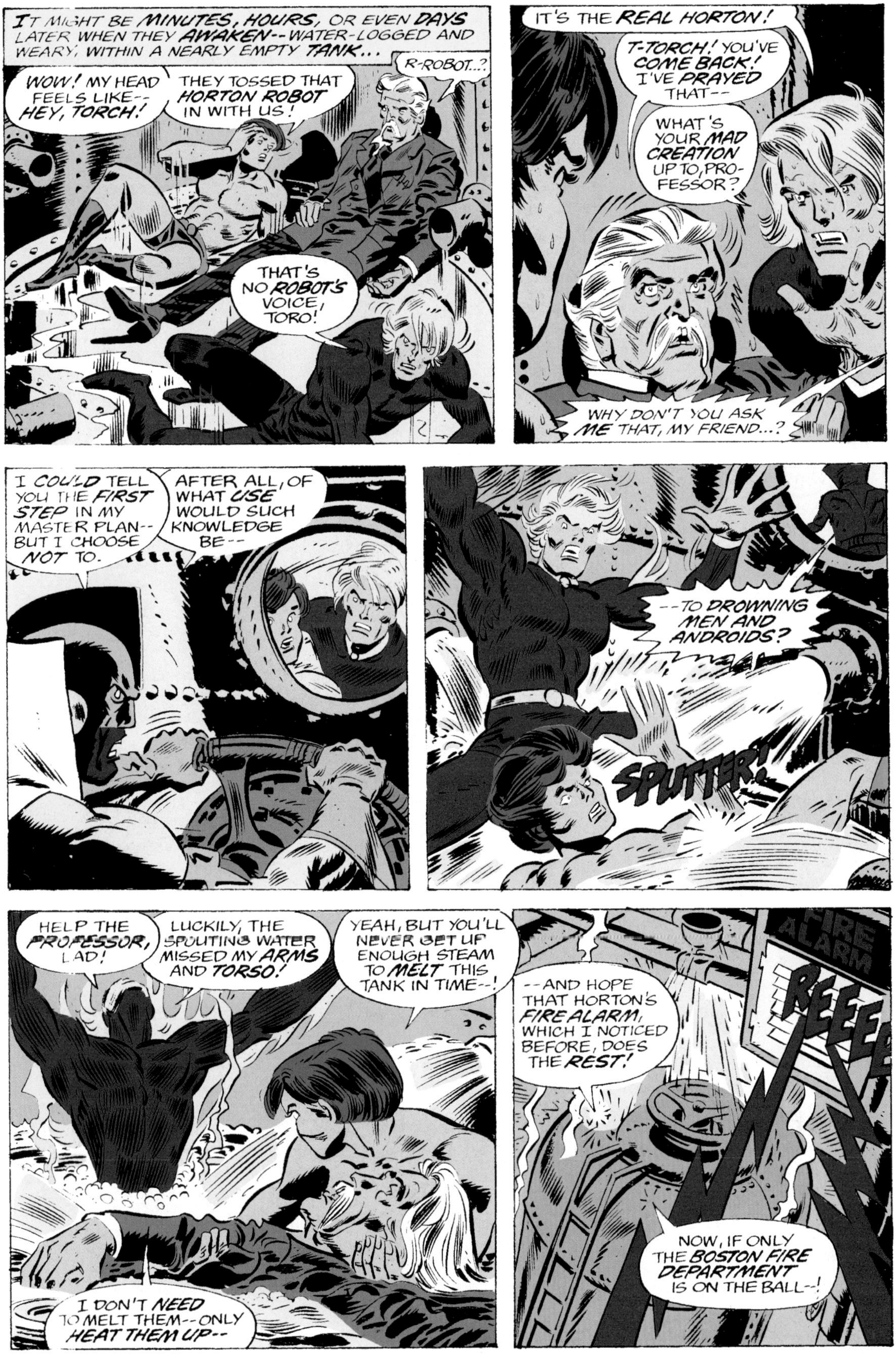

IT MIGHT BE MINUTES, HOURS, OR EVEN DAYS LATER WHEN THEY AWAKEN--WATER-LOGGED AND WEARY, WITHIN A NEARLY EMPTY TANK...
WOW! MY HEAD FEELS LIKE-- HEY, TORCH!
THEY TOSSED THAT HORTON ROBOT IN WITH US!
R-ROBOT..?
THAT'S NO ROBOT'S VOICE, TORO!
IT'S THE REAL HORTON!
T-TORCH! YOU'VE COME BACK! I'VE PRAYED THAT--
WHAT'S YOUR MAD CREATION UP TO, PROFESSOR?
WHY DON'T YOU ASK ME THAT, MY FRIEND...?
I COULD TELL YOU THE FIRST STEP IN MY MASTER PLAN-- BUT I CHOOSE NOT TO.
AFTER ALL, OF WHAT USE WOULD SUCH KNOWLEDGE BE--
--TO DROWNING MEN AND ANDROIDS?
SPUTTER!
HELP THE PROFESSOR, LAD!
LUCKILY, THE SPOUTING WATER MISSED MY ARMS AND TORSO!
YEAH, BUT YOU'LL NEVER GET UP ENOUGH STEAM TO MELT THIS TANK IN TIME--!
I DON'T NEED TO MELT THEM--ONLY HEAT THEM UP--
FIRE ALARM
--AND HOPE THAT HORTON'S FIRE ALARM, WHICH I NOTICED BEFORE, DOES THE REST!
REEEE
NOW, IF ONLY THE BOSTON FIRE DEPARTMENT IS ON THE BALL--!

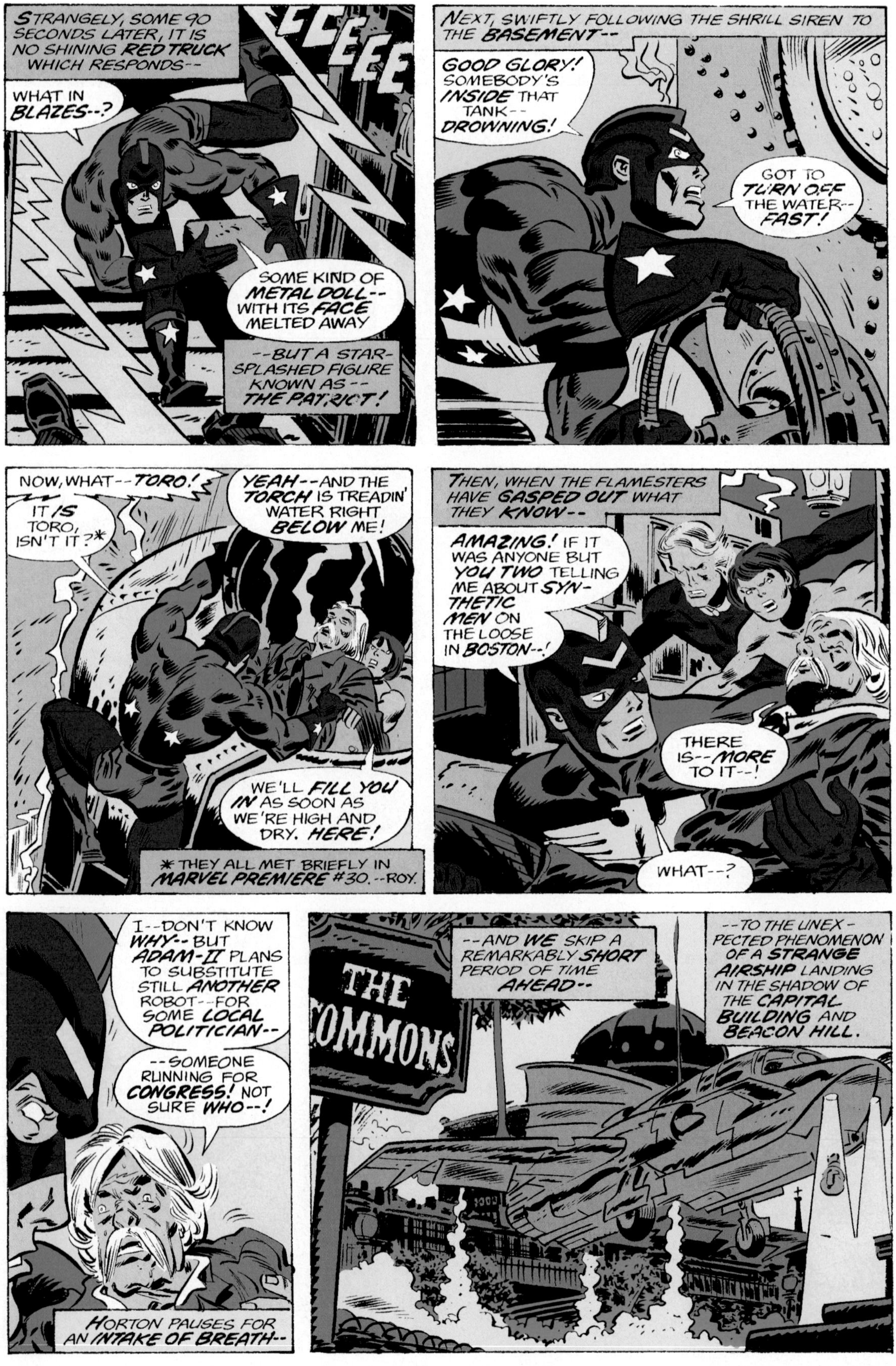
STRANGELY, SOME 90 SECONDS LATER, IT IS NO SHINING RED TRUCK WHICH RESPONDS--
WHAT IN BLAZES--?
SOME KIND OF METAL DOLL--WITH ITS FACE MELTED AWAY
--BUT A STAR-SPLASHED FIGURE KNOWN AS--THE PATRIOT!
NEXT, SWIFTLY FOLLOWING THE SHRILL SIREN TO THE BASEMENT--
GOOD GLORY! SOMEBODY'S INSIDE THAT TANK--DROWNING!
GOT TO TURN OFF THE WATER--FAST!
NOW, WHAT--TORO!
IT IS TORO, ISN'T IT?*
YEAH--AND THE TORCH IS TREADIN' WATER RIGHT BELOW ME!
WE'LL FILL YOU IN AS SOON AS WE'RE HIGH AND DRY. HERE!
* THEY ALL MET BRIEFLY IN MARVEL PREMIERE #30.--ROY.
THEN, WHEN THE FLAMESTERS HAVE GASPED OUT WHAT THEY KNOW--
AMAZING! IF IT WAS ANYONE BUT YOU TWO TELLING ME ABOUT SYN-THETIC MEN ON THE LOOSE IN BOSTON--!
THERE IS--MORE TO IT--!
WHAT--?
I--DON'T KNOW WHY--BUT ADAM-II PLANS TO SUBSTITUTE STILL ANOTHER ROBOT--FOR SOME LOCAL POLITICIAN--
--SOMEONE RUNNING FOR CONGRESS! NOT SURE WHO--!
HORTON PAUSES FOR AN INTAKE OF BREATH--
THE COMMONS
--AND WE SKIP A REMARKABLY SHORT PERIOD OF TIME AHEAD--
--TO THE UNEX-PECTED PHENOMENON OF A STRANGE AIRSHIP LANDING IN THE SHADOW OF THE CAPITAL BUILDING AND BEACON HILL.

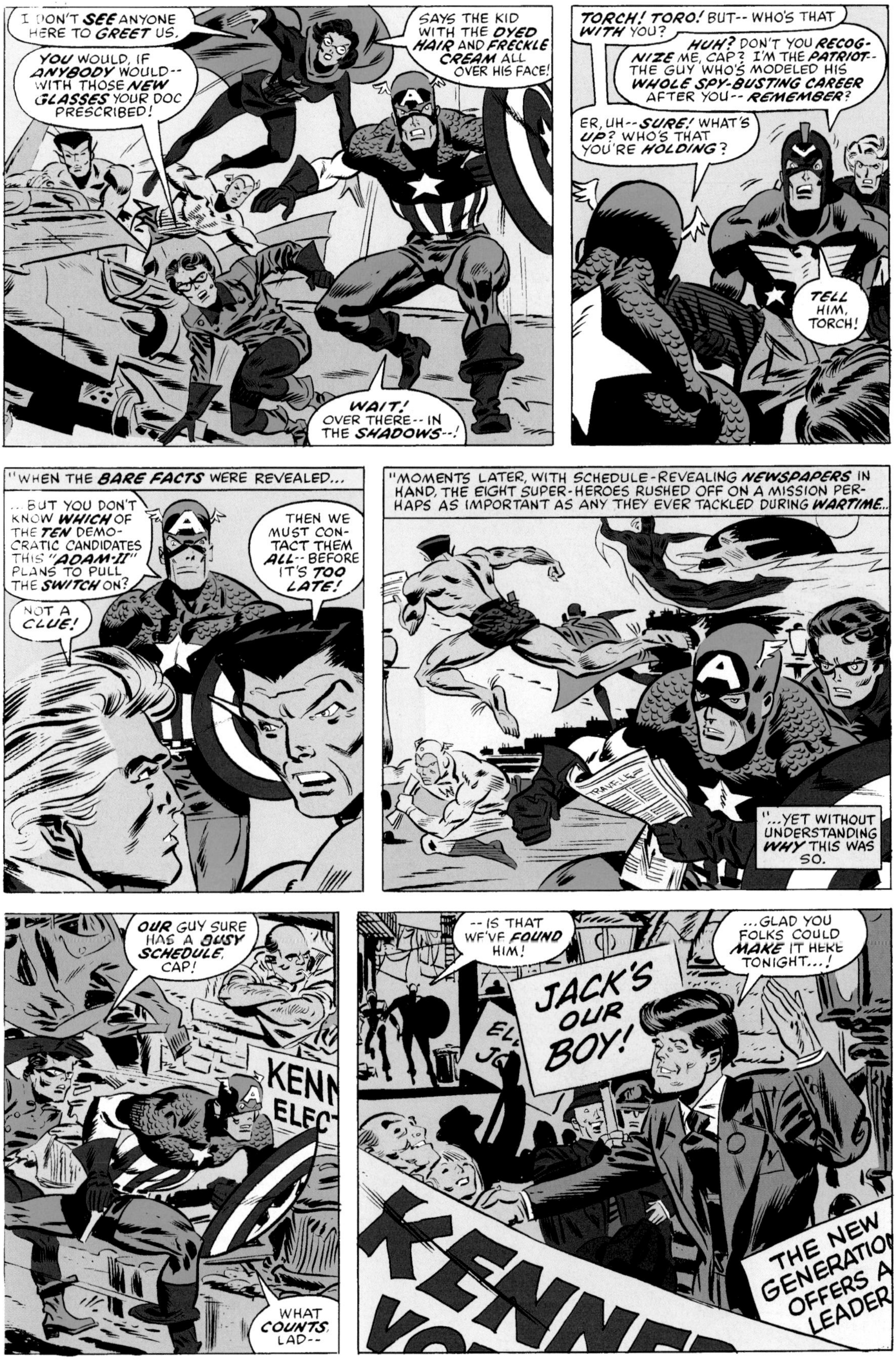
I DON'T SEE ANYONE HERE TO GREET US.
YOU WOULD, IF ANYBODY WOULD-- WITH THOSE NEW GLASSES YOUR DOC PRESCRIBED!
SAYS THE KID WITH THE DYED HAIR AND FRECKLE CREAM ALL OVER HIS FACE!
WAIT! OVER THERE-- IN THE SHADOWS--!
TORCH! TORO! BUT-- WHO'S THAT WITH YOU?
HUH? DON'T YOU RECOGNIZE ME, CAP? I'M THE PATRIOT-- THE GUY WHO'S MODELED HIS WHOLE SPY-BUSTING CAREER AFTER YOU-- REMEMBER?
ER, UH-- SURE! WHAT'S UP? WHO'S THAT YOU'RE HOLDING?
TELL HIM, TORCH!
"WHEN THE BARE FACTS WERE REVEALED...
...BUT YOU DON'T KNOW WHICH OF THE TEN DEMOCRATIC CANDIDATES THIS "ADAM-II" PLANS TO PULL THE SWITCH ON?
NOT A CLUE!
THEN WE MUST CONTACT THEM ALL-- BEFORE IT'S TOO LATE!
"MOMENTS LATER, WITH SCHEDULE-REVEALING NEWSPAPERS IN HAND, THE EIGHT SUPER-HEROES RUSHED OFF ON A MISSION PERHAPS AS IMPORTANT AS ANY THEY EVER TACKLED DURING WARTIME...
"...YET WITHOUT UNDERSTANDING WHY THIS WAS SO.
OUR GUY SURE HAS A BUSY SCHEDULE, CAP!
KENN ELECT
WHAT COUNTS, LAD--
--IS THAT WE'VE FOUND HIM!
...GLAD YOU FOLKS COULD MAKE IT HERE TONIGHT...!
JACK'S OUR BOY!
THE NEW GENERATION OFFERS A LEADER
KENNE

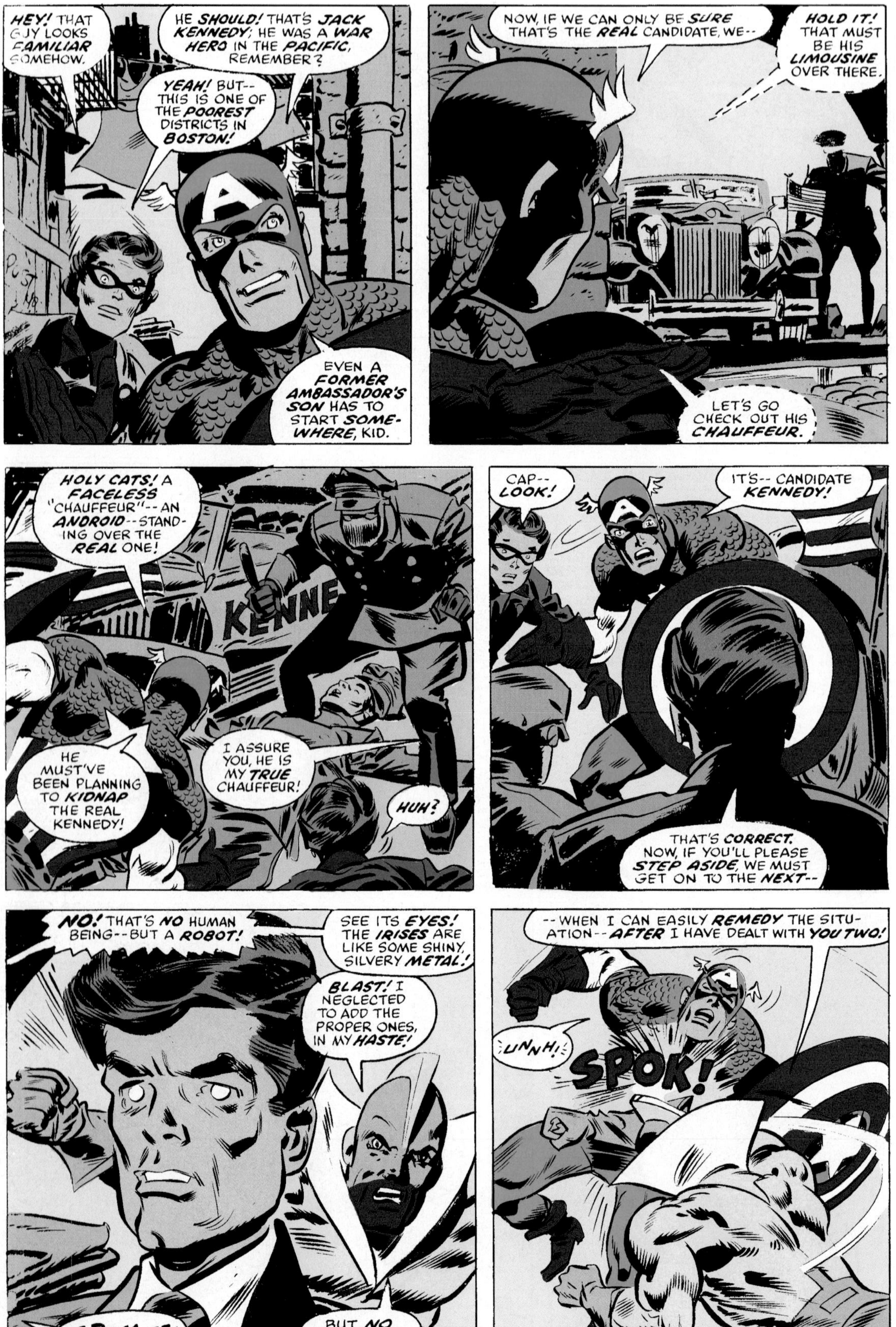
HEY! THAT GUY LOOKS FAMILIAR SOMEHOW.
HE SHOULD! THAT'S JACK KENNEDY; HE WAS A WAR HERO IN THE PACIFIC, REMEMBER?
YEAH! BUT-- THIS IS ONE OF THE POOREST DISTRICTS IN BOSTON!
EVEN A FORMER AMBASSADOR'S SON HAS TO START SOME-WHERE, KID.
NOW, IF WE CAN ONLY BE SURE THAT'S THE REAL CANDIDATE, WE--
HOLD IT! THAT MUST BE HIS LIMOUSINE OVER THERE.
LET'S GO CHECK OUT HIS CHAUFFEUR.
HOLY CATS! A FACELESS "CHAUFFEUR"-- AN ANDROID--STAND-ING OVER THE REAL ONE!
KENNE
HE MUST'VE BEEN PLANNING TO KIDNAP THE REAL KENNEDY!
I ASSURE YOU, HE IS MY TRUE CHAUFFEUR!
HUH?
CAP-- LOOK!
IT'S-- CANDIDATE KENNEDY!
THAT'S CORRECT. NOW, IF YOU'LL PLEASE STEP ASIDE, WE MUST GET ON TO THE NEXT--
NO! THAT'S NO HUMAN BEING--BUT A ROBOT!
SEE ITS EYES! THE IRISES ARE LIKE SOME SHINY, SILVERY METAL!
BLAST! I NEGLECTED TO ADD THE PROPER ONES, IN MY HASTE!
ADAM-II!
BUT, NO MATTER--
--WHEN I CAN EASILY REMEDY THE SITU-ATION--AFTER I HAVE DEALT WITH YOU TWO!
UNNH!
SPOK!

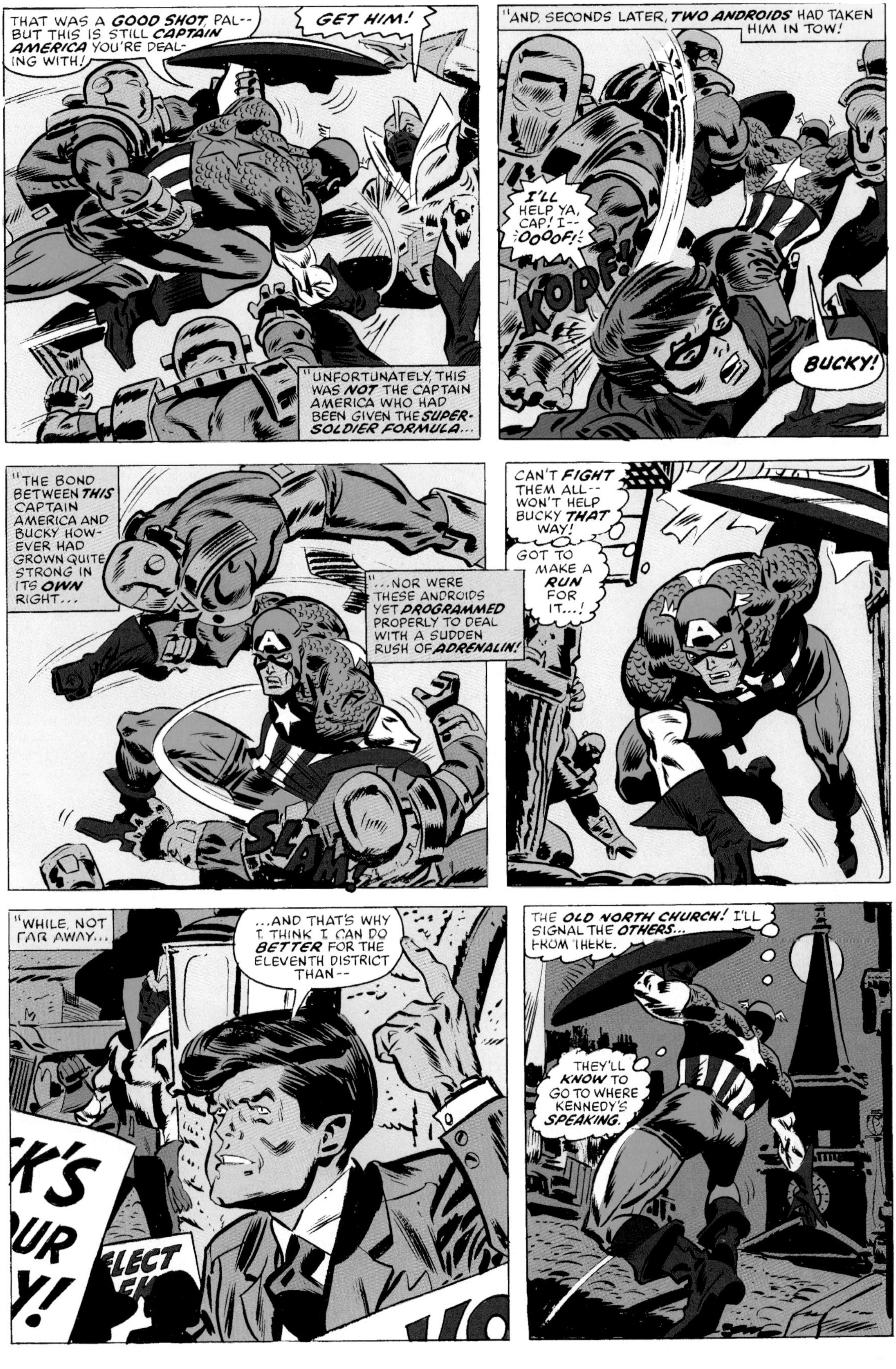

THAT WAS A GOOD SHOT, PAL-- BUT THIS IS STILL CAPTAIN AMERICA YOU'RE DEALING WITH!
GET HIM!
"UNFORTUNATELY, THIS WAS NOT THE CAPTAIN AMERICA WHO HAD BEEN GIVEN THE SUPER-SOLDIER FORMULA...
"AND, SECONDS LATER, TWO ANDROIDS HAD TAKEN HIM IN TOW!
I'LL HELP YA, CAP! I-- OOOOF!
KOPF!
BUCKY!
"THE BOND BETWEEN THIS CAPTAIN AMERICA AND BUCKY HOWEVER HAD GROWN QUITE STRONG IN ITS OWN RIGHT...
"...NOR WERE THESE ANDROIDS YET PROGRAMMED PROPERLY TO DEAL WITH A SUDDEN RUSH OF ADRENALIN!
SLAM!
CAN'T FIGHT THEM ALL-- WON'T HELP BUCKY THAT WAY!
GOT TO MAKE A RUN FOR IT...!
"WHILE, NOT FAR AWAY...
...AND THAT'S WHY I THINK I CAN DO BETTER FOR THE ELEVENTH DISTRICT THAN--
ELECT
THE OLD NORTH CHURCH! I'LL SIGNAL THE OTHERS... FROM THERE.
THEY'LL KNOW TO GO TO WHERE KENNEDY'S SPEAKING.

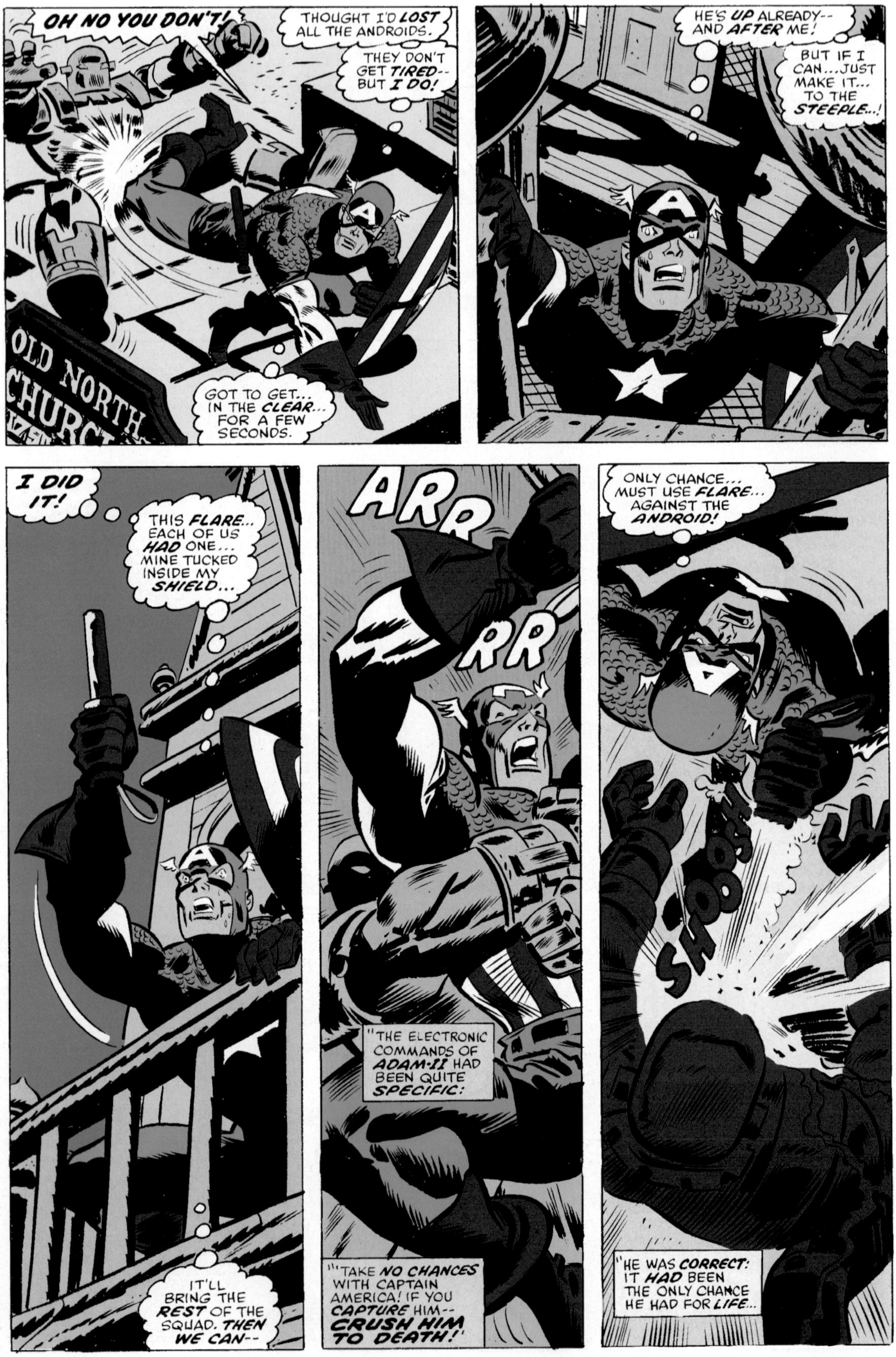

OH NO YOU DON'T!
THOUGHT I'D LOST ALL THE ANDROIDS.
THEY DON'T GET TIRED-- BUT I DO!
OLD NORTH CHURCH
GOT TO GET... IN THE CLEAR... FOR A FEW SECONDS.
HE'S UP ALREADY-- AND AFTER ME!
BUT IF I CAN... JUST MAKE IT... TO THE STEEPLE...!
I DID IT!
THIS FLARE... EACH OF US HAD ONE... MINE TUCKED INSIDE MY SHIELD...
IT'LL BRING THE REST OF THE SQUAD. THEN WE CAN--
ARRRR
"THE ELECTRONIC COMMANDS OF ADAM-II HAD BEEN QUITE SPECIFIC:
"'TAKE NO CHANCES WITH CAPTAIN AMERICA! IF YOU CAPTURE HIM-- CRUSH HIM TO DEATH!'
ONLY CHANCE... MUST USE FLARE... AGAINST THE ANDROID!
SHOOSH
"HE WAS CORRECT: IT HAD BEEN THE ONLY CHANCE HE HAD FOR LIFE...

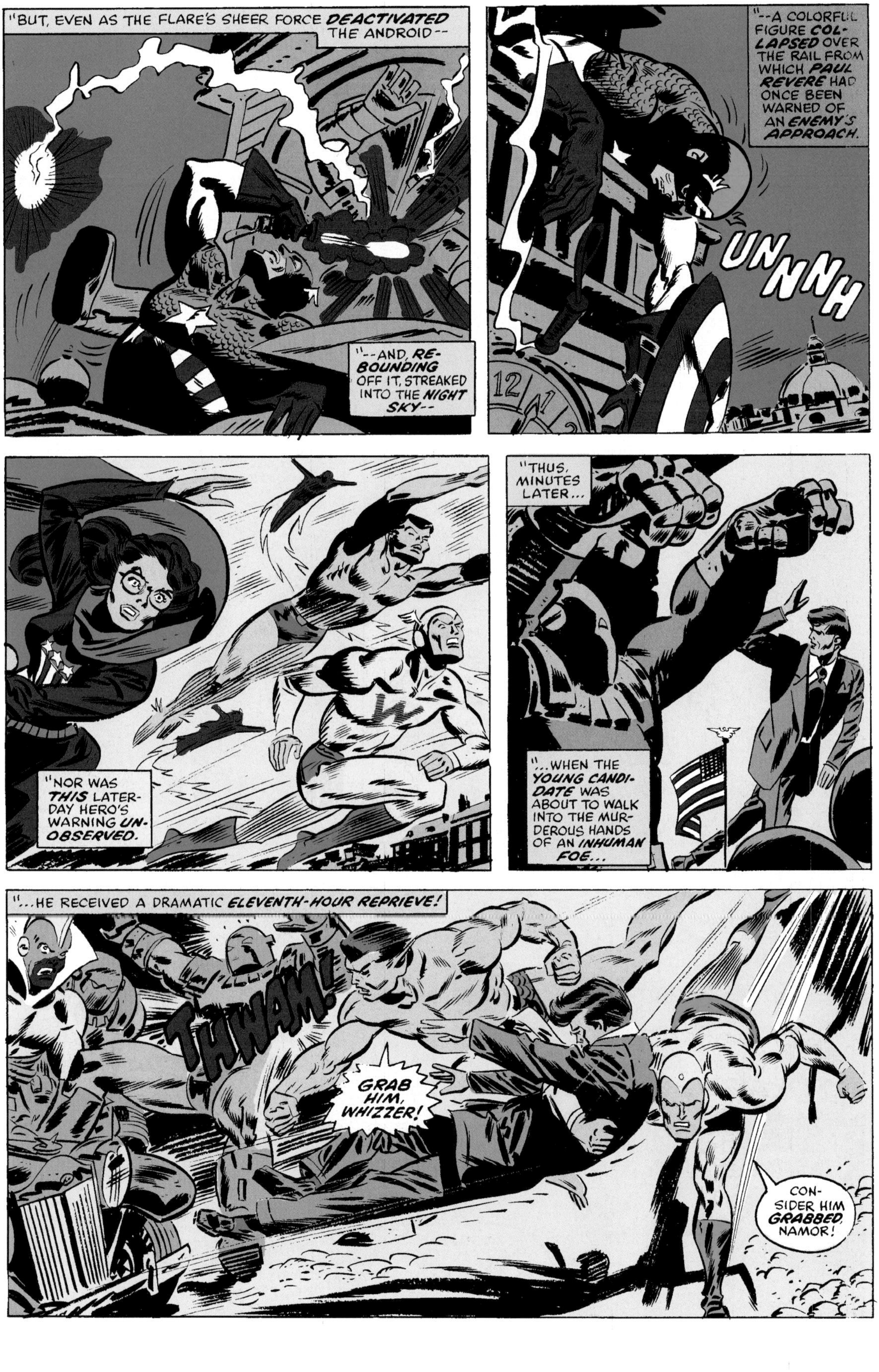
"BUT, EVEN AS THE FLARE'S SHEER FORCE DEACTIVATED THE ANDROID--
"--AND, REBOUNDING OFF IT, STREAKED INTO THE NIGHT SKY--
"--A COLORFUL FIGURE COLLAPSED OVER THE RAIL FROM WHICH PAUL REVERE HAD ONCE BEEN WARNED OF AN ENEMY'S APPROACH.
UNNNH
"NOR WAS THIS LATER-DAY HERO'S WARNING UNOBSERVED.
"THUS, MINUTES LATER...
"...WHEN THE YOUNG CANDIDATE WAS ABOUT TO WALK INTO THE MURDEROUS HANDS OF AN INHUMAN FOE...
"...HE RECEIVED A DRAMATIC ELEVENTH-HOUR REPRIEVE!
THWAM!
GRAB HIM, WHIZZER!
CONSIDER HIM GRABBED, NAMOR!

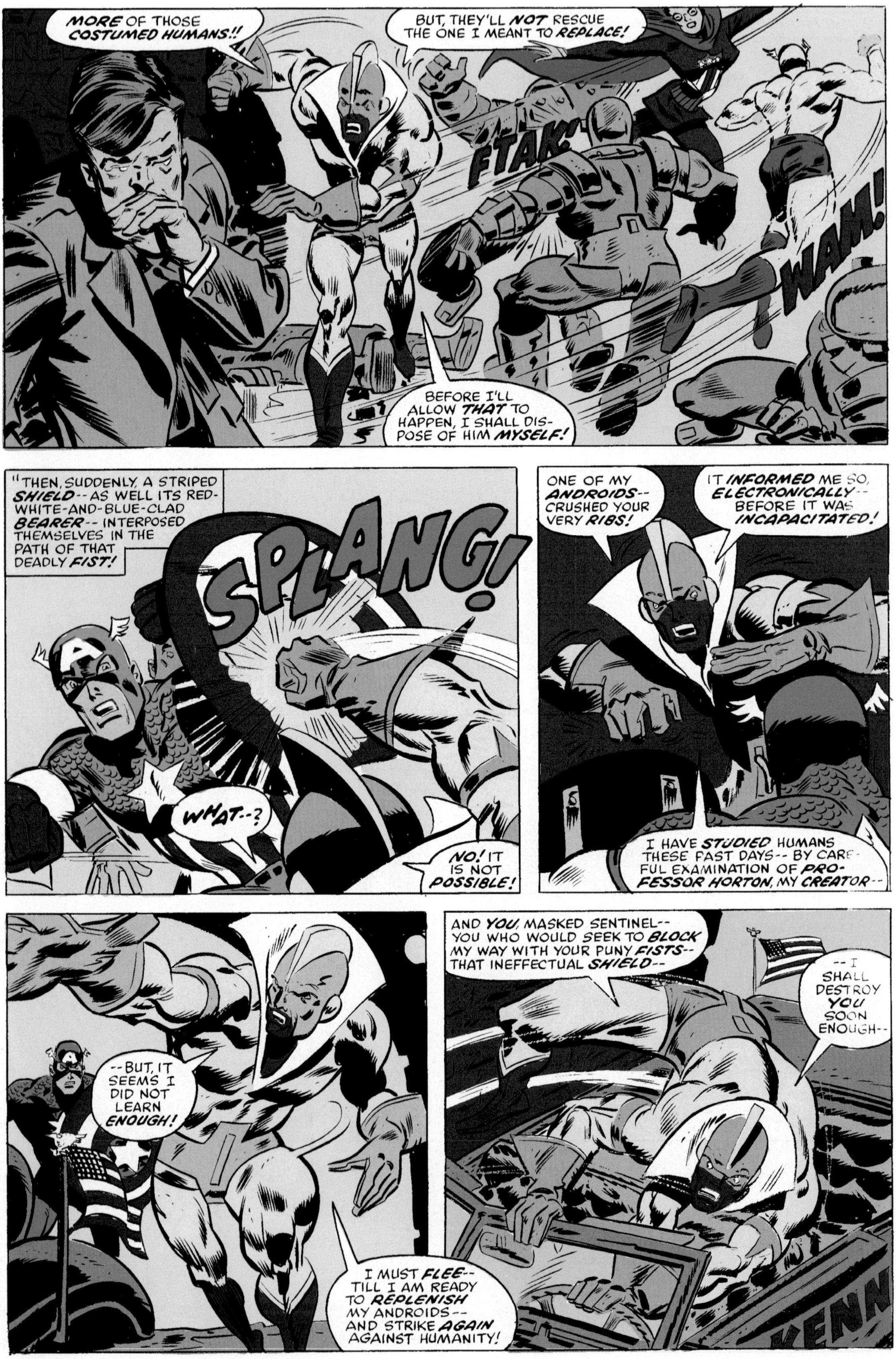
MORE OF THOSE COSTUMED HUMANS!!
BUT, THEY'LL NOT RESCUE THE ONE I MEANT TO REPLACE!
FTAK!
WAM!
BEFORE I'LL ALLOW THAT TO HAPPEN, I SHALL DISPOSE OF HIM MYSELF!
"THEN, SUDDENLY, A STRIPED SHIELD-- AS WELL ITS RED-WHITE-AND-BLUE-CLAD BEARER-- INTERPOSED THEMSELVES IN THE PATH OF THAT DEADLY FIST!
SPLANG!
WHAT--?
NO! IT IS NOT POSSIBLE!
ONE OF MY ANDROIDS-- CRUSHED YOUR VERY RIBS!
IT INFORMED ME SO, ELECTRONICALLY-- BEFORE IT WAS INCAPACITATED!
I HAVE STUDIED HUMANS THESE PAST DAYS-- BY CAREFUL EXAMINATION OF PROFESSOR HORTON, MY CREATOR--
--BUT, IT SEEMS I DID NOT LEARN ENOUGH!
I MUST FLEE-- TILL I AM READY TO REPLENISH MY ANDROIDS-- AND STRIKE AGAIN AGAINST HUMANITY!
AND YOU, MASKED SENTINEL-- YOU WHO WOULD SEEK TO BLOCK MY WAY WITH YOUR PUNY FISTS-- THAT INEFFECTUAL SHIELD--
--I SHALL DESTROY YOU SOON ENOUGH--
KENN

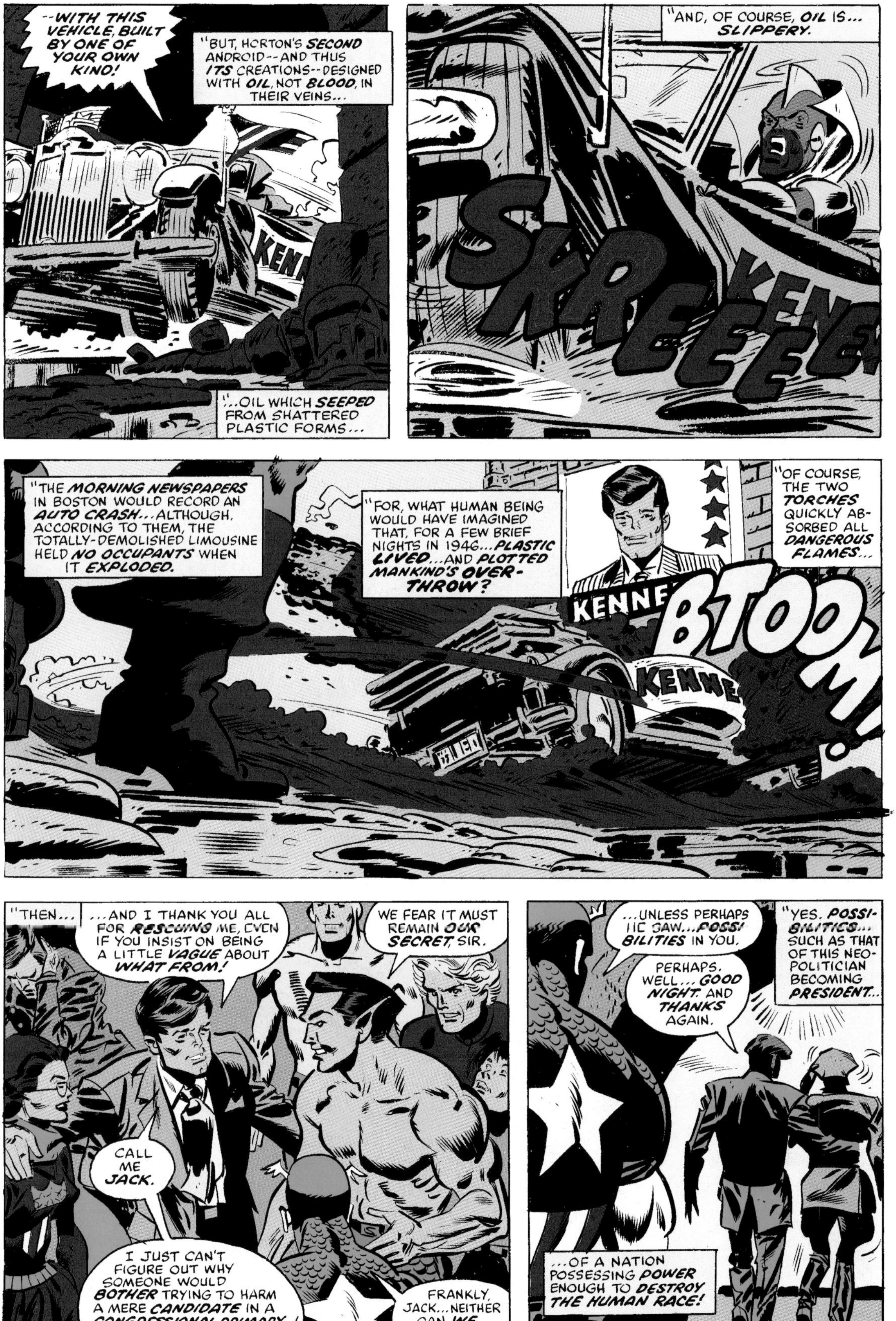
--WITH THIS VEHICLE, BUILT BY ONE OF YOUR OWN KIND!
"BUT, HORTON'S SECOND ANDROID--AND THUS ITS CREATIONS--DESIGNED WITH OIL, NOT BLOOD, IN THEIR VEINS...
"...OIL WHICH SEEPED FROM SHATTERED PLASTIC FORMS...
"AND, OF COURSE, OIL IS... SLIPPERY.
SKREEEEE
KENNE
"THE MORNING NEWSPAPERS IN BOSTON WOULD RECORD AN AUTO CRASH... ALTHOUGH, ACCORDING TO THEM, THE TOTALLY-DEMOLISHED LIMOUSINE HELD NO OCCUPANTS WHEN IT EXPLODED.
"FOR, WHAT HUMAN BEING WOULD HAVE IMAGINED THAT, FOR A FEW BRIEF NIGHTS IN 1946... PLASTIC LIVED... AND PLOTTED MANKIND'S OVER-THROW?
"OF COURSE, THE TWO TORCHES QUICKLY AB-SORBED ALL DANGEROUS FLAMES...
KENNE
BTOOM!
KENNE
"THEN...
...AND I THANK YOU ALL FOR RESCUING ME, EVEN IF YOU INSIST ON BEING A LITTLE VAGUE ABOUT WHAT FROM!
WE FEAR IT MUST REMAIN OUR SECRET, SIR.
CALL ME JACK.
I JUST CAN'T FIGURE OUT WHY SOMEONE WOULD BOTHER TRYING TO HARM A MERE CANDIDATE IN A CONGRESSIONAL PRIMARY...!
FRANKLY, JACK... NEITHER CAN WE...
...UNLESS PERHAPS HE SAW... POSSI-BILITIES IN YOU.
PERHAPS. WELL... GOOD NIGHT. AND THANKS AGAIN.
"YES. POSSI-BILITIES... SUCH AS THAT OF THIS NEO-POLITICIAN BECOMING PRESIDENT...
...OF A NATION POSSESSING POWER ENOUGH TO DESTROY THE HUMAN RACE!

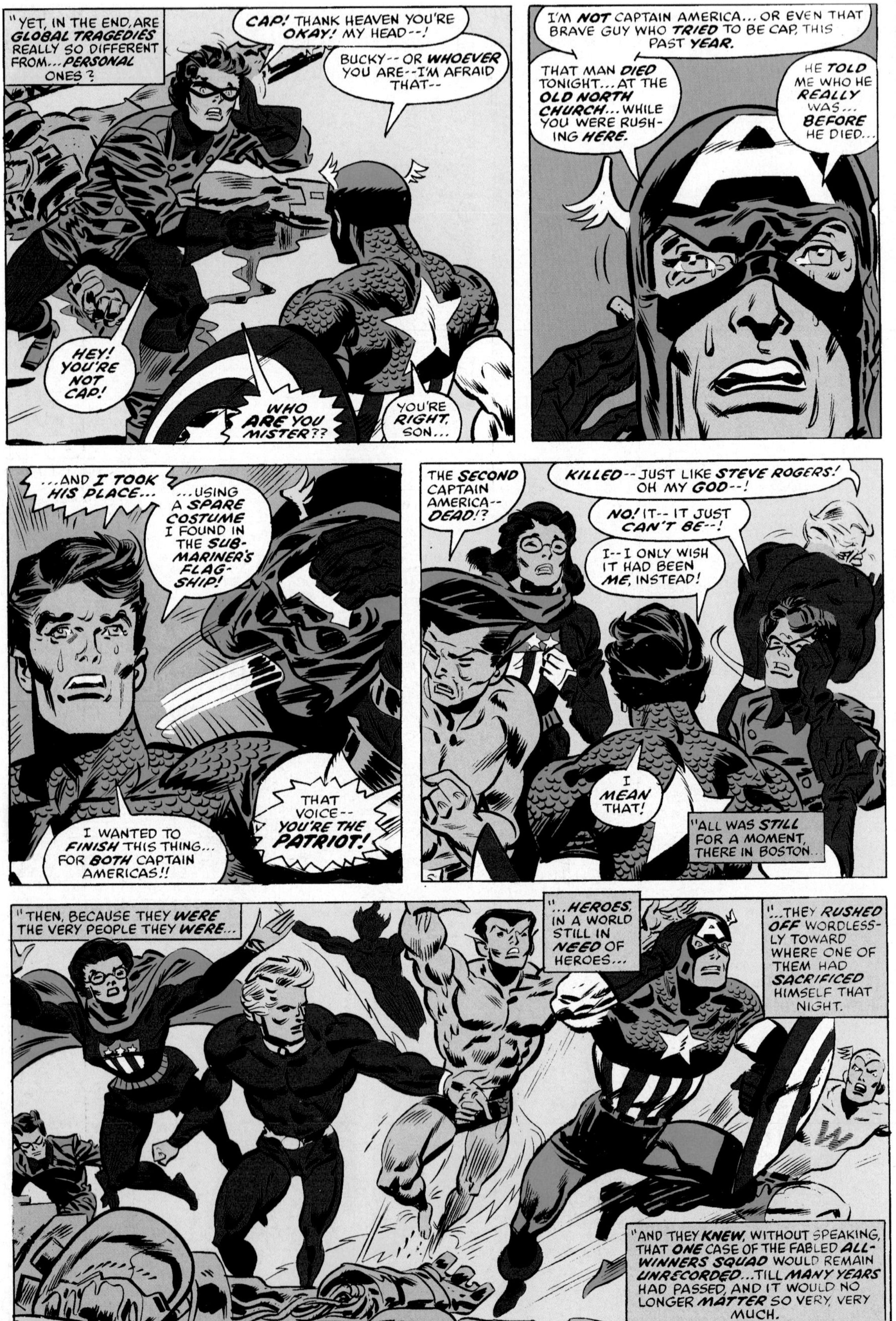

"YET, IN THE END, ARE GLOBAL TRAGEDIES REALLY SO DIFFERENT FROM... PERSONAL ONES?
CAP! THANK HEAVEN YOU'RE OKAY! MY HEAD--!
BUCKY-- OR WHOEVER YOU ARE--I'M AFRAID THAT--
HEY! YOU'RE NOT CAP!
WHO ARE YOU MISTER??
YOU'RE RIGHT, SON...
I'M NOT CAPTAIN AMERICA... OR EVEN THAT BRAVE GUY WHO TRIED TO BE CAP THIS PAST YEAR.
THAT MAN DIED TONIGHT... AT THE OLD NORTH CHURCH... WHILE YOU WERE RUSHING HERE.
HE TOLD ME WHO HE REALLY WAS... BEFORE HE DIED...
...AND I TOOK HIS PLACE...
...USING A SPARE COSTUME I FOUND IN THE SUB-MARINER'S FLAGSHIP!
I WANTED TO FINISH THIS THING... FOR BOTH CAPTAIN AMERICAS!!
THAT VOICE-- YOU'RE THE PATRIOT!
THE SECOND CAPTAIN AMERICA-- DEAD!?
KILLED-- JUST LIKE STEVE ROGERS! OH MY GOD--!
NO! IT-- IT JUST CAN'T BE--!
I-- I ONLY WISH IT HAD BEEN ME, INSTEAD!
I MEAN THAT!
"ALL WAS STILL FOR A MOMENT, THERE IN BOSTON...
"THEN, BECAUSE THEY WERE THE VERY PEOPLE THEY WERE...
"...HEROES, IN A WORLD STILL IN NEED OF HEROES...
"...THEY RUSHED OFF WORDLESSLY TOWARD WHERE ONE OF THEM HAD SACRIFICED HIMSELF THAT NIGHT.
"AND THEY KNEW, WITHOUT SPEAKING, THAT ONE CASE OF THE FABLED ALL-WINNERS SQUAD WOULD REMAIN UNRECORDED... TILL MANY YEARS HAD PASSED, AND IT WOULD NO LONGER MATTER SO VERY, VERY MUCH.

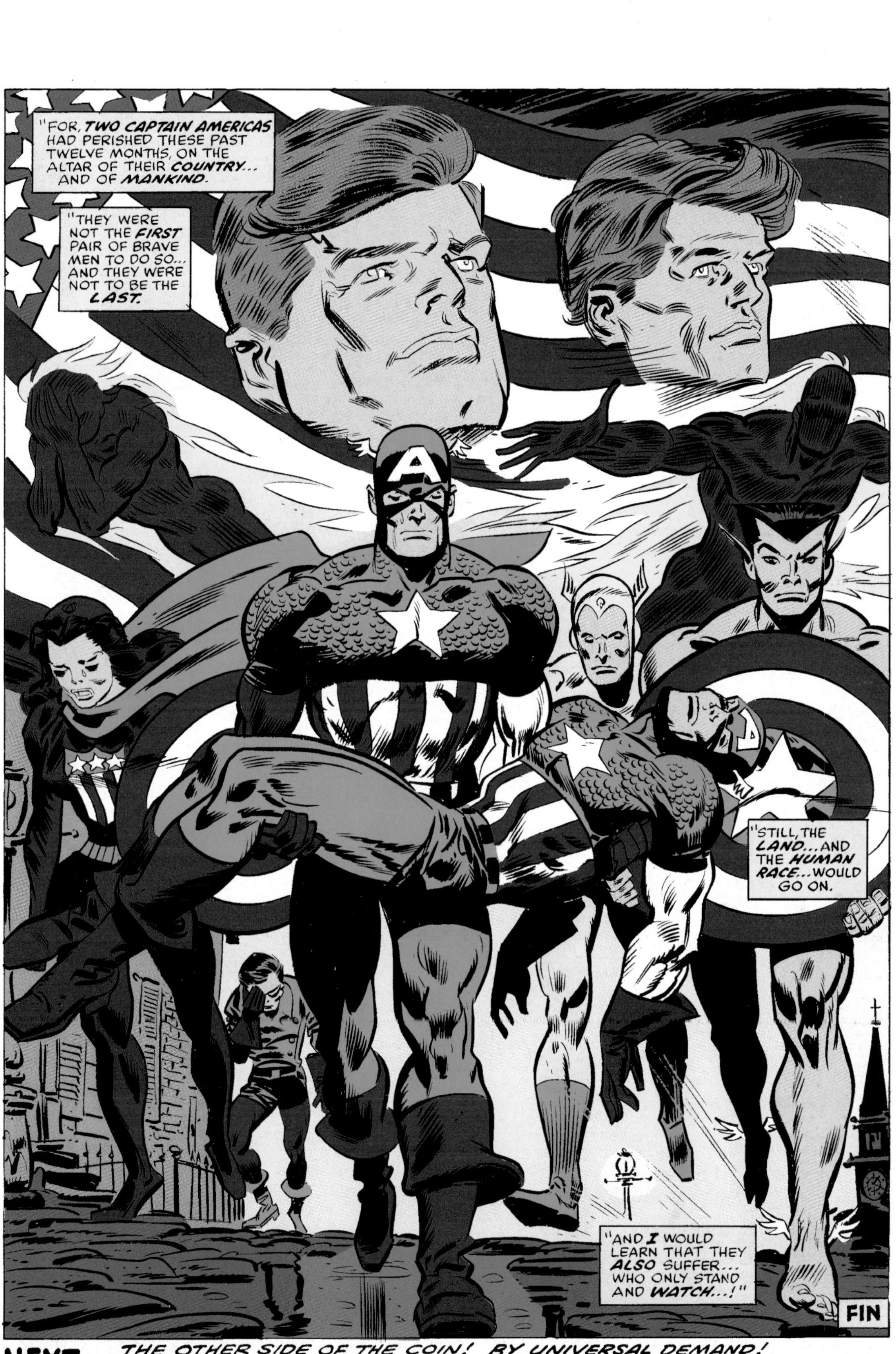
"FOR, TWO CAPTAIN AMERICAS HAD PERISHED THESE PAST TWELVE MONTHS, ON THE ALTAR OF THEIR COUNTRY... AND OF MANKIND.
"THEY WERE NOT THE FIRST PAIR OF BRAVE MEN TO DO SO... AND THEY WERE NOT TO BE THE LAST.
"STILL, THE LAND... AND THE HUMAN RACE... WOULD GO ON.
"AND I WOULD LEARN THAT THEY ALSO SUFFER... WHO ONLY STAND AND WATCH...!"
FIN

THE OTHER SIDE OF THE COIN! BY UNIVERSAL DEMAND!

NEXT ISSUE: WHAT IF CAPTAIN AMERICA HADN'T VANISHED DURING WORLD WAR II?

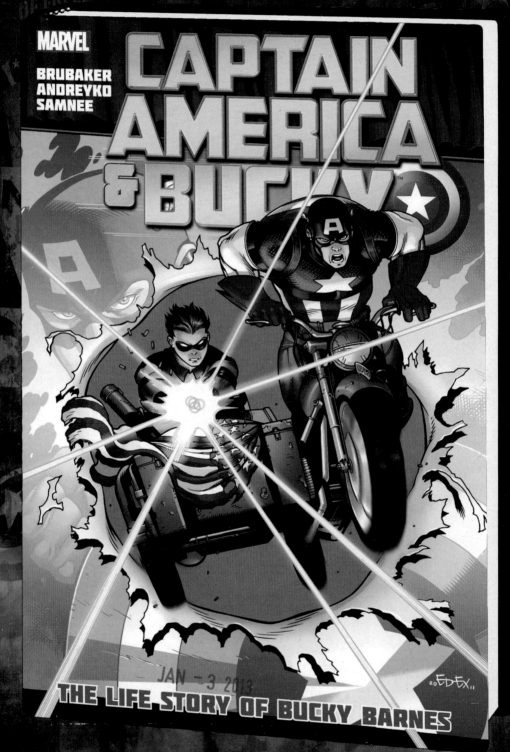